YoungWriters

My Favourite Person

Edited by Young Writers

A collection of
poems about the people
that make our lives special

First published in Great Britain in 2005 by
Young Writers
Remus House
Coltsfoot Drive
Peterborough
PE2 9JX
Telephone: 01733 890066
youngwriters@forwardpress.co.uk
www.forwardpress.co.uk

Foreword

Our company, Young Writers, was established in 1991 to promote the written word amongst successive generations. Now, in 2005, we are still striving to encourage today's youth to put themselves forward and to challenge their own talents.

The competition resulting in this compilation was a new one for us and we were astounded by the quality of, and enthusiasm in, the entries. Each hand-picked entry was carefully chosen from a massive amount of entries nationwide. It was then showcased in this volume, to appear alongside other sparkling tributes to fellow writers; and each author should be proud to be within these pages.

Within this volume are poems themed around teachers, famous people, parents, grandparents and many more favourite persons besides; all of whom should be proud to be such an inspiration to the generation to come. As a team, we thoroughly enjoyed discovering who inspires our budding authors and we hope you, as a reader, feel the enthusiasm radiate through the pages to follow.

A to Z of Poets

The Poems

Memories Of Grandad

Me and my grandad were an inseparable team,
We'd play hide-and-seek among bushes of green,
We'd chase each other through shallow brooks,
And bring bags of bread to feed to the ducks.
Sometimes we'd sit cross-legged on a sandy seashore,
With not a sound to be heard, we didn't need to speak anymore.
As we could sense what each other was thinking about,
There was no need to yell and shout.
Those times were perfect, both day and night,
Through the dark midwinter to the early spring light.
But nothing has changed since those past few years,
Though the pain is still felt and the tears
Are still shed, as we are still an inseparable team,
And we still play hide-and-seek among bushes of green,
And we still chase each other through shallow brooks,
And we still stand by the pond and feed the ducks.
I just rely on the memories and there I am,
A four-year-old girl holding her grandad's hand,
Though at the present he's not with me,
He's there in my heart and always will be.

Shona Jackson (11)

Winner!

Well done Shona! Your poem about
your grandad was our favourite in
the whole book! You win **£100** worth
of **Toys 'R' Us** vouchers!

You're A Star

I was living in a hole
With no way out
No one saw me cry
No one heard me shout
I was living in a circle
Same days, same nights
Same fear, same hatred
Same pain, same fights
I was living a lie
I was stuck in the mud
I covered up the bruises
I wiped away the blood
Then came the day
Where you entered my life
You resurrected my smile
And blew away my strife
I looked at my past
And I knew what was true
I started living
The day I met you
You took away the demon
Who took away my youth
With you by my side I won
And the jury knew the truth
Even when you're not around
No matter where you are
I think of you all the time
Because Ziggy, you're a star.

Helena Power (16)

Runner-up

We loved this poem so much that we made it one of our runners-up! Helena, you win **£25** worth of **Toys 'R' Us** vouchers!

My Mum

I love my mum
So very much,
I love the way she hugs me
And her gentle touch.
I love the way she tucks me into bed
With a hug and a kiss goodnight,
I love it when she reads me a story
Before she turns out the light.
She helps me with my homework
And plays the PlayStation too,
Sometimes I may beat her
And others she'll thrash me too.
She takes me to the park
On my bike or skates,
She will also serve my dinner
On my favourite plates.
When I'm sick or poorly
She'll tuck me up in bed,
She'll sit and never leave me
And gently stroke my head.
And when my brother and sister
Are asleep in their bed at night,
We sit and have our quiet time
Before I say goodnight.
So yes, I'm not embarrassed
To say Mum, I love you,
Because there is no one in this world
Who could ever replace you.

Lewis Hudson (10)

Runner-up

You are our second runner-up Lewis!
Your fab poem also wins you **£25** worth
of **Toys 'R' Us** vouchers!

19

My Favourite Four

Commended

I have a special message
it goes out to my mum
because she's a special person
and we have lots of fun

I have a special message
it goes out to my dad
because he's the greatest father
a girl could ever have

I have a special message
it goes out to my two bros.
I know you don't mean it nastily
but it's your job, I suppose

I have a special message
it goes out to you four
because you're my favourite people
and I love you most of all.

Lucy Dexeter (12)

Poppy

My favourite friend is furry
With big brown trusting eyes
When she wants rides on my skateboard
She hops on and down she lies.

Poppy loves fresh parsley
Dandelions and broccoli
But she's a really happy bunny
When it's locust beans for tea.

She likes chewing up Mum's flowers
And sunbathing by her hutch
Sometimes we share a secret
That no one knows but us!

Lee Morgan (9)

Commended

My Lovely Gramps

Hmmm ... to write my favourite person
Is hard you see
Because there are so many
From A right to Z!

The person I chose
Is not here today
But deep in my heart
He will always stay.

He loved to play games
And take me on trips
I loved to tell secrets
And he kept sealed lips.

He would take me on outings
To the museum and to the beach
And would lift me up high
To things I could not reach.

He had big blue eyes
As deep as the sea
He was as cuddly as a bear
And still means the world to me
And that is my lovely gramps.

Jasmine Morris (11)

Who Is My Favourite Person?

This poem is about my favourite person
But who will that person be?
As I sit here today thinking of all those I love
We'll just have to wait and see!

Is it my mum because she is always there for me?
Maybe it's my dad because he always cooks my tea?
Or is it my brother who plays games and makes me smile
Even if we do argue once in a while!
Perhaps it's my nan, gran and grandads too?
Or aunties, uncles, cousins and friends both old and new?
Teachers in my school have taught me a great deal
Doctors and nurses who helped me when I was ill.

After much deliberation it's time for me to choose
Who will be my favourite one? What would be your views?
Big, small, large or tall it really doesn't matter to me.
You see I do not have a favourite person,
Because everyone is special to me!

Rebecca Robinson (10)

Commended

Weeping Willow

(Dedicated to my uncle Jack)

Weeping Willow do not cry
For watching those who start to die.

Weeping Willow you look so bare,
So please don't stop and start to stare.

Why did you go when life's so tough
And leave me up and rough?

You will always remain where my life's in pain
And be a part of my golden heart.

I love you forever, no matter what the weather.

Bethany Stead (11)

Commended

My Favourite Person

Commended

My favourite person is my grandad,
He's so loyal and so kind.
He used to hold me in his arms,
And never was a bind.

A special person was he,
Who used to sit me on his knee.
He told me stories of long ago,
Oh I used to love it so.

But my dear grandad has now parted
To the heavens above.
An angel he has now become
Sending out lots of love.

Oh how I miss my grandad so
I thought you all should know.
He will always remain in my heart
So we will never be apart.

Jessica Laws (11)

Baby Brother To Be

Commended

I have a little baby brother waiting for me.
When we lay eyes upon each other how happy we shall be.
When he crawls about the world with everyone beside him,
All these feelings he shall feel going about inside him.
And when he's all grown up, making such a fuss about a game I have won
I'll tell him, 'You know what, as a baby you were much more fun.'
And when he grows old with skin all baggy and lighting his fire with the turf
I'll say, 'Brother I love you dearly and wouldn't swap you for the earth.'

Finan Rodinson (11)

My Auntie Carol Is The Best

My auntie Carol who I love the most
She's a Geordie, the best but I don't want to boast
She kisses, hugs and tickles me
She lights up my life like a Christmas tree.
She makes me happy all the time
When I'm with her I always smile
She's my auntie Carol. the very best,
She's full of life and full of zest!

Charlotte Smith (11)

You

My favourite person is hard to describe,
This is because it changes from time to time.
Sometimes it has blond hair, others red or brown,
Some of the time it smiles, some of the time it frowns.
It can change gender going from boy to girl
It loves to cook, play football or dance in a twirl.
This person helps me, gives me inspiration,
This person shows me what's important in the world.
He is caring, sensitive but unhelpful,
She is loving, clever but hates socialising,
See, this person is anyone and everyone,
People on the street, in a shop or on a bus,
Any race, religion, gender or type,
I will value you wherever I go
My favourite person is ...
    You!

Zoe Fox (14)

Bulging Bootsie

My cat is called Bootsie,
He has a bulging belly,
He's fat and chubby and very, very hungry,
His tummy is like a ball
Ready to bounce up a wall.
We play with him, but he's too hot,
He rolls about in the sun,
I love to tickle his tum,
His noise is terrible, it's really loud.

*You'd be amazed
   He can snore!*

Zoe Hyde (9)

My Favourite Person

My favourite person is Harry
He makes me smile a lot

When I'm in a bad mood
He cheers me up with jokes

When I'm in the sick bay
With a migraine, he comes and cheers me up

In the playground he backs me up
And talks to me when no one else will

He sits next to me in class
And we work together

This is why my favourite person is Harry
The Harry who makes me smile.

Toby Phillips (10)

My Special Person

Not long ago my life went through a change,
I was no longer the youngest,
I thought I would go insane,
But the trouble I had, was soon to be solved.
I was going to have a baby sister.
Or at least that's what I was told.

As soon as I saw her I was very excited,
She looked so cute, cuddly - I was not broken hearted.
Soon she became more cute and would learn how to talk,
I enjoyed making her smile and seeing her first walk.

I felt silly when I felt muddled,
I can't imagine life without her,
I love her and being cuddled.
My life changed, I'm very happy,
Although this person makes a mess in her little nappy,
But I love it when she copies me like a parrot,
She copies every word.
When I sing she sings - it's kind of absurd.
I like to play games with her like hide-and-seek
She comes behind the door to peek,
Now you heard my poem - you know what I love most
Please send me the £100 voucher straight in the post.

Afzal Hussain Kamrul

Mr Gareth Hughes

At first sight he didn't seem too good
Unlike any regular teacher should,
But during these two years of fun,
A perfect oh too perfect, friendship begun.

Behind these eyes of his I saw,
Life, humour and kindness, nothing more.
But no, there *was* more; there was cleverness too,
So weepy reader, it is all too true.

As months passed, I realised I *knew*
That Mr Gareth Hughes was one of the few,
One of the few that could make me smile,
One of the few that could make life worthwhile.

But time flew by like a bullet from a gun,
Unfortunately this was the end of the fun,
For I left school, but have you heard the news?
I will miss my jolly teacher, Mr Gareth Hughes.

Dale White (11)

My Friend's A Bit Different

My friend is like any other friend,
There is one thing different about her.
She always sticks up for me,
We can always share secrets.
The best thing about us is we never fight,
We are like two pieces of paper stuck together.
   Never will we leave each other's side.

The different thing about my friend is ...
When I talk to her people think I'm talking to myself.
They think I'm cuckoo in my head,
But I know I'm not mad because she is there.
If I can see, hear my friend,
We don't care what people think,
   For we will be best friends forever.

If you think really hard,
You know who my friend is.
The question is do you know?
If not have a little think.

A: My friend is an invisible friend.

Ravitta Suniar (11)

Great Best Friends

Best friends forever
And never break up.
We've had a bit of sand kicked in our face,
But we've come through
And we can go shopping together
And we go places really nice and far away.

Kershina Russell (7)

My Best Friend

My best friend is kind and caring
She plays with me every day
She always likes having fun.

My best friend always makes me feel happy
She never gets me into trouble at school
And her name is Katie.

Coral Gilbert (10)

My Favourite Person

My favourite person begins with an N and ends in an E.
Can you guess who that person might be?

She likes to sing to Justin,
She loves to dance to J-Lo,
Her favourite food is ice cream,
Strawberries and marshmallow.

She likes it when it's sunny,
She hates it when it rains,
Her jokes are never funny,
But she tells them all the same.

She is sometimes nice,
She is sometimes neat,
She is sometimes good,
She loves sweets.

Her eyes are brown,
She has black hair,
She hardly frowns,
And never swears.

My favourite person begins with an N and ends in an E.
Can you guess who that person might be?
... It's me!

Nicole Charles (9)

Yayo

I remember him,
As thin as a pole,
And as tall as a tower,
Looking into my pram like a little toy flower.

I remember him,
Calm like the summer sea,
In lovely, sunny Spain,
Running like a horse in my game,
And hiding like a little grain.

I remember him,
Fierce as a Titan when it came to maths,
But soft as a feather when it was time to play,
Reading away into the night,
Helping me to enjoy my day.

I remember him,
As skilled as Mrs James,
Painting tiny figures of lead,
Making every moment unique,
And then, with a great sigh, carrying me off to bed.

I remember him,
Waving my plane away,
He and Granny like two dots far down below,
Their faces full of warmth and glow,
I will always remember him.

Alexander Fanourakis (10)

Hannah Flood Is My Best Friend

Hannah Flood is my best friend
Hannah Flood is my best friend
I play around with her all of the time
And I love the sneaking and running
And the adventures that we do
So Hannah Flood is my best friend
Hannah Flood is my best friend.

Hannah Bloxham (7)

S Club Number 1

Rachel Stevens is her name,
Singing songs is her game.
Practising all day and night,
I hope she won't give you a fright.

When she's on stage her heart is pumping,
Then a quick blink and she is jumping.
'Sweet Dreams' was her first song,
It was great to sing along.

Her latest album is 'Negotiate With Love',
She has been known to wear a black velvet glove.
Trying out new moves each day,
She's the best people say.

Rachel Stevens is her name,
Singing songs is her game.
Rachel Stevens is the best,
She is better than all the rest.

Jennifer Hesketh (9)

My Dog Molly

Molly has fur as soft as candyfloss,
Her nose is as black as a dark cave,
Her eyes are like a mud bath,
Molly is as cuddly as my teddy bear,
Her complexion is as white as snow,
She jumps around as if she is a spring lamb.
Molly eats as fast as a cheetah runs,
But she chews her chews as slow as a turtle,
And she can sometimes be as lazy as a sloth.
Molly has puppy eyes as cute as a newborn baby,
I love Molly as far out in the universe
Like no one ever knows.

Anna Tormey (11)

Untitled

1, 2, 3 who is she?
Brown hair, blue eyes,
Can you guess, who is she?
Her nose is round but not pointy
I met her in Spinney
But who is she?
She is the kindest person you've ever known
But who is she?

Who is she?
  Megan.

Omega Russell (9)

My Favourite Person

My favourite person is my mum
She loves to eat creamy buns
And when I ask her to come and play
She says she feels too fat today.

My mum has short brown hair,
And looks after me with great care,
She is quite tall and slightly fat
And loves to play with a tennis bat.

She washes, cleans and cooks for me
And works as busy as a bee.
She takes me to school in the car
Or any place near or far.

Ethel is my mum's name
She loves her children all the same
When we have a tummy bug
She gives us a great big hug.

She tucks me into bed at night
And cuddles me, oh! so very tight
My mum is my best friend
And we'll love each other to the end!

Victoria Graham (9)

My Parents

My dad is so cool
His name is Peter
He always takes me out
And to the theatre.
When we go shopping
I always beg for stuff,
But when I ask for a swimming pool
He says well that's tough.
Sometimes he goes crazy
Sometimes he goes mad
But deep down inside
He's a brilliant dad.
My mum does the washing
My mum makes the tea
She also does ironing
And bed making for me.
When we go on holiday
She really is quite fun
Especially when there is
A lot of lovely sun.
She really is the best mum
A mum I'd never hate
That's definitely not a lie
Cos she's really, really great!
So now you know my parents
The ones that look after me
They really are the best
As good as parents can be!

Jennifer Cook (11)

My Sister

Gangly legs and nobbly knees,
Long frizzy hair that's full of fleas,
Hairy armpits full of nits,
Big wide eyes and big red lips,
Spotted face and hairy toes,
Leaves a smell wherever she goes,
But ...
She's my very favourite person really,
Because I love her dearly.

Alice Brown (11)

My Mum

My mum is my favourite person
She helps me every day of every week
She is always there for me
I love her very much
Though I am cheeky and chubby
It doesn't matter to her
She'll love me however I am
And I will never stop loving her.

Libby Moutter (9)

Pippin My Dog

I have a dog called Pippin
She's ace from head to toe.
Sometimes she's playful,
But sometimes she doesn't want to know.

When she barks, it's so squeaky
And when her ears flop up and down
She looks like a king or a queen,
Wearing a golden crown.

Pippin is like a fantasy or dream,
Waiting to be opened like a door.
She pounces like a lion,
And ends up on the floor.

So now it's the end of my poem
And Pippin says bye too.
I hope I'll write some more,
So see you later toodoloo!

Robyn Bulpitt (10)

My Hamster

His lovely golden hairs,
His little twitching nose,
His lovely little ears,
His little arms and toes.

His big, black eyes,
His long nails,
His sharp, sharp teeth,
His whiskers tickling me.

Heather Eggelton (8)

My Favourite Cat: Pharaoh Midas McFlurry

P haraoh is my Persian cat,
H is eyes are shiny amber glass
A nd he has a pancake nose
R ound his body black fur grows
A ll who see him have to smile
O h we love his catty style
H e's like a king of the ancient Nile.

M ost of the day he sleeps and eats
I f he spots a spider up he leaps!
D ancing around trying to catch his prey,
A ll this excitement's turning him grey
S o he's off to visit his litter tray.

M y little cat is simply the best
C ute, cuddly, playful: with him I'm blessed
F orget PC games, toys and possessions
L oving my pet has taught me these lessons:
U nderstanding, kindness, patience too
R espect for all creatures smaller than you!
R eally I don't possess my cat,
Y ou see he owns me, that's a fact.

Naomi McAdam (10)

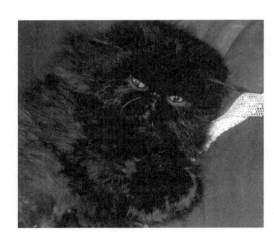

My Dog Billy

His name is Billy,
He's not fluffy nor frilly.
He's tall and hairy,
He's really, really scary.
He is funny and he's nice,
And he loves to eat ice.
He's brown and white,
And he is afraid of heights.
He barks at the man,
With a letter in his hand.
Woof, woof, woof,
He's the greatest thing around.

He is brother to Tikka,
A white and ginger cat,
Who chews my mother's handbag
And my father's hat.
My Billy is gentle,
And he's nice and kind,
When the postman shall go past,
He'll chew his fat behind.

Charlotte Edge (10)

My Pet Rottweiler

(Dedicated to Taigey)

Your warm furry body,
Always makes me itchy

Your big scratchy paw,
Always makes me fall

Your pink slobbery tongue,
Always makes me laugh

Your wet sniffing nose,
Always makes me giggle

Your short waggling tail,
Always makes me happy

Your soft brown eyes
Always make me smile

Your inquisitive face
Always makes me stay

Your mischievous mood
Always makes me say ...

'Come here you little rascal!'

Kirsty Lam (11)

The Best Mum Race

The best mum race has just begun
But my mum has already won
She started off through the gates
The others on a silver plate
If it was a running race
She'll still win that
So in your face!

Jessie Rourke (10)

My Mum

My mum she loves to have a laugh
She also loves to have a relaxing bath
I think she likes to scream and shout
She will wake the babies that's no doubt.
She also likes to shop and look at all the tops
It takes ages and then I end up playing with the babies
She loves to chat
Sometimes she just can't stop that chitter chat.

Emily Markham (8)

My Favourite Person

My favourite person she is always there
Even when she's doing her hair
When I'm sick she always cares.

My favourite person is always happy
Even when I am unhappy
Yes, you've guessed it,
My favourite person is my mum!

Ariana Flynn (10)

Summer Has Come For My Mum

Summer is here
Summer has come
Summer is so hot
The blossom thinks it's too hot
The flowers are out
The trees gently sway in the breeze
The air is so hot
But the best thing of all
Is to have some fun with my mum
I love my mum
Summer has come for my mum.

Will Nangle (8)

Zoe, Zoe, Zoe

Zoe, Zoe, Zoe - full of joy
Zoe, Zoe, Zoe - full of fun
Makes me laugh, till the break of day
Zoe, Zoe, Zoe - so imaginative
Zoe, Zoe, Zoe so fun and good to make up games
She has a good mind.
Zoe, Zoe, Zoe, so intelligent
Has a great mind at speed,
Zoe is a good joker
Zoe sometimes helps me with maths.

Kelly Flanagan (9)

Ami

Sitting on the ground
I see her,
Jumping up and down
I see her,
Never making a sound,
I see her,
Always there,
I see her,
It's Ami,
It's Ami,
Who else would it be?

Lucy Cole (10)

My Sister

My sister is so sweet
She really is a treat.

She makes me laugh when
I want to cry,
Every time she says, 'Hi.'

She's only one yet still full of fun,
When it is raining she is my little sun!

Her skin is very soft to touch,
And I love her very much.

Jade D'Cruz (8)

White And Grey

White and grey - the softest fur
Cuddle up close, a satisfied purr
Pointed ears smooth as silk
Rough pink tongue lapping milk
Dark, still night, silent creep
Home again for another sleep
Wraps around my cold, cold feet
Warmer now I sense the heat
White and grey - the softest fur
The best of friends - me and her.

Elizabeth Simon (8)

My Nan

My favourite person is my nan
She is an Eddie Stobbart fan
She follows their lorries along the road
To see the name on the front, she's in detective mode.
I love eating at Nan's, she's a really good cook
Guess what, she doesn't need a recipe book.
Sometimes I stay over at night
And if I get frightened she turns on the light.
That's why my favourite person is my nan
I love her lots, I'm her number one fan.

Tayla Roostan (9)

My Friend

My friend is pretty
My friend is cool,
My friend is trendy,
My friend's got it all.

My friend is nice,
My friend is great,
My friend is good,
My friend is my mate.

My friend is always there for me,
We're as happy as can be.

And together we will stay
Always, forever and a day!

Chloe Lewis (9)

My Grandma

My grandma's old and very sick
Can't walk around even with a stick.
My grandma wears glasses, but cannot see.
My grandma wears a hearing aid,
But cannot hear.
I love her so dear.
My grandma doesn't smile a lot, but she smiles for me.
If anything happens to my grandma where would I be?
My grandma likes chocolate and all things sweet.
When I see her it's such a treat.
I look at my grandma and shed a tear
I love her so dear.

Sarah Shilson (11)

Confusing Sisterly Love

Sisters have to love each other
Don't they?
Because if they didn't they wouldn't
Be sisters.

But they always quarrel
Like when my sister dared me
To jump in the lake. I did.
So I dared her back.
We ended up all soggy and dirty.
That was all her fault.
Not mine.

When we tried to steal the biscuits -
That was a disaster.
When we finally got them off the shelf
We argued about who got the first one.
Mum heard and told us off.
Well. That was mainly my sister's fault.

But if we didn't quarrel, we wouldn't love each other
As much as we do.
We can't live with each other
But we can't live without each other.

Confusing, really.

Yasmin Rai (10)

My Little Sis

Disco balls, hearts, glitter, gloss and lots more.
A fluffy pink 'Stay out!' hanging on her bedroom door.
Short skirts, high boots that she never would lend,
For a seven-year-old she sets quite a good trend.
She is cute, kind and loving - always in need of a hug.
Screams at the sight of a big scary bug.
She's my little sister and I'm proud of her too,
Because every day of her life she says, 'Annie I love you.'

Annie Fitter (10)

Dad/Mam

Dad

My favourite person is my dad
He makes me laugh when I'm sad
He looked after me when I was in nappies
Now he makes me very happy
That's my dad, he's the best.

Mam

My favourite person is my mum
She shines on me like the sun
She fed me, bathed me,
Can't you see
My mum's the best you ever did see?

Emily Perry (10)

Pebble My Pony

Pebble races like the wind
One day I'll be on her galloping over the moor
With her warm flanks underneath me
In the green field a I scrub her ears
She'll hug me with her head.
I love the feeling of her sweet grassy breath against my shoulder
We're so lucky to have each other
Pebble is the sweetest pony ever
With her dappled grey, brown and white body
And her soft velvety muzzle
Nuzzling my hand for peppermints
As we finish our daily lesson
We will always trust each other
I enjoy watching Pebble frolicking in the field
Lying in the grassy field with my Pebble
Dreaming of our future as we learn together.

Tabitha James (9)

My Favourite Person

B eing kind
R eally good
E very time he plays with me
T otally cool
T erribly great.

Kennan Thompson (7)

My Favourite Person Is Rosa

R osa is funny, laughs a lot
O ur cousin Rosa laughs because I make her
S he is a lovely girl
A lovely girl is so fun to play with, and she laughs a lot.

Freddie Playford (7)

My Favourite Person

R osie is kind
O n my team she always plays
S he is very funny
I ce cream is Rosie's favourite
E very day Rosie is wonderful.

Molly Johnson (7)

My Favourite Person

I still remember Clarise
My best friend
She played with me
But our friendship broke
When I had to move.

Sarah Carpio (7)

The Longest Poem I've Written In Five Minutes

She's in a rock band
The opposite of me
Even though she can't sing
She feels so free.

I love her to pieces
As much as can be
She has black hair
So why can't she see?

She plays electric guitar
She has but not two
I love to listen
To all she can do.

She gets on my nerves
But all sisters do
Please listen to me
And get in the queue.

Listen to her music
It will do you some good
Hear all the words
As much as you could.

Have you guessed
My sis is the fave
It's what we've got
So please just save!

Nicole Sarahs (12)

Mother

Mother you filled my life with colourful lights
Fairy tales and sweet dream nights
If I don't receive your kiss
All day in my lessons I will miss
Mother you get me everything I need
But also you plant loads of seeds
You always stay in my heart
And in everything you give me a part
You cook and clean for me
I feel so thankful for every morning tea
Mother you are the best
But why do you live in the west?

Aroosa Akhtar (10)

My Guardian Angel

Whenever I am troubled and I close my eyes
I call my guardian angel who I know is very wise.
She stands by my side so loving, gentle and kind.
She is completely surrounded by a soft, golden light
And she wears a long dress which is the purest of white.
When I talk to her she smiles at me
And I can feel and I can see
That she is lovingly protective of me.
Whenever I am happy or in despair
I know that she is always there.
Whether I am on the rickety bridge of life
She guides me across until she knows I am safe.
My guardian angel is so much part of my life
That she is forever with me in joy, sadness or strife.

Isabella Fernandes (10)

My New Baby Niece

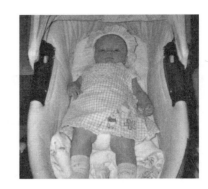

Oh what a wonderful day Friday the 13th of May
When my cute little baby niece was born.
Her name is Rianna
Her mummy's Allana
And her daddy is Andy MacKay.
She's such a tiny creature
With lovely little features
Tiny fingers, tiny toes, bright blue eyes,
And a button nose.
I love my little niece.

Laura Kelman (9)

My Monkey

Soft and snuggly
Brown and adventurous
Brave and fearless
What are we being today monkey?
An explorer or a footballer?
I love my monkey.

Mark Guise (8)

My Favourite Person, My Mum

She helps me with my homework
She has taught me right from wrong
She keeps the place clean and tidy
And sometimes bursts into song.

Chocolate is her favourite treat
She can eat a bar really quickly
After work she is sometimes tired
And dozes off very easily.

She buys me things I need
Although I get pocket money on a Friday
She enjoys her day at college
Which happens every Wednesday.

She has encouraged me to do well
And aim high at what I want to become
But the most important thing of all,
I like her because she's my mum!

Mhari Macdonald (11)

My Mum

My favourite person is my mum,
She likes to sing and likes to hum,
She's mostly happy but sometimes sad,
She's my mum and I'm so glad.

She takes me here, she takes me there,
She takes me nearly everywhere.
She listens to what I have to say
About the things I've done that day.

My favourite person is my mum,
She likes to sing and likes to hum,
She loves me even when I'm bad,
She's the best mum and I'm so glad.

Rebecca Faulkner (11)

My Favourite People!

My favourite people are ...

Daddy because you're just like me,
And you're fantastic company,
Daddy and I go in the countryside for long strolls
Where we sometimes see newly born foals.

Mummy because we have long chats
And she was so supportive during my SATs,
She really is the best cook ever,
And she is extremely clever!

Nanny because you're practically perfect in every way,
And you're bright and cheery every day!
You make the best carrots,
And your nickname is 'Mrs Parrot!'

Grandad because you're absolutely great,
You're never a minute late!
Grandad you're interesting and busy
Always tending your busy Lizzies.

Nanny W because you give me sweets,
When we play games you never use cheats,
You're kind and never firm,
Which is what I love about you!

Emily Green (11)

My Favourite Person

My friend Ben, yes, he's the best
He would give anything that I request
He makes me happy when I feel down
But he likes to be a bit of a clown
He lets me play on his new Game Boy
And believe me, that's one cool toy.
I'd get invited to his house to play
But the only thing is, I'd want to stay
He cheers me up even when I feel sad
Even if his day has gone quite bad
We've been friends ever since primary school
Even though sometimes I've been a bit of a fool
My one request is that we will stay
The best of friends to the end of our days!

Robert Boyd (11)

My Favourite Teacher

Thank you Mr Beards for teaching me this year
I've really enjoyed your lessons, without getting a clip around the ear
You're always funny but can be strict at times
Which we all respect you for, even the children that whine
This season I really hope that Wolves go up
You never know, they may even win a silver cup
I hope you have a lovely holiday, good weather all the day,
I love being in our class, I wish I could *stay!*

Elise Hart-O'Hagan (8)

Mum

Mum she's clean.
She's never mean.

She likes to shop.
She'll never stop.

Her name is Kirsty.
She's always thirsty.

She loves my dad.
She's never sad

Because she's got me
And my sister!

Ashley Bell (11)

My Grandma

My grandma has lots of grandchildren
And still she is very special to all of us
She takes us places, gives us treats
Buys us presents and just makes us
Have a wonderful time with her
Wherever we may go
My grandma is very special.

Gabrielle Aitchison (11)

My Cat Katjie

My cat is so soft and fluffy
She sleeps in bed all day,
And wags her tail when she wants food,
She is a bit confused, you know,
She thinks she is a dog!

By night she scampers out the door
A hunter she becomes
Beware little creatures,
Because by the light of the moon, she stalks her prey
And once again, when daylight comes
She sleeps in bed all day
My soft and fluffy cat ...

Sarah Rattray (10)

My Favourite People

My favourite people are special to me,
In every single way.
They've loved me so much, for the whole of my life,
Each and every day.

They help me with homework and other things too.
Keeping me safe and healthy,
They want me to grow up and become something new
And also be wise and wealthy.

I think I should tell you who these people are,
Thinking of the fun days we've had,
For my favourite people in the whole world are,
My mum and my dad.

Henna Chauhan (10)

My Best Friend

H er smile lights up my day
E very day she is waiting there at school for me
A t break time we have fun and laugh together
T he school day really whizzes when she is with me
H ome time comes too quickly
E ven when we're apart, there's a bit of her in my heart
R eally good friends will never be apart.

Can you guess her name?

Kate Green (9)

My Friend Lydia

Lydia can help me when I'm sad,
Lydia doesn't often drive me mad.
We have never fallen out,
But sometimes I just wanna shout.
My friend Lydia, I've known so long,
My friend Lydia, she helps me along.
My friend Lydia never lets me down,
But once or twice has made me frown.
My friend Lydia can understand and see,
My friend Lydia just wants to be ...
  My friend.

Lucy Wordsworth (9)

My Favourite Teacher

My favourite teacher is Jacquline
She is the best teacher I have ever had
She is as sweet as honey
She is always listening to what you have to say
Her hair is ginger and her skin is white
Just like the soft, cold snow
With freckles on the skin
She is kind and caring
And is an excellent PE teacher
She will always give you a smile
And say hello!

Tejal Purohit (9)

My Best Friend

My best friend
Is very special to me,
When I laugh, when I cry,
She's always there for me.

I met her not long ago,
We've not known each other long,
But now we're especially close
And our friendship is very strong.

We fall out but we make up
We're as best as friends can be
She makes me smile, I make her laugh,
We make each other happy.

No one could replace her,
Because she is my best friend,
We're very close, she's so special to me,
We'll be friends until the very end.

Emily Haigh (12)

Peter Rabbit

I found this poem a struggle,
I had to think of my favourite person,
I like all my friends the same,
I love all my family the same,
Have several favourite authors,
No favourite sports players,
Two pets I love the same,
So I chose someone, or rather something,
That in my head is a person.
I was given him on the day I was born,
Have cherished him ever since.
He never minds being squashed in my bag,
Willing to go anywhere,
Always soft and cuddly,
This possession is my toy rabbit,
Peter Rabbit,
His familiar blue waistcoat,
And his once orange, now pink, carrot
Clutched in his tiny paws,
Make me feel safe.

Nicole Hendry (10)

My Teacher

My favourite person is my teacher,
She is really kind, go and meet her,
My favourite person is Miss Nichols,
She always gets herself in the giggles,
My favourite person is very kind,
A little bit crazy, but has an open mind,
My favourite person makes me smile,
It never takes an hour, it never takes a while,
My favourite person likes to talk,
She would rather run than go for a walk,
My favourite person likes to sing songs,
She would carry on if she could, all day long,
My favourite person has those looks,
That make you wonder, what's next in the book!

Ella Williams (11)

Grandad

My grandad is very loving,
Makes me laugh all the time,
I'm glad that he is my grandad,
He's mine, mine, mine!

When I go to visit him,
We play with his walking sticks,
He sits me on his lap and tickles me,
And he's always showing me clever card tricks!

I don't see him very often,
As he lives a long way away,
So when I do get to see and visit him,
I make it a very special day!

When I walk down the stony path,
And up to his plain, white door,
He opens it with a smile and arms out wide,
And I hug him, till my arms are sore!

Jasmine Bradbury (11)

My Favourite Person: Grandad

Loves to tend his garden
Loves my nana's cake
As clever as a wise man
You should see what he can make.

Rings the church bells on Sunday
Twice more during the week
Mends the ropes when broken
Which keeps the ringing sleek.

He loves the cat called Sheba
He feeds the tortoise called Fred,
He used to keep a number of goats
In the back garden shed.

He reads the Sunday paper
When he isn't reading a book
He loves to read Harry Potter
And I like to take a look.

He loves his bar of fruit and nut
And the occasional oatcake too,
He likes his Sunday dinner of
Roast potatoes and Yorkshire too!

Kate Harwood (10)

Lily Is Number One!

I met Lily when she was one
It was obvious we were going to have fun
She took away my dummy and blanket when she was two
But she got told off by her mum, Sue!

We used to live closer but now I have moved,
I was determined to keep in touch, with this cool dude,
We meet up for fab days out
We laugh, we cry, we scream and shout!

I have friends at my new school,
But none of them are as cool.
She has passed the best friend test,
Lily is the very, very best!

Lois Brennan (10)

My Favourite Pet

My favourite pet is Bart,
A hamster who loves to play.
He drinks water from a bottle,
And munches seeds every day.

He's small and soft and cute,
And has small pink paws.
He sniffs at everything in sight,
And scratches with his claws.

Sometimes he bites my fingers,
And sometimes he makes them bleed.
That's a sort of sign,
That he's ready for a feed.

I love Bart very much
And hope he never dies,
Because if he ever did,
I would have big tears in my eyes.

Heather Bradbury (9)

My Favourite Person

My favourite person is cute but bold
My favourite person is six months old
My favourite person laughs and giggles
My favourite person can't walk, she wriggles
My favourite person has just discovered her toes
Her fingers, her thumbs, and her nose
My favourite person has a smiley face
If I were to grade her, she would be ace
My favourite person is special to me ...
　　She is my sister, *Emily!*

Danielle Green (12)

My Best Friend Charlotte

My best friend Charlotte always made me laugh
We always followed the same path
When we played hide-and-seek we used to peek
When we played with each other's toys,
We played catch the boys
Charlotte had apple-blonde hair
And freckles on her face.

Amber-Louise Diskin (8)

My Favourite Friend

She shares,
She's kind,
That's my favourite friend.

We hang out at school,
We wait for each other,
Yes, my favourite friend.

She likes me, I like her,
She gives things to me,
My favourite friend.

We do a lot together,
We're in the same class,
Me and my favourite friend.

Michelle Ngwenya (9)

My Favourite Person

My favourite person is as quiet as a mouse
But when you get to know her ...
She is the loudest in the house.

She is only four foot three
But she can always outrun me
She can jump the highest in the school
I think she is really cool.

She is kind and thoughtful
And makes me laugh a lot
Becase she is so silly,
That is why she is my favourite person
My best friend, Milly.

Amelia Pickles (11)

My Baby Brother Harvey!

My baby brother Harvey is a bundle of joy
In a number of different ways,
His eyes are as blue as a summer's day sky,
His nose is as dinky as a button,
His smile is as loving as a big, snuggly bear,
His hair is like strands of freshly cooked spaghetti,
When I touch his skin, it feels as smooth as silk
His legs are so skinny, they look like a pair of matchsticks,
His laugh makes my heart beat to the rhythm
Of his happiness rushing through my body,
When he looks at me, I get a warm, glowing feeling in my heart,
My baby brother Harvey is a bundle of joy
In a number of different ways!

Lucy Oldfield (11)

I'm Glad

I'm glad to have a dad like mine,
He's loving and kind
He's motorbike mad
He cheers me up when I'm sad,
When I see him it makes me smile
I love him loads
My mum and dad have filled my life with love,
He's made me what I am now and that's why
I'm glad to have a dad like mine.

I'm proud to have a dad like mine
He's caring and cool
He's the best too
There are only a few,
Like my dad,
Actually there's only one of him
And he's mine!
And that's something to be proud of and I am
Proud to have a dad like mine, but
Also lucky to have a dad as great as mine.

Charlotte Mills (9)

Lily-Dot

Cute and cuddly
Bright eyes wide
Loves adventures
All the time.

You can blow
On her tummy
And ticket it too.

That's no cat
That you
Already knew.

Louise Raper (10)

My Best Friend

I always dreamt of a best friend
A best friend I'd look after and tend
And then she came my way.

We went and visited her
And decided she was the one
I could see it was gonna be fun!

Soon she was there
All I could do was stare
And our adventures
Have always gone on!

I love my little doggy,
Even when she's soggy
Can you see my dream has come true?

I hope I won't be parted from my bundle of fun,
My little treasure sent from the sun.

Claire Scott (9)

Wayne Rooney

Wayne Rooney is the best yes!
He scores goals for England for Man U,
He scores them for me and for you
He scores an excellent goal then passes it to Andy Cole
And his shot hits the pole.
When it's the big day he shouts out *hooray*!
Then has another good footie day.
So listen to me this is how it's going to be,
Wayne Rooney is the best, yes, so don't mess with him or with me.

Megan Davies (10)

My Rabbit And I

I could tell her everything
My secrets and mistakes
She listened and understood
She was one of my mates

When I walked out the door for school
I knew she was at home
Waiting for me to get back
I'll never be alone!

My friends thought I was weird
I didn't really care
She was my friend and is always there!

I never wanted her to leave
She always was at home
But when she did die
I was alone.

I still talk to her
She is always there
I tell her my feelings
And she will always care.

Siân Green (11)

My Sister

She's pretty
She's bright
Sometimes we fight

She's slim
She's blonde
And of her I am fond

She's kind
She's funny
She's my special sister.

Andrew Davies (8)

Me And My Mum

Me and my mum went shopping
We went to Lidl's one day
And then we went to Farm Foods
Which wasn't too far away
I like going with my mum
Sometimes she treats me nice
She will go into the sweet store
To spend a little more
Me and my mum.

Carrisa Eddelston (10)

Super Dad

My dad's real name is Super Dad!
He runs around being super mad.
He's always crazy, and he sings funny rhymes,
All the memories I have of him are all funny times.
He tickles me until I die of laughter,
Every day he gets dafter and dafter!
He tells me stories, then writes them down,
He prances in my room and pretends he's a clown!
He plays football with me in the backyard,
So when I'm happy, I'll make him a special card.
He plays games with me, and I always win,
Then after we've finished,
You can see his stupid grin!
He makes me tidy up,
As a tiresome chore,
But he's the one that leaves his smelly socks on the floor!

Abigail Harrison-Henshall (10)

My Pony Flash

My pet pony Flash is
Quite greedy but inside
He's cheeky
He troops around
The field, showing
Off to my friends!
He swings his tail
Like a swinging monkey!
His skin is softer than a feather!
His eyes are big and bold
Like a big ball!
And that is
The end of my poem about my
Pony, Flash!

Mehrnoosh Maddah (9)

Faye

F riendly Faye always plays with me
A lways is kind and generous
Y et loving and caring
E specially when I feel sad.

Keeleigh Goldring (9)

Christmas Surprise

Sam is my pet dog,
We got him for Christmas
I'd wanted one for ages,
But Mum just said *'No!'*
But still each Christmas I'd wait to see what I got,
Each Christmas that I didn't get one, I'd moan a lot,
Then one Christmas my mum must have given in,
We went to the kennels to see what they had in,
A cute puppy spaniel with big soppy eyes,
That even my mum can't resist when he cries,
But ... I've got to admit that it's hard to deny
That it's got to be his long droopy ears that are
What makes him the best
   Christmas Surprise!

Katie Goodwin (10)

It Is, Lenny Henry

It is a field of blue, full of floating sheep that move,
Sometimes there are no sheep.
I speak of the sky and the clouds.
It is an ocean of green, full of multicoloured fish that stay stationary.
When winter arrives the fish disappear.
I speak of a field and flowers.
It is a sky of blue, the clouds are multicoloured,
The clouds live there all the time, but they need protecting.
I speak of an ocean and fish.
It is brilliant, the sound continues through all of mankind,
It is always there, it blocks out sadness.
I speak of laughter.
He is my idol, the one who creates laughter, my hero.
His impressions are fantastic,
I speak of Lenny Henry, a comedy genius,
He is the famous person I look up to.

Libby McCollom (11)

My Mum

My mum is kind and caring
And she is always sharing
I may get on her nerves sometimes
But I will always love her no matter what
She loves me and I love her
And that will never change.
She gave birth to me
She made me, she created me,
And I will always appreciate that.
No matter what I do or say,
I'd be lost without my mum.
She makes my tea,
And finds the remote control.
I don't have a boyfriend
But who would need one
When I have my number one mum?

Danielle Rainer (10)

My Best Friend

My favourite person has to be
The wonderful, magnificent Kate

She watches the best runner, me!
But her favourite person is Miss B

She's my best ever friend
The best thing is her trend

She has beautiful blonde hair
Also her great big blue stare.

Jessica Lacey (8)

Danny Jones (McFly)

Danny may be in a band
But he's still so sweet
He may be working all the time
But he doesn't miss a beat

The band he is in
McFly is the name
He does all he can
And he is still the same

He's a right laugh
He can make you smile
He jokes all the time
You couldn't wait a while.

This is my favourite person
This is why it's about his life
He's the best in the world
And he still hasn't got a wife.

Shannon Adams (11)

My Dog Monty

Monty is not just a dog
I don't treat him like a frog

He's like a best friend to me
With Monty - that's where I want to be

Even though Monty is at my nan's
I still go and see Monty when I can

But still I'll never give away
My lovely dog Monty.

Jessica Hawthorn (11)

Choices, Choices, Choices

My favourite person, who could it be?
Any relative like my auntie?

My mum's very nice,
Like sugar and spice,
I wonder, who can it be?

My favourite person, I wonder who?
Of course my dad, he's very nice too.

And my sisters all three
Are also kind to me,
I wonder who it can be?

My favourite person, I think I now,
She's lovely and really gentle somehow.

So careful she is,
And nowhere near tall,
I wonder who it can be?

Of course it's Nanny!

Shaylea Merrick (11)

My Brother George

My brother George is my favourite person
He is funny and silly like a monkey
He is as good at golf as Tiger Woods
He cheats like a cheetah
He can run as fast as a leopard
He eats like a pig
He sleeps as long as a tortoise.

He is the best brother in the world!

Keith Ragon (8)

My Favourite Person

I love my mum's hug
She makes me as snug as a bug in a rug
My mum is a special lady
She hugs me every day
Sometimes when I'm naughty
She still lets me out to play
Her hair is fair and beautiful
She has sparkling eyes
And when I've been especially good
She buys me a nice surprise
I love my mum so dear
And I know she loves me too
Me and my sister Shannon
Mean the world to you.

Jordanne Wozencroft (8)

My Favourite Person

My mum is my favourite person
I don't know what I would do without her.
She cooks and cleans,
Makes the house sparkle and gleam
She'll feed the sheep,
Keep me upon my feet,
She washes the sheets inside out,
Because she's the best mum ever without any doubt.

My mum is my favourite person
I don't know what I would do without her.
She waters the plants,
Picks me up from dance
In the morning she'll do up my hair
She might even play a few truths and dare,
She's really clever,
Because she's the best mum ever!

Charlotte Knowles (10)

My Favourite Person Is ...

Sir Alex Ferguson
He's the man,
I've got to like him
I'm a United fan.

When I see him
Shout at the others;
And they co-operate
Just like brothers.

It puts a smile
On my face
To see United
In first place.

It's all the work
Of my favourite person,
The one, the only,
Sir Alex Ferguson.

James Turner (11)

My Mum And Dad

My mum is the best
But she's a real pest
She is a grown up
And she does stitching up
She does lots of typing
But she would not do hiking.

My dad is mad
And he's very bad
He has a new job
His boss is called Bob
He drinks a lot of beer
But his head is not in gear.

Victoria Davison (9)

My Little Sister Hollie

My little sister Hollie messes up my stuff,
I go to my mum and she says it's too late - its tough.

My little sister Hollie smacks me on the face
And when I chase after her she thinks it's just a race.

My little sister Hollie likes to pull my hair
And when I scream she just doesn't care.

My little sister Hollie chucks my shoes in the bath
And when I shout at her all she does is laugh.

My little sister likes to wave goodbye,
But when I go to school all she does is cry.

My little sister Hollie is naughty still
But I love her and always will.

Lorna Dalziel (10)

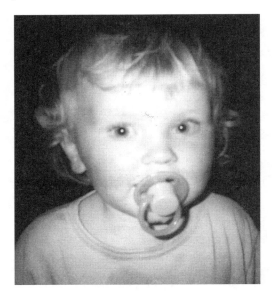

My Great Friend

I like the person because he always plays with me,
He is nice and always friendly,
He's got a brother and curly hair,
When I'm lonely he is always there
I can run fast but I never leave him behind,
Because he's my best friend and always kind
When he's around and never bored
Together we create great games, of this I am sure
He never hurts my feelings, and when I am down
He makes me happy and acts like a clown
He's good at his work, and never bad at school,
He is the number one best friend
And he is *super cool!*

Omeiza Haruna (7)

Steven Gerrard

Steven Gerrard is my favourite person,
He is captain of my favourite team,
And when that team is feeling sad,
His presence is like a shining beam.

Liverpool is the team he leads,
Every day closer and closer to victory he proceeds,
He gives you hope where there is none,
And treats every boy like the boy's his son.

Steven Gerrard is the man,
Leading Liverpool further as much as he can.

Adeiza Haruna (10)

Dolphins

How gracefully they jump
And how alive they splash
How high they leap
And how low they dive
These lovely creatures
So proud with pride
They're three metres tall
And sneakily they hide.

Larissa Dempsey (8)

Yeah That's My Grandad

He's a funny person that I can always turn to
His vests are always clean like new,
He'd never support a football team that's blue
But whatever he says is always true

   Yeah, that's my grandad.

Whatever he planted always grew
And he'd use the herbs in Sunday stew,
Then he'd sit and have a chat with you
And maybe play a game or two,

   Yeah, that's my grandad.

Charlotte Craig (9)

My Favourite Person

My mum is brill,
She is as active as a drill.
My mum is cool,
She likes playing pool.
My mum is fun,
She is as nice as a cherry bun.
My mum is kind
And will always find a kindness within her.
My mum is amazing,
She always has that little 'zing'.
My mum is my favourite person.

Cameron Gardner (10)

Gold Winner

She won a gold medal in 2004
The race was stunning - too hard to ignore
Britain was on edge as she ran the race
The drum was thudding and the 'ding' of the base
The first lap of 400 metres had finished - we're on the last
Then that lap went really fast
Then the last straight went really slow
We weren't gonna win, we know
Then she started to speed up
Kelly Holmes got to the front in time
Then she crossed the finish line.

Amy Hawthorne (9)

My Best Friend Ele

My best friend Ele
Likes to watch the telly.

My friend Ele is cool
And likes to swim in the swimming pool.

My friend Ele always makes a cake
My friend Ele likes ice cream with flakes.

And best of all my friend Ele is the best friend ever
Who also happens to be very clever.

Isabelle Lee (8)

The Person I Like The Most

The person I like the most
Is someone who does not boast

The person I like the most
Is someone who tells jokes.

Her favourite hobbies are
Watching racing cars.

Her favourite hobbies are
Looking at sparkling stars.

Amy Warner (9)

My Favourite People ...

My favourite people are my friends at school,
One thing I know is they are really cool.
Whenever I am down with problems on my mind,
They are always there and are always kind.

When the school bell rings and it's time to go
It's now the half term and we shout 'Cheerio!'
But we know we'll see each other tomorrow again,
Walking round the shops at half-past ten!

Lorna Shufflebotham (11)

My Mum

My mum gives me sweets
My mum gives me treats
My mum gives me toys
But best of all my mum gives me love.

My mum gives me bikes
My mum gives me cars
My mum gives me pens
But best of all my mum gives me love.

My mum gives me footballs
My mum gives me swings
My mum gives me games
But best of all my mum gives me love.

Daniel Morris (8)

My Brother

My brother is Jamie Lynch
He likes the grumpy Grinch
His favourite food is rice
But does not like a lot of spice

Every day Jamie likes to play
But then he would probably say
Can we please go to the park?
I don't want to play in the dark

He is five years old
So he is not growing bald
Everyone thinks he is cute
But I think he is a brute

When my brother cries
I have to say my goodbyes
Because I don't want trouble
I have to run at the double.

In the end I like my brother
And I also like my mother
I think we make a good pair
And then after we go to the fair.

Matthew Lynch (11)

My Aunty Lou

My aunty Lou is the best
She makes me feel blessed.
My aunty Lou is as silly as a clown
She cheers me up when I'm feeling down.
My aunty Lou is oh so funny
She makes the world so bright and sunny.
My aunty Lou loves everything shiny and pink,
Even if it was a kitchen sink.
My aunty Lou plays the piano really well
She's had lots of practise you can tell.
When she passes her driving test, she'll buy a pink car
She'll take me on trips, near and far.
My aunty Lou makes me smile,
I love it when she stays a while.
My aunty Lou is the best
She makes me feel blessed.

Grace Broome (9)

My Grandad

My grandad is so special
He takes me on his walks
And even to the sea
He takes good care of me
We feed the birds
And water the plants
My grandad means the world to me.
He is fun
I love him.

James Clare (9)

If I Didn't Have A Sister

If I didn't have a sister,
I really would miss her,
She's awfully clever
And makes sun shine in any weather.

She's kind in every way
Although we argue every day,
She looks out for everyone
And is second to none.

Cos I'm three minutes older,
I've always told her,
That I'm the boss
Though she gets cross.

She's my twin
And she makes me grin
And she's always going to be
Number one to me.

She's the best sister
By a huge amount
I love her so much
I want to shout.

I love my sister,
She's the best,
That's all the good things
So I'll leave the rest!

Chloe Wells (9)

Me And My Grandma

Grandma looked after me every day
And treated me special in every way.
I really miss her lovely smile
And because she always waited for me a while.
Grandma taught us how to bake a cake
And was always there to lend a hand.
Now she has gone to Heaven to watch over us
And guide us through each and every day.
I really miss her lovely drawings that caught my eye
On Sunday mornings.

   My wonderful grandma.

Rebecca Reynolds (9)

My Friend's Life

My life has been a beautiful day
From my best friend Bethany.
So what I am going to do is give her a present
Because she is beautiful.

Jasmine Butt (5)

My Old Hamster

I had a hamster just last year
She had a cut in her ear
She was only young
And smelt of hamster dung

My hamster went on the wheel
And spat out a load of home meal
It almost glowed in the night
What a disgusting sight.

Katie Handley (9)

Belle

My best friend is soft and fluffy,
She's very tidy and not at all scruffy,
With floppy ears and a cold wet nose,
She has a wiggly-waggly tail and scratchy toes,
She has many different habits,
She chases birds and also rabbits,
There's so many more things I could tell,
But most of all ...
I love my dog Belle.

Alexander Warren (10)

My Mum

She makes me laugh
She makes me smile
She knows me like a fact file.

She knows my age,
She knows my name,
To her my life is not a game.

So as I've seen over the years
She has patched up all my rips and tears.

My mum's always having a cup of tea
But still, she really cares for me.

Ruth Muleya (10)

My Funny Family!

My grandma May has got a brain like a sieve,
She forgets where things live in her bedroom.
She has perfume in the bed, bedclothes hanging out of the window,
And slippers on the bedside table.

My brother Jack has got tricks up his sleeve.
He's got creepy things, spiders and bugs to make you heave.
He once flicked a baked bean which fell on Grandpa's head,
Poor old Grandpa didn't know until he went to bed.

And finally,
My cousin Elizabeth has got ears like cauliflowers,
She listens to the neighbours chat for hours and hours.
She can hear an ant whistling from miles and miles away,
And butterflies beat their tiny wings and little woodlice snore.

Anna-Marie Hart (9)

Big Brother Daniel

He makes me laugh all the time
And he makes me cry.
But on the trampoline he bounces me high.

I know he must like me
As he makes me cups of tea
But I don't like him when he hits me.

But now he's seventeen and much older
He hardly sleeps over.
He likes mini moto's and going fast
When he's on his motorbike he waves when he goes past.

He lives with his dad in his house
But he doesn't have a mouse!

Ben Sharp (9)

My Cousin Who's The Best

My cousin is normally rough
But I don't care.
He likes motorbikes
He likes plants
But the best thing about him
Is the fact he likes me.
He cares for me
He may only be fifteen
But he still cares for me.
I'm so lucky to have a cousin like him.
He has a motorbike,
He only uses it when he goes out with his friends
But if he doesn't need to he'll play with me.
I love my cousin and he loves me,
He's always been my best cousin in the world.
He couldn't get any better I tell you
He gives me rides on his quad bike and motorbike.
I wish he could be here right now
He used to have braces and be mean,
But when he lost those braces
He was the nicest person,
I had ever seen.

Carter Scott (8)

Good Old Harry

Harry was a good pet,
From the first day we met.
He was a scruff ball,
But nobody's fool.
He liked dandelion leaves,
And climbing up people's sleeves.
One day we had to move,
It was a better place we had to prove
In the next part of his life,
We managed to find him a wife.
When the children came,
We had the dilemma to think of a name.
They were called Rainbow, Susy and James,
My good pet Harry always liked to play games,
Fun, laughter and amusement, is what he gave,
Now he's in his grassy grave.

Good old Harry.

William Young (11)

My Rabbit Robbie

My rabbit is a ...
Sharp, painful nipper,
A warm, wet licker,
A silent, peaceful sleeper,
A constant, mad eater,
A deep, razor scratcher,
A high, jolly jumper,
But most of all, my rabbit is
A warm, cosy fluff ball.

Kathryn Everington (9)

The King Is Gone

The King is gone
The King is gone, long live his name.
Although apart from all
His fame his life was just a game.
August the 16th 1977,
He left this Earth and went to Heaven.
God knew that he needed rest
As He always takes the very best.
Because he had to say goodbye,
Elvis is now a star up in the sky.

Stephanie Fitzgerald (11)

My Brother William

My brother William is nice
And he likes rice
But sometimes we fight
But most of all
We play at night.

Joshua Begent (8)

Nico

He is my best friend
We play together
Short hair
Skinny belly
Nice boy.

Jack Bruhin (7)

Best Friend

He makes me laugh
Being such a fool
He's not really
He is cool!

We play football and ride our bike
These are the things we really like.

Trampoline bouncing is really fun
Backflips and somersaults
Have got to be done.

A game on the PlayStation
A game of pool
That's enough for one day
My best friend the fool ... !

Max Sharp (10)

Harpreet

Harpreet, Harpreet - furry like a peach
Her hair smells like coconut
Eyes like chocolate.

Chelsea Bell (7)

Jack

His eyes are nice
Better than spice
He smiles like a heart
Funnier than his tummy
We play together each day
We have lots of toys
But we both like lots of boys
We have lots of joy
He is my brother!

Freya Bruhin (7)

Manon

Manon! Manon! You are so mad
You have a go when I am bad.

You are my auntie
That's why I am proud
To be your nephew.

You look like Nanny
And have small ears.

You smell magnificent.

Alfie Barker (11)

My Sister Sadie

S adie is my sister
A nd no one is sweeter
D on't know what I would do without her
I s more lovely than anyone else
E yes as green as the sea.

Sherrilee Kenward (10)

Super Duper Dad!

My dad, he's really funny,
He gives me loads of money.

So he gives me bags of dosh
But he doesn't regularly have a wash.

He loves Shredded Wheat
Definitely not outdated meat.

He's got piles of paperwork but they're really neat,
But if I must say he's got cheesy feet.

Ha, ha, ha, ha.

But if I must say you are super duper Dad.

    Love you
      Dad
        Forever
          Your daughter
            Nadia
              Shazadi
                Xxx.

Nadia Shazadi (13)

My Best Friend

My best friend is sweet,
My best friend is nice,
She's called Hannah
And she doesn't like rice.
She always plays with me,
I'm even in her class,
The teacher never splits us up,
Well only in maths.
She's full of fun and laughter,
She's got a big, big pool,
She comes over most weekends
And I think that's cool!
I like her and she likes me,
We're like a happy family,
It's like she's my sister,
A sister of a kind,
But if she was my sister,
She'd have a different best friend.

What do you think?

Emily Baxter (9)

Our Fishy Friends

Fish can live in a tank,
Fish can live in the sea,
Or sometimes battered on a plate,
All for your tea.

My fish don't live in the garden,
Or live in the sea,
My fish live in a tank,
There for you and me.

We have two wonderful fish,
And look after them day by day,
They must miss their friends and family,
Who live down by the bay.

Christopher Hunt (11)

My Mum

M y mum is very kind, if
Y ou want a hug go to my mum.

M iss her if she goes away
U nder the sheets I cry
M aybe she will too, nearby.

I love my mum more than anything
S he's funny, no one could replace her.

G reat to have her as my mum
R unning around after me
E verybody likes her
A loving parent
T hat is what she is.

Johanna Mason (11)

My Favourite Person

My first is in Grandad but not in Mum
My second is in Carr but not in Mylonas,
My third is in Dad and also in Auntie,
My fourth is in Uncle and also in Ben,
My fifth is in David but not in Elaine,
My sixth is in McFly but not in Good Charlotte,
My seventh is in Girls Aloud and also in The Faders.
Who is it?
I have used the names and the surnames of my friends and family
And my favourite pop bands.

Georgina Myers (11)

David Beckham

B eckham plays for England
E ngland are the best
C helsea are the worst
K ick the ball Beckham
H e scores loads of goals
A golden trophy in his cupboard
M adrid is who he plays for now.

Georgia Main (10)

The Best Mum In The World

My mum is the best mum in the world
Her hair is a little bit curled.
She likes it when it's sunny,
At night she gets really funny.
She has friends as gay blokes,
She tells really good jokes.
She goes out and has fun,
So hey, that's my gorgeous mum,
There's nothing more to say
About the best mum in the world.

Jean-Paul Rama (8)

Grandad

Sitting in his caravan nice and cosy,
My grandad's face is red and rosy.
He's like a snow-white polar bear,
He even has the chalk-white hair.
He loves to have fish and chips,
But they always seem to go to his hips.
He is like Peter Kay, very funny,
But always loves to spend his money.
'Have I to?' he would say
In a deep broad Yorkshire accent, that's his way.
Cruising he loves, in his superstar car,
But never seems to go very far.
He always comes to support me,
And that's why the best grandad is he.

Joshua Garlick (11)

My Favourite Person

L auriece is her name
A nd it is not lame
U nder her great dance moves, she's a
R eally funny mathematician-a
I mpressions she's brilliant at,
E ach person you meet couldn't say better than that.
C lever she is and trendy as well,
E very day she activates, in her body, each single cell.

M cCluskie is her surname
C leverness I've mentioned but I can't be blamed.
C lumsy she can be and I mean it
L aying in bed until 12 midday is her worst habit
U ntil she tells what they act like I'll tell you,
S he has three dogs called Pepsi, Chilli and Blue.
K atie Ainsworth is her friend, so are Jemma and Paige,
I know that Lauriece has a pet rat in a cage.
E ach week, at least once, I think about how Lauriece and I became best friends.
   Ta-da that's the end.

India Oldfield-Cherry (10)

My Mum

Mum you are a fast horse,
You are a tasty bacon bap
A cuddly woolly jumper
And the beautiful gardens of Trebah.

Mum you are the lightest blue in the world
You are a gentle singing of a violin
A lovely red rose
  And Mum you are
    the best.

Robert Lynes (9)

A Special Someone

My mum's the best
She's always being funny
As long as she's got money.

My dad's always late
But I'll know he'll be my mate.

My stepdad's the best
He's above all the rest.

My brothers and sister
They're all the same
They're nothing but a bunch of pains.

My nan is grand
I'm her biggest fan.

My grandad's tops
Guess what?
He always pops!

Hey there's someone missing

  That's me!

Amy Allen (8)

Billie

I love my budgie Billy.
Hi I'm ten years old and I'm called Lilli.
We gave my budgie a nickname, Babie Nin.
We keep her seeds in her own little tin.
Her feathers are yellow and green
She's the most beautiful bird I've ever seen.
She barks and sings all day long
She even barks when EastEnders is on.
She often goes on her little swing
Or got her head tucked under her wing.
On her cuttlefish she scrapes her beak
I wish I could teach her how to speak.
She's my little budgie, Billy
I love her, she's Babie Ninny.

Lilli Green (10)

Turtle On The Beach

The turtle crawls slowly on the rippled sand, turquoise and cream,
Like a crispy green leaf, floating gently to the ground.
Like a green current blending in with the blue ocean.
Like a coconut cracking and spreading out its white creamy milk.
Like a Granny Smith apple rolling out of the fruit bowl,
Turtle as slow and gentle as a butterfly.

Emily Stock (9)

My Favourite Friend

Out of my friends, my teacher, my aunt,
My dad, my nan, my mother,
My grandad, my cousins, my neighbours,
My sister or my brother.

From all of these people I had to choose one,
Difficult for me to decide.
But finally I made my choice,
For he's always by my side.

My friends think it's silly,
My friends think it's weird,
They may have teased behind my back,
Laughed, joked and jeered.

But I know deep inside my heart,
He will always be my friend.
He's been with me forever,
And will be there to the end.

His head now tilts to one side,
His skin the colour of frost.
His fluffy fur has faded,
And his hat and scarf are lost.

But however he appears,
He always makes me smile,
I always go and hug him,
And stay with him a while.

My favourite friend who I've described,
For whom I really care,
My best buddy in the world is ...
My special teddy bear.

Thomas Loe (10)

109

My Father's Workshop

In my memories of my father's workshop
Is clear to me and always will be.
I can still see the horseshoe on the door
And me playing with the sawdust on the floor.
It was painted blue and then green
And now it is brown and it's still standing on the ground.

Caoimhe McClean (11)

Ian Thorpe

I   ntergalactic, swims fantastic
A   nd a world champion too
N   o one can catch up to you.

T   horpe is my last name and swimming's my game.
H   ave you guessed who I am?
O   nly my supporters probably can.
R   ound and round I go and when I retire nobody knows.
P   odium here, I come to get, gold, silver, bronze, I
E   nd my career with my medals round my neck
      Just like when I became world champion in Sydney 2000.

      You now know who I am, I'm Ian Thorpe.

Alice Pearson (10)

I Love My Mummy

My mummy has a big bummy
But I love my mummy
She has a little tummy
That's why I love my mummy
I hate my mummy's bummy
But I love her tummy
I love my lovely mummy
Even if I don't love her bummy.

Fay Oxby (9)

My Sister

Sometimes people's sisters can be boring,
Weird or dumb,
But my sister is loads of fun.
She is very funny, she's funny it is true
She puts on weird voices that I could never do.
When I'm feeling down she is always around.
She makes me feel so much better
So I can be a winner.
We pick out songs for each other,
We make up a little dance,
We do the catwalk together
And then do a little prance.
She is the best sister ever,
Like none else could be.
I wish we could know each other forever
And invite her round for tea.

Jessica Potter (9)

111

Adam Stocks

My favourite person is Adam Stocks
Because he is my friend.
When people are feeling blue
He is always there with you.

He is always beside you
Even if he does not like you
He is always funny even if he likes honey
He always cheers me up even if we are at the local pub.

George Bailey (10)

Untitled

My favourite person is my dad,
My dad tastes like love.
My dad smells like ginger.
I feel responsible if anything happened to him.
My dad feels like soft beds!
My dad looks like ten thousand handsome men.
My dad sounds like something cute.

Alexander Jack Carter (10)

Little Rani

L ittle Rani, oh so cute,
I cky, sticky bibs on,
T ouching everything she sees,
T ired head and wobbling knees,
L aying down her sleepy head,
E eking every word she said.

R aking up the garden leaves
A ching chest with Grandma's weaves
N appy changed to go to bed
I nnocent sleepyhead.

Cara Vaitilingam (7)

The Best Mum Ever!

My mum has eyes of brown
That twinkle in the day
She helps me with my homework
And I help with the housework.
Even when she is ill in bed
She still cuddles me a lot.
Every day we walk the dog
And talk about our day
Or something like that.

She really is my favourite person
For all the things she does
My favourite time with my mum is
When we go to the beach
Every night in the summer.

Holly Thorne (11)

Coldness To Warmth

There you were alone in the cold
Under the JCB, shivering and quivering in the snow.
Being eaten away by the hunger in your stomach
What a waste of a dog of four months old.

You were abandoned and left to die
By owners so mean and dry.
Your fur was matted with dirt
In your eyes all you could see was hurt.

As I walked by, you caught my eye,
The closer I got, the smell of my food drove you out,
It was like love at first sight.

Now four months on, you're mine,
You bark with joy instead of pine.
We named you Jess and some days I wish
You hadn't made all that mess!

Ashlee Matthews (11)

Just One Person

You ask me to name
My favourite person,
But how can I
When so many jostle
For space in my heart?
A naval hero, shining in glory;
A handsome poet, his words crafted with love;
A young actor, resplendent with talent;
My mother, special beyond words -
These and many more,
All unique,
Struggling for dominion
As
My favourite person.

Charlotte Meredith (15)

My Favourite Person

My brother Jordan
There is no other
Like my brother.
When he says things
He makes me laugh
When he's bad
He makes me mad
When he smiles
He makes me giggle
In his mouth he has
No teeth in the middle
There is no other
Like my brother Jordan.

Elisha Wharmsby (11)

My Grandad

My grandad was funny
He used to catch bunnies
He liked telling me stories
What used to cheer me up
He helped me with my homework
Thank you very much!
And that's the grandad who I lost
And loved so much.

Jade Brooke (10)

My Dog Ben

I have a dog called Ben,
He's better than a hen.

His name is really cool,
I want to take him to school.

He runs and fetches sticks
He can do lots of tricks.

He is a well-trained sheepdog,
And he is not as lazy as a log.

He has quite a lot of hair,
And I want to take him everywhere.

John Hatherley (10)

Memories Of My Grandad

He was around most of my life,
And all those days were good.
He worked and worked and worked all day,
But he never understood.

That working all that much
Would definitely wear him out,
And it just so happened that one day,
I heard my mother shout.

Not from joy or harmony
It was misery and doubt
Everyone was in despair
We could not work it out.

How could such a kind man just lose his life
Who never had done wrong?
My family just sat around saying,
We have to try and carry on.

Joshua Buckingham (11)

My Family

I love my kin they make me grin
I know I have their love within.

I love my mum, I love my dad,
They make me smile, they make me glad.

I love my sisters, they are so kind
They're the best in the world you will find.

I love my kin they make me grin,
Their love I know I have within.

Chike Oforka (9)

My Pet Lamb, Daffodil

Daffodil was born in spring,
She was the cutest little thing,
I fed her with milk.
Until she felt like silk
Now she has grown up,
The bottles of milk must stop.
I know she misses her mum
But she knows I'm her special chum,
When I call from the gate
She races to me, her mate.

I love Daffodil; Daffodil loves me!

Clarissa Cullinan (7)

My Baby Bro

C illian was born in Derry,
I think he is really cheerful and merry,
L ively, he can climb up his cot,
L ittle troublemaker crawls a lot!
I f you tickle his ribs he will laugh,
A nd he soaks the bathroom if he has a bath
N ow you've heard the highs and lows
of Cillian, isn't he just one in a million?

Ciara Cullinan (10)

Spencer Bear

My favourite person is Spencer
I like to have him there,
And you may think it odd,
But he's a nice, plump teddy bear!

His real name's Spencer Bear, of course,
But that's too long and wordy,
He's usually quite sensible,
Though he can act absurdly.

Spencer, he can be quite careless,
And often loses his map,
And as you can probably guess
It usually ends in mishap!

But he's done some really quite good things,
He once made a hot air balloon,
And now I believe that he's making
A rocket to go to the moon!

His favourite food is 'hunny'
And something I didn't say,
In the corner of my kitchen,
Is a magical doorway!

Only the toys can see it,
And its magical country inside,
But that's where a cat and two run-around dogs
He and a panda will hide!

Gabrielle Bianco (9)

Penny Is My Favourite Lamb

P enny is my favourite lamb,
E specially when she finds a scam,
N ever naughty or any trouble,
N ot quiet but full of bubble,
Y is my favourite lamb.

Eleanor Braithwaite (10)

McFly

McFly are great
The best to this date,
Their music is brill,
A perfect skill!

I buy TOTP mag at the stall
I stick their pics on my bedroom wall.
When I hear their songs,
I sing along.

So the McFly guys are a fab four,
I don't think you could ask for anything more!

Angelica Cullinan (10)

Reggie The Rat

My favourite person is Reggie the rat
He is cute and fluffy and very fat
I've had him a year - he's almost one
I never knew a rat could be so much fun
He eats a lot of food - sweetcorn is his best
But he's not all that fussy, cos he eats all the rest.
He is grey and white with a long pink tail
And he's pleased to see me without fail
He's intelligent and clever
And my best friend forever.

Freddie Cooper (8)

Day Tripper

(Inspired by The Beatles)

Yesterday I caught a train
That took me down to Penny Lane
A friendly fireman caught my eye,
He waved and smiled as I passed by.

I lay on the grass in strawberry fields
You know the place where nothing is real!
I gazed at the sky, was it diamonds I saw?
Lovely Alice, asleep on the floor!

Tangerine trees danced in the haze
Cellophane flowers waved in the breeze
Bent-back tulips swayed to the beat
Taking in their strength from the summer heat.

In fields of fragrant strawberries
Or under the coral seas
Visiting all these whereabouts
Is my favourite place to be!

Alice Barron (11)

My Favourite Person

Whether on the crusades
Or a pirate's mate
Playing the hero
Or a featherweight.

Just one look at his face sends my heart into space
He is so divine
I wish one day he could be mine!

Orlando Bloom
He makes me swoon!

Lily Aston (11)

Mum!

Mum, when I look at you,
I think that you are a real athlete.
You can swim, run, jump and throw,
All at the age of thirty-nine!

Mum, when I look at you,
I think you are a professional chef.
You can cook spicy chicken, chocolate pudding,
Sizzling sausages, and other delicious dishes.
All at the age of forty!

Mum, when I look at you,
I think you are a fabulous knitter.
You can knit hats and socks
And dresses and skirts
All at the age of forty-one!

Mum, when I look at you,
You are a talented author.
You can write fairy tales and fantasy stories,
Historical articles and poems,
All at the age of forty-two.

Mum, when I look at you,
I seem to see a glowing star.
It twinkles and glitters and sparkles and gleams,
For it knows that you take the first position in my heart ...

Sinthu Sridharran (10)

Hector

H ector is my cat
E xtremely lazy and fat
C ute and cuddly pet
T hat cat is asleep I bet
O h how soft is his fur
R eally loud is his purr.

Hector is my cat
He lies all day on his mat
I tickle his belly
It wobbles like jelly
Because he's so very, very fat.

Emma Foster (9)

My Favourite Person

There was a lady
Who seemed quite shady
But was the one
Who made everything fun.

Her hair's a tip
But she's thought of as hip
Her clothes are always matching
And very eye-catching.

I love this person like a friend
But she sometimes drives me round the bend.

Can you guess who this person is?
Her name's not Kim, her name's not Liz.

She's my mum and she's the best
Unlike all the rest!

Alexandra Harvey (11)

My Fave Pony, Speckles

My fave pony, Speckles,
Prances round and round,
She is very sweet,
And is grey and brown.
If you ever get to meet her,
Look at her and smile,
But if you get to ride her,
Then just think you're lucky,
And don't forget
To be proud!

Jenni Visuri (9)

My Mummy

My mummy loves honey
She might get me a little bunny
I might call my bunny sunny
My mum is sometimes funny
My mum hates chewing gum
My mum is very fun.

Lucy Wright (7)

My Favourite Person

My dog is called Jack,
He is fluffy and black.
He is a Jack Russell,
He loves all his cuddles.
He has a white patch on his eye,
He also has one on his thigh.
He is my lovely pet,
He loves it when he gets wet.
He loves to run and play,
He goes for a walk every day.
But he still gets tired and has to lay.
I hope you like this poem,
And I'll see you another day.

Coral Callaway (13)

Oh Georgia

Your tiny hands remind me of your tiny feet.
Your eyes remind me of the sea.
Your hair is so soft.
Your lips are like a rose.
Your bum is soft like singing birds.
Your ears are small like an ant.

   You're my best girl.

Ellie-Mae Matthews (10)

Friends Forever

Friends forever
Share and care
In the classroom and elsewhere
Friendship bracelets, necklaces
One with best and one with friends
And now the friendship never ends!

When one is soon into tears
The other one will strengthen their fears
And when you're best friends
You never break up
And when you're older
You'll still keep in touch!

Anna Sayers & Stephanie Killen (9)

My Teacher

A teacher is sky-blue
She is the happy springtime
In a fairy-tale cottage
She is a glowing sun, smiling and happy
A teacher is a velvet nightie,
She is a cuddly cushion
She is an adventure story
My teacher is a gooey chocolate gateaux.

Becky Duggins (10)

126

My Favourite Person

My favourite person is my mum
She really loves me all of the time
She helps me with my reading and writing storylines
She rubs my head when I am ill.
She takes me to the doctors to ask for a pill
She makes my bed
She hurries along
She sings silly, stupid songs
She does my dinner for me
She cooks me breakfast, lunch and tea
My favourite person, that's my mum,
I love her forever long.

Charlotte Gough (9)

My Best Friend

Daisy is my friend
From when we started school.
We always are together
And I think she's really cool.
We play together at playtimes
And dinner times at school
And after school on some days,
She comes swimming in my pool.
She stays around at teatime
And we all sit down to eat
Daisy is my best friend
And I think she's really neat.

Lois Byrne (8)

My Favourite Person

Since you have gone
The sun has never shone.
You're a special friend,
Our friendship will never end.
You're the best person I know
Since you've gone we've had snow.
You're like some kind of relation
Your body is always in motion
Your soft silky skin
Makes me feel thin
I love you Taz
Love from Bethany.

Bethany Smith (10)

Purrfect Pet

What's that purring noise I can hear?
It's coming from the bushes over there.
I wonder what it can be
I'll just tiptoe over and see.

It just looks like a ball of fur,
And I can hear it going purr, purr, purr,
Right now I'm feeling like such a wussy,
Wait a minute ... it's my pet cat Lucy.

Mica Sinforiani (11)

My Mum!

My mum is a star
I know she'll never go far.

She takes me to the park,
Tucks me into bed at night
If I'm afraid of the dark.

She likes to look good when going into town,
And if I'm naughty she'll just give me a frown.

She has multicoloured underwear,
I think it's over the top, she doesn't care!

She likes to read in the bath,
And we have a good laugh!

Mum!

Anya MacSorley-Pringle (8)

My Mum's Special!

My mum's special,
My mum's alright,
She's beautiful
All day and night.

My mum is so cool
But she makes me go to school!
She spoils my sissy
Who is a hippy.
My mum also spoils me
Even when I was very wee.
My mum's favourite food is Brie
But she loves me!
I love her too!

Sam Watts (10)

129

Friends Forever

A great friend
L oving and caring
I   ncredibly giggly
C an't stop talking
E xcitable

B atty
A nd wonderful
T en times better than all the rest
T he greatest friend in the world
E nergetic
N o way we'll ever break up

P ick up the phone
H aving fun
E nding a phone call is sad
L aughing all day
P retty as a picture
S taying friends forever

Alice Batten Phelps.

Georgia Duckett (11)

Friendship With My Mum

You are friendly, kind and caring,
Sensitive, loyal and understanding
Humorous, fun, secure and true
Always there ... yes that's you.

Special, accepting, exciting and wise
Truthful and helpful, with honest eyes.
Confiding, forgiving, cheerful and bright,
Yes that's you ... not one bit of spite.

You're one of a kind, different from others
Generous, charming, but not one that smothers
Optimistic, thoughtful, happy and game,
But not just another ... in a long chain.

Appreciative, warm and precious like gold,
Our friendship won't tarnish or ever grow old
You'll always be there, I know that is true,
I'll always be here ... always for you!

Nadine McNally (11)

Milly

You are eighteen weeks old
So lovely and cuddly to hold.

Your cute little smile
Makes my heart jump a mile.

In your pram you go for a walk
Soon you'll learn how to talk.

Your dresses are pink and oh so frilly
You are my baby sister, Milly.

Chloe Meiklem (11)

Cooler Than Felix

My favourite person is *not* a person but a cat,
In fact some people would say, 'Ooh fancy that.'

I love how he purrs to wake me in my bed,
I guess he's saying, 'Get up sleepyhead.'

He isn't really skinny and he isn't really fat,
I think he's just a normal middleweight cat.

He's black all over with little white toes,
So there're little pawprint splodges everywhere he goes.

I think my cat is the coolest in town,
In fact I think he deserves the coolest cat crown.

April Penman (11)

My Best Friend

She's always around when I need her,
With a huge smile and a warm cuddle,
She always makes me feel so special
Wrapped in her cosy arms,
Her face lightens up my day,
She can always make me feel safe and happy!
I must be so lucky to have a friend like her!

Emma Barrett (11)

My Friend, My Rainbow

Just like a shining pot of gold,
Have you heard the stories she has told?
Tales of warmth, of love, of fear,
Tales so special for you to hear.
I want to show that you're my best friend,
I want to be with you till the bitter end,
And there's something else you have to know,
I love you
You are my rainbow!

   My mum.

April Mullings (11)

My Brother

I have a brother called Aaron
And he is quite smart
Sometimes he could be naughty
But he is very good at art.

Sometimes he could be an angel
Helping around the house
But at times he could be a daredevil
He even tried to eat a mouse!

My brother is polite
My brother is cute
He is kind
But he doesn't like my flute.

My brother is the best
And he likes the sun
So that is the reason
I think he is fun ...

Sneha Sircar (9)

My Mum

She's loving and caring,
Generous too
Looking after me the best she can
I love her.

She takes me out shopping
Buys me new games,
Always there for me,
I love her.

She bought me a dog,
A TV for my room
Helps me with my homework
I love her.

James Royce (11)

Friends

F un that lasts forever
R emember all the good times
I nclude everyone
E xcitement when playing
N ew games to play
D oing things together
S taying friends forever
   Smiling all day long.

Laylaa Whittaker (11)

The Natalie Rap

Natalie is my best friend
She never drives me round the bend
We have loads of fun
Out in the sun
We have loads of fun
Not out in the sun.

Natalie is really kind,
She is always on my mind.

Yes we do have our ups and downs,
With tongues poking out,
And horrible frowns,
But nevertheless,
We always shake hands
And settle it with some Coca-Cola cans!

Hooray!

Hayley Taylor (10)

My Favourite Person

M y best friend is Ian
Y ou might ask me why

B ecause he often makes me laugh so much that I cry.
E very day we go out and play
S pring, summer, autumn, winter, night and day
T errible friends to the end.

F orever we will be the best of friends
R ule the world together
I nvent magical kingdoms
E ven fly above the Earth
N ever shall we leave each other
D espite getting into a lot of bother.

Micheil Russell Smith (9)

My Favourite Person

My favourite person is organised and quick
My favourite person is always my chum
My favourite person is helpful and loving
My favourite person is easily my mum!

My favourite person is cunning and clever
My favourite person is a joyful lad
My favourite person is fast and funny
My favourite person is obviously my dad!

My favourite person is cheeky and loud
My favourite person is very hard to miss
My favourite person is caring and sweet
My favourite person has got to be my sis!

My favourite person is very hard to pick
My favourite person has no time to lose
My favourite person could be anyone
My favourite person would be difficult to choose!

Baveena Heer (10)

My Mum

I love my mum so very much
And we always, always keep in touch.
I know my mum will never lie,
And she's more beautiful than a butterfly.
And if I ever get into trouble,
She'll always be there on the double.

My mum has a great personality,
Which matches her incredible beauty.
My mum is so smart,
She can make a strawberry tart,
And even when she's asleep,
She can drive a car and go 'beep beep!'

My mum's so strong,
She can even bend a prong.
When my mum embarrasses me,
I'll always still be a bit happy,
And even if she gets a bit out of hand,
I'll always still think of her as being grand.

Gavandeep Singh Nijjar (10)

My Kitten Nelson

Nelson, Nelson black and white,
There always is a big fight.

Nelson, Nelson black and white,
He wants to go out every night.

Nelson, Nelson black and white,
He doesn't like a faraway height.

That's my pet Nelson!

Isabella Fabbrini (8)

You Mean The World To Me

Nan I just want to say
To you on this sunny day
How much you mean in your own way
You mean the world to me.

You mean to me more than the stars
Even more than the planet Mars
I'd even go behind bars
You mean the world to me.

Now it is time to think
And say the truth, no wink.
I love you more than the kitchen sink
You mean the world to me.

Madeleine Hughes (10)

"You mean the world to me"

My Dog Tess

My dog Tess ...
She makes me laugh
She makes me smile
She plays with me
When I am sad
I love her to bits
My dog Tess.

Kirsty Shepherd (10)

My Favourite Person

My favourite person is my mum
She makes every day such fun,
She makes cakes that are yummy,
Which fill up my tummy,
She is my number one.

She takes me to school every day
Where I can see my friends and play,
I don't do much work,
So she goes berserk,
But I still get my own way.

Sian Powell (10)

My Sunshine

You love me
You care for me
You see me
You spend time with me.

You fed me
When I was little
You still do it,
With love and
Respect.

Now you have all
Been wondering,
Who this person is,
Well she's my mum
Who else do you think it is?

Amarpreet Thind (10)

My Great Grandad

My great grandad's like an old chair, fragile and slightly grumpy,
Like quiet time at the dead of night when everyone's asleep.
He's like a ripe banana, soft and easily bruised,
Sometimes like a cloudy day, but always looks on the bright side.
My great grandad's like a turtle, slow and can be hidden away,
A happy man, who's lived a long life and has even shed the odd tear.

Alice Norman (10)

My Best Friend

How many friends are there in this world?
But not a single one is like this girl?

Her smile is my courage
Her laugh is my strength
She's a lovely person
She's my best friend!

To cheer me up
Is her aim
My best friend is here
Anika is her name!

Gayathri Eknath (10)

My Favourite Person!

My favourite person is my friend Rebecca.

She's a very friendly and funny girl,
She has long blond, curly hair,
She has a horse called Ben, she enjoys riding Ben
It makes her chuckle when he gallops and neighs.
Rebecca has two sisters and goes to my school
We play together a lot
We go to each other's house, have tea, play and talk
My favourite person is Rebecca.

Emily Unsworth (9)

My Mum

I love the way my mum tucks me in
And cuddles me till I fall asleep.
Sometimes she falls asleep with me
She kisses me and says, 'Goodnight.'

She takes me shopping to Inverness,
To spend my pocket money.
I buy loads of clothes to wear to parties,
My mum shouts, 'Hurry up Laura!'

I love the way my mum loves and cares for me
And makes up funny jokes,
She makes me laugh,
No matter what.

I love the way my mum plays with me
We play tennis and go on the trampoline.
All kinds of stuff, I am so lucky,
To have the best mum

In the whole wide world!

Laura Macleod (10)

My Favourite Person!

My favourite person would be fun,
And won't just sit out in the sun,
They'd take me places I'd enjoy,
And wouldn't treat me like a little boy!

My favourite person would be clean,
He certainly wouldn't be mean,
He'd pick me up when I fell down,
He'd pull funny faces and look like a clown!

My favourite person would be happy,
And when I was a baby, changed my nappy,
They'd take me to the doctor's when I fell ill,
And covered me up in case I caught a chill!

My favourite person wouldn't be mad,
She would cheer me up when I felt sad,
She would fix a tap when it sprung a leak,
She would after dinner play hide-and-seek!

Daniel Johnston (9)

My Favourite Person Is My Mum!

My mum inspires me in so many ways
Her children are God's gift, that's why she prays,
Oh, yes, my favourite person is my mum
That's why to me she is my number one.

She's made of bronze, silver and gold
So answering your question, she's not that old,
Oh yes my favourite person is my mum
That's why to me she is my number one.

If you were her child you'll love her too
But this is me and it is not you
Oh yes my favourite person is my mum
That's why to me she is my number one.

I love my mum so much I may not show it,
So I'm sending this to you to say, 'Mum I'm a good *Poet!'*

Marissa Clarke-Ryder (10)

My Mum

My mum is the best
Better than all the rest
She is never a pest.

My mum is cool
She likes to play pool
Sometimes she is a funny fool.

Some mums are boring
But not my mum
She is a real fun chum

My favourite person
  In the world is
    My Mum!

Robyn Ffoulkes (11)

Sam

Sam is a dog
That means so much to me,
I love him,
A dog that is special to me.

He's so fun,
He loves to go on walks,
I walk him,
And love to take a ball on walks.

He is cool
The cutest in the world,
He is great,
Sam is the best dog in the world.

Makes me smile
And loves to play footie,
Fur is soft
He likes to paw and nudge the footie.

Sam is the best dog,
And always will be.

Ellen Smith (9)

You Are My Star

(For my mum)

You are my star, you shine
Brightly in the sky.
I love you.

You are my tree, you are
Steady in the ground.
I love you.

You are my beautiful fish,
You swim peacefully in the sea.
I love you.

You are my sweet-smelling flower,
You blow gently in the field.
I love you.

You are my perfect planet,
You sit silently in space.
I love you.

You are my pretty mum, I love
To hug you.
I love you lots.

Mollie Wilson (11)

My Dog Jess

My favourite pet is a dog
She's wilder than a wild warthog
Her fur is rough, protects her meat
I wonder how she stands the heat
Her favourite food is beef and ham
She's fiercer than a gun-armed man
She loves to run and is three years old
Her nose is wet and very cold.

Nathan Bull (10)

My Loving Mom

My mom is caring and also loving too
She always picks me up from school
And that's what I love to do.
She helps me with my schoolwork,
She helps me every day and when we have days off from school
She takes me out for the day.
My mom is trusting and a brilliant dancer too.
She is brilliant at cleaning and adventurous in her mind.
I love her so much, she helps me all the time.

Jessica Langridge (9)

My Favourite Person

My dad is kind and caring
He is my favourite person
My dad has a heart of gold
He is my favourite person
My dad loves me loads
He is my favourite person
My dad would do anything for me
He is my favourite person

And that's why I love him so.

Amy Hillier (9)

Christopher Who?

Chris made the Doc come alive
Chris and I had fun with episode five.

I told Chris that I was bored
Chris showed me the Tardis and said
'Welcome aboard.'

Chris is a northern lad like me
Would we be home in time for tea?
Chris explained to me the art of mime
And the relative distance in space and time.

My head was spinning all over the place
I didn't want to end up lost in space,
I know you enjoy poetry and your
Art Attack sketchboard.

But it doesn't compare with me,
Cos I'm a Time Lord.
Just like Christopher.

Dean Dawkes (9)

Holly Scott

Always smiling
Big and white
Lovely cheeks
Red lips rouge
Cheerful and humorous
Great for a mate
So Holly for a friend
Is really quite special.

Katy Lane (8)

My Best Friend Laura

Short brown hair,
Smiles everywhere,
She gets along with everyone,
And is as radiant as the sun,
She looks into people's souls,
And sees the real you,
She's only looking for the good things,
The things that are strong and true,
Even when people tease her,
She will never be unkind.
She always sticks with the faithful,
And to the bad she is blind,
She feels the world,
A happy place,
And in return she gives it grace,
She does the same with everything,
She takes the great,
And leaves behind the hate.
She's my best friend,
She's good and true,
Because she will never betray you.
Look inside, there is more to a person than you think!

Yasmin Burton (10)

My Mum

My mum she is the best
Much better than the rest.
As she tucks me in at night,
And deserves the things that are right.
She is there when I cry,
Making sure I don't sigh.
When I am in trouble, she is still by my side,
Even though she knows I have lied.
She gives me a gentle kiss,
Which feels like the summer bliss,
And because of her soft skin,
She wipes away my sins
And this is why my mum is my favourite person ever.

Daniela Frangiamore (10)

My Older Sister

Today is extra special
A very important date,
As I have an older sister
And it's time to celebrate.
We've been through lots together with so many memories to share
And even though she knows my faults
She still shows that she cares.
We have a very special bond
Which will always see us through,
And it's so good to know I can put my trust in you.
So I have an older sister
And today I hope she'll see
That she's both my sister and my friend
And she means the world to me.

Jade Hearne (11)

Link

My favourite person would have to be Link
He isn't real but he's cool, that's what I think,
He has a mighty sword, a green tunic,
A shield for blocking and an ocarina for music,
He's got blond hair and is kinda funny,
When he puts on his mask and turns into a bunny,
He's the greatest swordsman that's *never* lived,
But hey what do I know? I'm just a kid!

Blossom McAfee (11)

My Auntie Raine

My auntie Raine is taller than me
My auntie Raine is my mum's sister
My auntie Raine likes the sea
Because she likes the creatures in it.
My auntie Raine makes me laugh
She really likes to have a bath.
My auntie Raine is very kind
My auntie Raine has always got time.
But best of all my auntie loves me
And I love Auntie Raine.

Gemma Blackwell (8)

Ben Massey

Ben is very helpful
He is my friend
Our friendship can be never broken
Until the very end.

He supports Man U
I support Forest
Any of the teams we don't mind
Cause they're the very best.

We both like playing football
Ben scores ten goals
But every time I take shots
It always hits the poles.

Now it's time to say goodbye
'Cause I have run out of time
Now we say farewell
To mine and Ben's little rhyme.

Marcus Woollands (11)

My Mum

My mum is like a star
Shining brightly
In the moonlit sky
My mum is my sun.

My mum gives light
To the stars so they can
Shine brightly in
The resting night.

My mum is my knight
In shining armour
She's always there to protect me
From evil.

That's my mum
Forever.

Ruth Davies (11)

My Favourite Person

My favourite person is kind and funny,
My favourite person has a bunny,
My favourite person has a pet,
My favourite person wants to be a vet,
My favourite person has blonde hair,
My favourite person has cool clothes to wear
My favourite person never comes to an end,
My favourite person is my best friend.

Kelly Sambucci (8)

Georgia

G is for great girl
E is for Elsie who is her best friend
O is for outstanding knowledge
R is for reckless
G is for 'Grease' - she loves it
I   is for iguana - shaped eyes
A is for absolutely brilliant.

Elsie Elder-Smith (10)

My Mate Harry

Harry is like a surprise package
As he opens up,
Something new and entertaining
Is revealed.
I've never known him angry
No dark clouds and thoughts ever emerge,
Nothing but rays of hope and sunshine
Fill our time.
Since starting school, yes way back then
Our paths have crossed and intertwined
Both love football, adventure and bikes
No secrets.

They say we are inseparable
As our lives uncurl
Harry is a boy
And me, I'm a girl.

Sophie Robinson (10)

My Mum Is ...

My mum is fun,
She's like the shining sun
My mum is the best,
She never gives me a test.
My mum treats me like a guest,
Like a bird in a nest,
My mum gives me lots of ice cream,
She's never mean,
To me.

My mum is helpful,
She's the best at being careful.
Bugs can beat me,
But no bug beats Mum.
My mum can ride,
Better than you can go down a slide,
My mum is Karen,
Karen Pickering.

Clare Pickering (9)

My Mum

My mum is the best
Even when I'm a pest
She cooks me food
She's a real cool dude
That's what my mum is like.

My mum is so caring
And also quite daring
She gets me toys till my room is full
I've never seen her hardly dull
That's what my mum is like.

My mum is so kind
And also so smiley
She's the best in every way
Each hour, each day
That's what my mum is like

My mum is the best
Even when I'm a pest
She cooks me food
She's a real cool dude
That's what my mum is like.

Katie Brown (10)

My Favourite Person

My favourite person used to own the Plume of Feathers,
She gives me hugs and kisses even when I'm naughty
Even when I'm sad
She's very beautiful and she cooks me lovely dishes.
She's very smiley and that makes me happy,
(But one more thing I have to say she's very chatty).

   My favourite person is my mum
   Oh! I forgot to say I love her.
     Goodbye.

Zachary Baxter-Hill (8)

My Friend Mol

(For my best friend)

She's fun, she's cool, I met her at school,
She's my best friend, cos she rules,
Her kindness, her thoughts, her particular smile,
Can keep you happy for a very long while.

She's my best friend and she always will be,
Because she's different just like me,
She's an angel brought from Heaven,
She's amazing and nearly eleven.

Molly's my friend and she's God sent,
Me, Tin and Phee would be sad if she went,
Because she's the best, Molly you're the best,
And you always will be!

Amber Kaye-Kenyon (10)

My Mum

My mum is very special,
In every single way,
I love her more and more
Every single day.

She's cuddly and kind,
Truthful and pretty,
She's like a star that shines,
She's like a little purring kitty.

She's a bright sun,
Which always wants to have some fun.
She plays about,
But never ever shouts.

My mum is a wonderful mum,
In fact she's a super mum.
When you need her she comes,
She'll always be a special person.

That's my mum.

Rebecca Philpot (11)

My Favourite Person

My favourite person is my friend Kayleigh Covell.
She always makes me laugh.
She always wishes we were sisters.
She is like a clown when she comes round to stay.
Kayleigh invited me to go to the beach with her.
Kayleigh and I will be friends forever.
We will never break up and argue.
Kayleigh is the best ever!

Jessica Fraser (9)

My Best Friend

She helped me when times got rough
I had a shoulder to cry on
When things got tough
Or when my joyful feelings were gone.

If I needed someone to confide in
No one could be better to give advice
Care was what she was showing
I wouldn't have to think twice.

Now things are better than before
No more bad times or hurting
And I'm going far
Good times I am finding.

A big thanks for my best friend
Who I'll be there for me 'til the end
Things are not so bad
And no more feeling sad.

Louise Smith (16)

My Furry Friend

My friend is a cat,
He helps me in most ways,
He lies on the mat
He hates rainy days.

But when it's sunny,
We come out and play,
He used to chase the bunny
Now the bunny's died anyway.

I taught him how to come,
When I whistle very loud,
And I love him very much,
When he follows me around.

He licks me when I'm sad,
And makes a lot of fuss,
He's never ever bad,
My furry friend is sussed.

Sophie Farmer (10)

My Mum

My favourite person is my mum
The way her hair shines in the sun,
Her teeth are always pearly white,
All through the day, all through the night,
Her job as a lifeguard may sound dim,
But it can mean I get a free swim.
In the winter, when it's cold,
She's always bright, she's always bold,
She's always happy, never glum.
But that's her job as a mum.
When I'm naughty she'll shout quite loud,
Which makes me happy, it makes me proud.
So when the nasty robbers come
They will be afraid of my heroine mum.
So there's my poem, please take a look,
I hope it gets published in every book
To everyone around the globe
Everyone must read it from rag to robe.

Bethany Pearce (10)

Mothers

Mothers are like flowers
Beautiful and have always got bright colours.
Passionate with a sense of love and tenderness.
Sweet and innocent but yet so powerful inside.
Always growing strong and never willing to give up.

Silva Gashi (15)

159

A Secret Friend

I have a secret friend,
Who it is you'll never guess,
Jumping, sleeping, crawling, purring,
She really is the best.

Oh I've got a secret friend,
And surely you can't know,
Scratching, pouncing, eating, loving,
My best friend is Flo!

Sam Mills (10)

Mummy

Mummy's cuddly
Warm-hearted and sweet
Kind and helpful
And loves a treat.

My mum irons
My mum cooks
She loves to sit,
And read her books.

I love Mum
And she loves me,
With Sarah and Dad,
We're a happy family.

Emma Loughran (8)

One Of My Favourite People

My favourite person, that's a tough one to call,
For all of my family and friends, I admire them all.

But I suppose I have to choose one, so let's go,
I choose my dad who often makes me feel I glow.

He's part of my family and a wonderful friend,
I know the bond between us will never ever end.

We both love to travel and walk,
And also we like to just sit and talk.

When Mum's away, my brother, Dad and I turn the house into a mess.
Then when she's coming home, we transform it back before being put to the test.

We do tough things that make us try our all,
Dad is always there to catch me when I fall.

I love him so much and also along,
With my other family and friends who also keep me strong.

Madeleine Maloney (11)

My Mum

I love my mum because ...
She cooks
She cleans
She never burns the beans.

I love my mum because ...
She's clever
She's pretty
She's always witty.

I love my mum because ...
She's kind
She's cool
She's on the ball
And that's why I love my mum!

Millie Jones (10)

Who

Who is kind
And who has a sensible mind?
Who's sweet
And cooks me lovely food to eat?
Who's caring
And loves sharing?
Who's a nurse
And always digging in her purse?
Who's brown
And never frowns?
Who's chatty
And always happy?
Who's always around
And keeps my feet firmly on the ground?
Who is it?
I bet you want me to give you a clue!
Or can you guess?
Yes ...
It's my mum!

Shauna-May Gordon (10)

My Wonderful Cousin

Elizabeth is my cousin
I love her very much
She's that special kind of cousin,
With that special kind of touch.

When I'm sad or feeling blue,
I ask my cousin, 'What should I do?'
She always answers just the same
'Feeling blue is just a game,
Get over it little cuz.'

Next year my cousin will learn to drive
She says that she might drive me to school,
I hope her results will jump and thrive.

Even though we live miles apart
She will always be in my heart,
Just one phone call to hear her voice,
Can put a big smile on my face!

Sarah Aldridge (11)

My Favourite Person

The one who always shares with me
The one who helps me when I'm stung by a bee

The person who tucks me in at night
The person who never has a fright

The one who has a great sense of humour
The one who believes in no rumours

The person who makes me laugh a lot
The person who makes sure my teeth don't rot

The one who makes sure I'm glad
The one who calms me down when I'm mad

The person who lets me buy toys
The person who made me a boy

The one who helps me when I'm sad
My favourite person is my *dad*!

Andrew Laws (11)

Why Is My Dog So Wonderful?

Why is my dog so wonderful?
Why is she so great?
Why do I like her so much?
Why is she such a really good mate?

Is it because she is big and furry
Or is it because of her lovely big brown eyes?

Is it because she is big in width
Or is it because she is small in size?

Is it because she is so cuddly
Or is it because she is so playful?

I think it's all of these and one more thing
Her great big heart in that very small body.
The love that it gives out to everybody.
Even though some people just ignore it.

It sometimes sounds like she cries
Some other people and some other dogs hate her.

But Sophie's perfect in my eyes.

Jennie Joyce (11)

Mummy, Mummy

Mummy, Mummy, when it's sunny,
She is looking hot,
I will try to find her a lovely shady spot.

Mummy, Mummy, with some money,
Going down to town,
When she's skipping all around she looks just like a clown.

Mummy, Mummy, looks so funny,
When she plays with me,
When it's time for me to stop she calls me for my tea.

Mummy, Mummy, watches me dance,
When I do my tap.
When I'm in a dancing show she always starts to clap.

Mummy, Mummy's very kind,
She always buys me sweets,
And when I get my pocket money we go out and buy treats.

Isabel Adams (7)

My Best Friend

M is for mine - she's my best friend!
Y is for yes - I'm just making my point!

B is for best. She's the best ever friend.
E is for ever - we'll stay friends for ever.
S is for Sophie. That's her name.
T is for time 'cause we like time together.

F is for funny. She makes me laugh.
R is for running - which we like to do.
I is for in - we sometimes live in our own land.
E is for every - I see her nearly every day.
N is for naughty - naughty but nice!
D is for daft 'cause she plays the fool a lot.

Chloë de Lullington (10)

My Grandad

A shock arose a few weeks ago
When I was feeling very low
My grandad was in a lot of pain
So the ambulance came
I thought he'd be in until the end of the day
But for three weeks he was away
When my nan came down
On her way back from the town
I went to make her a cup of tea
Without thinking I got a mug for my grandad's coffee
I could not believe he was so ill
But the worst was yet still
Major surgery he had, had
I felt very sad
For the sake of my grandad.

A couple more weeks passed
He's come home at last
Luckily he is on the mend
I don't have to write a letter to send
As I can visit to let him know
Just how much I love him so
And now when my nan pops in
I can go into the kitchen
When I get a mug for her cup of tea
I can also get one for his coffee.

Daniel Parsons (10)

My Favourite Person

She is rather pretty,
Tall but slim,
But sometimes can be amazingly dim!
She's got a mum and a dad,
A cool sister too,
Everybody loves her,
Wouldn't you?
She has many good friends,
Quite a few.
Eileen and Imogen,
Emily too,
Selena and Kelly
Amy as well
And last but not least don't forget Danielle.
When it comes to interests it's all a blur,
Writing, arcade games, even Sim City Urbz,
She's mad about computers,
Her family has two.
But she's even more crazy about Chinese tattoos!
But you see the thing is,
When it comes to my favourite person,
I am stuck for words,
My favourite person you see,
Is me!

Claudia Rozier (10)

My Cat

My cat is black
My cat is white
Even its eyes glow in the night.
My cat is purple
My cat is pink
Don't laugh, it looks like a sphinx.
My cat is orange
My cat is red
When it's tired it goes to bed.
Yes, I know my cat is multicoloured.

Dane Hodgson (10)

My Guinea Pigs

G etting them was fun.
U nusual behaviour sitting in the hay rack and knocking it down.
I really will enjoy them.
N ever will forget them.
E ven when they die.
A pproaching footsteps make her scuttle nervously away.

P atterned black and white fur like a zebra crossing.
I nconveniently pooing all around our garden in the run.
G enerally found chewing juicy green dandelions.
S pectacularly special guinea pig called Lilly!

Emma Collier (7)

My Brother

My brother Joshua is nine months old,
Sometimes he can be as good as gold.
He's got blue eyes and ginger hair,
He's big and cuddly, like a teddy bear.
Shuffling along trying to crawl,
Then he starts to bang and bawl.
He's just learnt to clap his hands,
I can't wait till he stands,
So we can go outside and play football,
'Cause he's the bestest brother of them all.

Kyle Liddle (10)

A Poem To You Mummy

Mummies are sweet as sweet as the honey
Mummies are as soft as silk,
Mummies are loving as loving as I
And mummies are as beautiful as a
bird in the sky.

I love my mummy as Mummy loves I
Because she is only mine
She is my beauty and she is my song
Because she, oh she is my mummy.

Mary Montgomery (9)

My Guinea Pig

My guinea pig is cute
but she is a little minute.
She is a ball of fur
when running - is a little blur.
Her cage is wooden and metal
which you have to clean
with animal Dettol.
The hay she sleeps in is soft.
It looks like a little loft
which is a room on a
double-deckered hutch.

Her fur is a mixture of colours
with tan, brown, black and white.
Like a suntan in different places
with white in the little spaces.
She is quite inquisitive like a little cat
with eyes that are sapphires when
They twinkle in the light.

I never will forget her
as long as I live!

Jonathan Collier (9)

My Auntie Sinead Is The Best

My auntie Sinead, simply speaking, is cool
Real trendy for her age I think.
There are words to describe her such as loving and kind.
Listen to this, there's truth you will find.
As I said simply speaking she's cool.
If you don't know who it is, you're a bit of a fool!
The legend, the queen, ruler of all,
Champion of the universe, Auntie Sinead!
The coolest, the best!

Aislinn FitzGerald (8)

I Love My Mum

I love my mum when she tucks me in bed
I love all the things she says.

I love my mum when she smiles,
I love her laugh all the while.

I love my mum when she buys me things,
Books, sweets and pretty rings.

I love my mum when she takes me on trips out,
And she makes us live in a tidy house.

I love my mum when she takes us on holiday to see the sea
But most of all I love my mum because she loves me!

Shannon Tiernan (11)

The True Best Friend

My best friend has to be
The girl who is almost identical to me
She's really clever and funny too
And she always thinks of something fun to do.

There's never a time when she leaves me alone
Whether it be at school or at home
She's there for me if I cry
So there's more to my friend than meets the eye.

My best fiend is exciting too
And our friendship will see us through
For she is my one true friend
And she will be there till the end.

Charlotte Hall (11)

Emma My Cousin

When I see Emma my heart skips a beat
Smiling all the time
Brown hair overlapping her shoulders
Her eyes sparkling with delight
Kind, caring, sweet too
Emma is the best ever
I love her.

Kelly Averill (9)

My Guinea Pigs

My favourite people are my guinea pigs
Around the middle they're mighty big.
Sometimes they run, sometimes they hop
Sometimes they look like they're going to pop!
Chocolate, Chip and Cookie
Sometimes look a bit mucky.
Running around the garden
No excuse for pardon.
Sometimes they bite me
Sometimes they eat a pea.
My little chums
Eating lots of crumbs.

Christopher Goult (10)

Chocolate, chip and cookie.

My Best Friend

My best friend is Bethany because she looks after me and she plays with me.
My best friends are my brothers because they play with me and they make me feel
  nice inside.
They play with me at school and they play with me at home.
My best friend is Chanice because she is funny nd she plays with me.
My best friends are all of the school and my mum and dad are too.

Rebecca Burke (10)

Pawson

My favourite person is a dog I know,
Who goes by the name of Pawson.
He's soft and cuddly and always wants a hug,
He runs and jumps and does funny things.
He's always bouncy and makes everyone laugh.
He's a number one dog and that's why
He's my favourite person in the doggy world.
My friend, Pawson the dog.

Lauren Newsome (10)

My Horse Redcurrent

My horse, Redcurrent,
Is cheeky and jolly.
She is also lovable and lively.

My horse, Redcurrent
Loves jumping and racing.
She also eats like a pig.

My horse, Redcurrent,
Listens and does what you say.
She also loves having fun.

My horse, Redcurrent,
Loves being ridden.
She also knows where she stands.

This is my horse, Redcurrent.

Gabrielle Ryland (11)

My Friend Lauren West

My friend Lauren West
Would never hurt a fly
She is the best
Lauren is kind and a really good friend.

I don't see her much
Because we don't share schools
She lives down my close
Lauren is cool.

Nobody on planet Earth
Is like this wonderful girl
Nothing, in any shape or form
Diamond rings, not even a pearl.

Lauren West, is the best
With a dog, a cat,
Her little brother Thomas,
A purple bathroom mat.

My friend Lauren West
Would never hurt a fly
She is the best
Lauren is kind and a really good friend.

Kristy Britt (10)

Pickles

Pickles my hamster likes to snuggle in his tiny house,
He's very greedy, his favourite food being celery,
With a golden coat of fur and large black eyes,
Here's a hamster melody ...

He's sly, secretive, cute and small
Liking everyone he meets
Not forgetting his tiny hands
And weeny feet!

So there's the hamster melody
Being my best friend (of course)
A bum wiggling when he's running
And a tiny pink tail wobbling
I just hope he stays forever and ever!

Sophie Cornish (11)

My Dog Barney

I love my dear dog Barney,
He really is a gem,
He loves the fields and woodland,
But is scared of the sheep in the pen.

Most of the time he obeys me,
But sometimes he is bad,
He runs away, I yell and yell,
And then he knows I'm mad.

He trots back, his head held low,
Behind him a wagging tail,
He licks my hand, I understand,
He didn't mean to go.

Emily Guthrie (10)

Mr T Rhyme

You are great 'cause you pity the fool.
You are great 'cause you are so cool.
You are great 'cause you wear gold chains.
You are great 'cause you call people names.
You are great 'cause you're very well known.
You are great 'cause your fame is shown.
You are great 'cause you don't like planes.
When you fight people, they feel the pain.
You are great 'cause you're on TV.
You are great 'cause you're called Mr T!

Chris Bint (11)

My Dog Bonnie

If I'd have found her in a ditch, on the side of a road,
If I'd have found her as a rock on a mountainside,
If I'd have found her on some bubblegum stuck under a chair,
My puppy would still be a part of me.

If she'd have been a hamster or a fish,
If she'd have been an elephant or a rhino,
If she'd have been a fingerprint on a windowpane,
I'd still love her, my little pup.

To conclude this poem, I just want to say ...
Don't judge a dog by her fluffy white tail!

Emily Dixon Fallon (11)

Mutley

Every time I ring the bell
Mutley comes running, roaring by the door
Once I sit on the couch he comes up with his smiling mouth
And slobbers with saliva!

Even though it sounds rancid
A dog's saliva has antiseptic in it
I love his cool fluffed up hair
Which I love putting into quality styles.

It's really funny when he looks at me
While his minute head is looking in the other direction.
When he runs, it looks really dappy
And he sometimes keeps running in and out of the house!

And at the end of the day, my mum starts walking up the stairs
Then he rushes after her and slips under the bed
After we all go to sleep Mutley has his doggy dreams.

Justin Francis (11)

Grandad

My grandad is called Joe,
I am also called Joe,
My grandad was a Royal Marine,
His stories are always cool,
My grandad is my hero,
The greatest in the world,
I want to be like Grandad,
The greatest in the world.

Joe Housley (10)

Bono

Bono is the best,
He is better than the rest,
He sings really well,
And he is in a cool band.

He played in Live Aid
Twenty years ago,
He was in Live 8
A couple of weeks ago.

His band is so cool,
He is the best singer in the world,
He makes brill songs,
And sings them with his cool band!

Bono is the best,
He is better than the rest!

Hattie Dowling (11)

My Best Friend

My best friend is John Glover,
And so he has been for many years,
But he's hardly any football lover,
His mother's handy with her shears,
I just like going and popping in
To play and have some fun with him.

Oscar French (9)

My Brother Jack

We argue a lot
When it gets hot
But we should not,
He has mad hairs
And is too young to wear flares,
He has lots of toys
Which he enjoys,
Jack is three
And he can't climb a tree,
He looks like me
And he's a big part of my happy family.

Lauren Allen (9)

My Favourite Person

My favourite person is my mum,
Every time I see her I stick up my thumb,
She's tall and great,
She's my best mate!

She buys me things which I love,
I hear angels singing high above,
She drives me places I need to go,
Even when it's in the snow.

You should realise she is the best,
She is better than all the rest,
She is my favourite for many reasons,
And many more for the four seasons.

Ashleigh Irwin (9)

Rosie

My best friend is Rosie my cat,
She is white, brown and black
She is so sweet
And ever so neat.
When I am sad, she makes me smile
And all that love makes life worthwhile.
She has little white socks, not pulled up right,
But that doesn't matter, it is all right.

Rhiannon Pike (10)

My Aunty Shell

My auntie is the greatest,
She takes me all sorts of places,
Like shopping, to the cinema and bowling!
My auntie Shell is my pal ...
Cos she always makes me smile!

But if I have problems,
She is the one I can tell.

My auntie is the greatest.

Sophie Tredwell (11)

My Dog Spike

Every morning when I get up he greets me like a long-lost friend
When I am down he'll always put a smile on my face.
We play for hours in my garden running round and round
Until I fall over dizzy.
Then he jumps on me licking my face and wagging his tail
He runs like lightning across the garden.
Then suddenly, just like puppies do,
He curls up in a ball and falls asleep
At two months old he is a fluffy bundle of fur
Black with a white collar and a white tip to his tail
My friend lives up to his name, which is Spike.

Michael Cooke (8)

My Favourite Person

I haven't got a favourite person,
It's really clear to me,
Because I have loads of favourite people,
It's my whole *family!*

Well there is my daddy,
He is Newcastle mad,
He's glued to Sky Sports,
And we think he's quite sad!

There is my mummy,
She shops quite a lot,
My daddy says,
'This has got to stop!'

Then there is Charlotte who's seven,
A sister asleep equals Heaven,
Oh ... I don't really mean it,
OK then ... maybe I do just a bit.

Last of all are my pets,
There's Woody, my dog who hates the vets,
There's Custard and Cream, the noisy birds,
We think they want to join us
'Heards'.

Georgia Heard (9)

My Best Friend Ellie

Me and my friend Ellie
Do competitions together
Even though I never win
We have great fun
If it's a football challenge
To dancing - we do it
It could be writing
It could be drawing.

Amy Springett (9)

My Crazy Friend

My crazy friend
She drives me round the bend.
She can run round the playground,
And also have time to go to the fairground.
She is one hell of a chick,
And she isn't (thank God) as thick as a brick.
My crazy friend.

Alison Robertson (9)

Gizmo

My cat Gizmo is grey and white
She has a pink nose
But she doesn't like to fight
She has sharp claws
She has a thin tail
But when she's cross
Her fur sticks up like candyfloss
She likes to purr
And she has lots of fur
I like my cat Gizmo
She's a bundle of fun
And she's the prettiest cat I've ever seen.

Bethan Gregory (10)

My Best Friend Molly

She's as bright as the sun
As nice as a cherry bun
She's as good as gold
If there's a secret, she can hold
She's as wild as a flower
Climbing up a big tall tower
That's why she's my best friend!

Ellie Bond (9)

My Best Friend Bethany

My best friend has a smile as big as a melon
My best friend has a heart as warm as fire
My best friend is as kind as can be
My best friend is as pretty as a princess
My best friend is as small as a mouse
My best friend is as best as a friend can be
My best friend is as polite as can be
My best friend couldn't be a better friend.

Gemma Butler (9)

My Precious Mum

What on earth could I do without my mum?
Everything except from my mum seems dumb.
Thanks be to God who gave my mum power
My mum's life is as precious as a flower.
I love my mum, she has a heart of gold
Bad or good she is always bold.

Esther Idowu (10)

My Mum

My mum is amazingly great,
She's the greatest mum ever and my best mate.
She's funny and kind,
The best you'll find.
Her hair flicked out and lipstick on,
For best mum awards she'll win number one.
She's carrying my sibling in her tum,
She's full of fun, that's my mum.
My mum is the best, I cannot lie,
To be the best she doesn't have to try.

Toni Morton (11)

The Best Dog In The World

My dog is my mate
I love her so much
Her heart has a special rate
Her lick has a certain touch
If I could be you
It would be so good
It is so true
Our love is stronger than wood
Nothing can stop our relationship
Even if she's broken my best cup
Even if I lived in a tip
She can always keep my chin up
I play with her every day
When I walk her
I just want to say
She seems to get smaller and smaller
But less of the old
And more of the new
She loves her food (I'm told)
She doesn't know I've done this, *(Phew!)*
That is part of our secret bond
It can't be broken, never!
Even if her hairs were blonde
I would still love her forever and ever!
To my loving dog, Biscuit.

Daniel Barry (11)

My Dad

My dad is funny,
He likes lots of money,
He's an inventor on cars
And likes chocolate bars,
I'm very glad
That he's my dad!

Kathryn Edmondson (11)

My Fave Cousin

My fave cousin
The best out of ten dozen.

She is really cool
And wants a pool.

She is the best
And is never ever stressed.

She's so funny
Even when it's not very sunny.

She is quite tall
Not very small.

She is my best mate
Definitely really great.

She is so fast
And will never be last.

She is a party girl
And wants a pearl.

That's my cousin
Hermione.

Alice Crawshaw (10)

My Best Friend

M any fun times we've had together, but now she's getting old
Y ou'll never get a better dog than her so I'm writing it in *bold*.

D irt is what she likes to play with along with her fluffy toys
O n every occasion I give her a bath she makes a lot of noise
G oing on long walks up the park and grooming her hair.

L oving every minute we have no time to spare
U ndoing her lead so she can run wild and free
C all her back and she'll run back to play with me
K ind and loving she always makes me smile
Y ou'll never find a sweeter friend then her, that makes my time worthwhile.

I f I'm feeling down she always cheers me up
S he will roll on the floor just like a pup.

My friend to the end.

Jodie Tryphena Dolloway (11)

My Fab Dad

My dad is my mate
We both go on adventures together
Which are so great
My dad is so funny
And makes me smile every day.

I love my dad so much
We both stick together like glue
Then we play hide-and-seek
Dad finds me and says, 'Boo!'

I am always playing out with him
When the boiling hot sun is out
We are always there for each other
The best thing I like about my dad
Is he does not *shout!*

Bethany Lea Wild (10)

My Dad

My dad is ...
My dad is as strong as a tornado.
Wrecking all that gets in its way.
As loving as a kitten asleep on a warm bed.
As playful as a puppy running about with children.
Because that's my dad and that's what I think about him.

Emily Dalton (10)

My Mum

My mum is busy then she goes dizzy.
My mum used to be a doctor.
My mum is weak but if you're naughty she will get as strong as a lion.
My mum cooks every meal in the house.
My mum is having a baby.
My mum goes to Jack Hunt swimming.
My mum is kind.

Kyle Seaton (8)

The People I Like

My favourite people are Mum and Dad
They're the best people I've ever had,
My mum is small
My dad is tall
What a perfect family I have.

My favourite people are Rachel and Scott
They're nice and make me laugh a lot,
I like my friends they're nice and kind
They're the best people I'll ever find.

Jade Inman (9)

My Mum's Simply The Best

(This is dedicated to my mum)

My mum's simply the best
She does everything for me.
Every time I look into her eyes
I see a sparkling blue sky staring at me.
My mum's simply the best.

Her lovely shiny and smooth hair
Her hair's simply the best.

Her clothes are lovely and pink
Her clothes are simply the best.

My mum's lovely, isn't she beautiful?
I love my mum, she's so perfect
She will always be in my heart!

Sophie Fahey (11)

Mitten Ingham

Mitten is a cuddly cat,
Who is very far from fat,
She loves being tickled
Under the chin, and that's
When the fun begins.
Purring all day,
Purring all night,
She jumps into bed and gives you a fright
But don't be shocked
'Cause she's my Mitten.

Eloise Ingham (9)

Chestnut

Chestnut is my rabbit,
She lives in a green and red cottage,
She uses a grass box as her bed
Her blanket wrapped round her,
When she sleeps she makes no sound.

When she was little she rolled on her back,
Like my aunt's dog did while sitting on a log,
She's the best pet in the world,
And maybe even my friend, my rabbit.

Harriett Wragg (9)

Nan

We love our nan
We love her so
But when I fall
She doesn't want to know,
She looks after me
So tenderly
After she has laughed at me!

We love our nan
We love her so
But when she sleeps over
She's got to snore
When she farts in the middle of the night
She gives us such a terrible fright!

Jonathan Edwards (9)

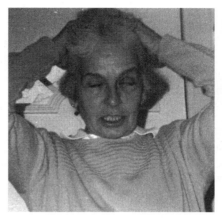

My Best Friend

Whenever I'm down she's there
We're definitely a troublesome pair
She's always putting a smile on my face
When I'm sad it's always the case.

She makes me happy all the time
She's the one that makes the sun shine
She makes me laugh until I need a wee
Because she's the greatest friend to me.

We never ever fight
She's the one who brings the world light
She's the kindest person I've ever known
When she needs me she knows where to phone.

I know her inside and out
And I know what she's all about
Because she's the greatest!

Tasha Tucker (12)

My Dad Is The Best

My dad is so cool
He helps me with school
He is the best
In the south-west.

My dad works all day
At Lockleaze Kellaway
He comes home at four
Unlocking the door.

My dad likes Stephen King
And likes the film 'The Ring'
He loves to watch 'Time Team'
And likes the Roman theme.

My dad has brown hair
Like a large fluffy bear
He loves me and my hamster
Whose names are Chloe and Hamper.

He sends me to bed
And says, 'Goodnight sleepyhead'
He takes me to the park
But not when it's dark.

He loves his family loads
And supplies us with nice clothes
He loves me
And I love he.

Chloe Nicholls (10)

My Mum

My mum is my favourite person
I adore my mum!

My mum is a faithful, peaceful alarm clock
Waking me each morning with a kiss.
My own personal organiser!

My mum is a stretched golden limousine
Dropping me off and picking me up.
My own personal chauffeur!

My mum is my favourite teacher
Chasing away dull, hard homework.
Appearing at the turn of every page!

My mum is a soft loving teddy
Comforting me when I cry.
My loyal best friend!

My mum is a silver star
Shining through the moonlit sky.
Hanging on my wall every night!

I adore my mum
My favourite person is my mum!

Nikhil Mair (12)

My Sister Lois

Lois is not just my sister
She is also my best friend
She's always there when I need her
On her I can depend.
She fills my days with laughter
Shouting and tears too
Lois my little sister
I will always love you.

Laurie Plant (10)

My Wonderful Mum

Who loves me so?
Who holds me tight?
Who tucks me into bed
And says goodnight?
Who looks out for me?
Who makes me bright
Who gives me toys
And stops my fights?
My wonderful mum.
She buys my food
She keeps me fit
She makes my bed
But she doesn't mind one bit.
She likes my dance
She likes my style
She helps me bake a cake
And it makes her smile.
My wonderful mum
I make her laugh
I make her cry
Once we even made an apple pie.
My mum and I go to see a movie
I think my mum is really groovy
My wonderful mum.

Hayley Diamond (9)

My Mother

My mother is silver
She looks like an angel from Heaven
And sounds like a mouse squeaking 'hello'.
She tastes like a chocolate cake
With extra chocolate coating
And smells like a hot dog with fresh bread
My mum is like a thousand pound note to me.

Connor Godwin (10)

Everlasting Friendship

I wake up each morning to see my friends,
I hope our friendship never ends.
They make bubbles and seem to smile at me
Have you guessed yet?
They're pet fish I like to see.

I wake up each morning to see my friends,
I hope our friendship never ends.
Their names are Tickle and Patch
After a TV show I used to watch
They're pet fish I like to see.

I wake up each morning to see my friends,
I hope our friendship never ends.
But one night in October at seven o'clock
Their heart beat stopped going, *tick-tock*
Now they're RIP.

Claire Dent (10)

Dylan

Dylan is my bestest brother
I love him more than any other
Even though he is adorable
He can drive me up the wall
He can be fun
I'd pick him over a bun
But best of all
I love him, he loves me
I know it's true
Cos even Dylan says it too
But I love him, he loves me
That's all that matters.

Connor Foxon (10)

My Dog

My lovely dog he is as furry as a jumper.
His eyes are as green as the grass in the summer.
He loves to be fussed all over the place and especially on his tummy.
He is as black and white as the clouds and the dark sky.
He chases anything like foxes.

Laurianne Dudgeon (8)

The One, The Only Aunty Nancy

I've got an aunty called Nancy,
But she's not my aunty, she's my mum's
Her house is always very fancy
And I like the way she hums.

I love to go and visit her,
To her house on the prom,
Where we bake yum-yum biscuits and
Watch the boats into the harbour come.

My aunty goes to school, to work not to learn
She helps the cooking class for her pennies to earn.
She wears her school specs on the end of her nose
To read the recipes and to keep them on their toes.

Nancy has a dog, Kayleigh is her name,
They go for walks down the beach - to have some fun and games,
She comes back a wee bit smelly so my uncle gets the blame.

My aunty is kind, my aunty is patient
My auntie's an inspiration,
Wouldn't it be nice if everyone had an Aunty Nancy?

Charlotte Eason (9)

Best Friend

Becca is my bestest friend
Even though she's round the bend
All my school friends think she's great
I'm so glad she is my best mate
Whenever I feel dreary
She makes me feel all cheery
It's nice to stay up late
And chat with your best mate!

Hayley Jones (10)

My Supercalifragilistic Mum

My mum is special to me in many different ways,
She cares for me and comforts me in every single way.
When I am with her she tells me to be careful,
When I am sad she makes me cheerful
My mum smiles all through the day,
Even when she is sad in different kinds of ways.
My mum is the best mum in the whole wide world ever.

Sophie Dunne (9)

Our Pet

We have a pet called Nibbles
He really loves his food
His favourite colour is green
We think he's a cool dude
We've had him for three years
He always is so good
But when we get him out
He'd escape if he could
We're near the end of our poem
Our pet has grown quite big
But although you have to guess what animal he is
Of course he's a guinea pig.

Naomi (10) & Hannah Stanaway (6)

My Baby Brother

My brother is the best,
Though he never lets us rest!

He runs but doesn't walk,
And shouts but doesn't talk!

He always dribbles,
And when you tickle him, he giggles!

He puts a smile on your face,
But I'd stay away from him,
Just in case!

But overall he's the best,
And is extremely cute!

I will love him forever,
And hate him never!

Khimi Grewal (11)

Simply Great

Hi, my name is Kate
And I know someone who is simply great.
Big blue eyes and long blonde hair,
Pink is the colour she loves to wear.
A delightful dancer.
A fantastic footballer.
An amazing musician.
She gives good advice
And is especially nice.
Kristina is her name,
Helping everyone is her aim.
I'm so glad she's my cousin!

Katie Lapping (9)

My Mum

Mum you do everything for me,
You shop and make me tea.
I wish there was a way I could repay
I hope this poem will stay
You help me when I am ill
And pay every single bill.

Mum, Mum you pick me up from places
And used to tie my laces
You wash all our clothes
And used to admire my little toes.

Mum, Mum you do all the ironing
And calm me down when I am crying
You take me on holiday every year
And dried my first tear.

But best of all you love me so
You get rid of all my woes
You care for me every day
I hope it will stay this way
Forever and ever.

Natasha Thornton (10)

The Twins

The twins are two great people
Mary-Kate and Ashley they're called
They're my favourite actresses
They're just so cool.

It would be great to be like them
Acting in films
Being so popular
Being so cool.

They're so perfect
Their fashion so great
What would I give to be like them?
Anything at all.

Esther Stanesby (10)

My Marvellous Mum

M ost parents spoil their children
Y ou ask them for sweets, they say 'Yes.'

M y mum feeds me the right kinds of food,
A nd will nourish my work to the best.
R ooting for me on sports day,
V ersatile in things she can do.
E ven in times of trouble
L oving and caring for you.
L oves me lots,
O f course my mum is marvellous,
U ntil the end of day.
S till my mum will love me.

M aking me laugh when I'm old and grey.
U nderstanding and thoughtful
M y mum is special in her own unique way.

Darrell Coker (10)

My Mum

My mum, my mum
Is my favourite person
She has lovely black hair
With blonde streaks.

My mum, my mum
Is my favourite person
She's a personal trainer
At Esporta.

My mum, my mum
She was a beauty therapist
And once an artist
She's just the best.

My mum, my mum
Can sometimes be annoying
But I love her because she's my mummy.

Tia Simran Dhaliwal (11)

My Mum

My mum smells like roses
My mum is so lovely that
I love her more than the universe.
She is the best in the world.
She is kind to people and nice.
She's so fit and she works at Kiness High School.
She is the best cook in the world.
She is enjoyable to have a laugh and fun with.
She is always busy on some days but I love her.

Harry Bayne (11)

Beyoncé Is My Star

My favourite person's Beyoncé
I love her booty shake
I like the way she dances
And nothing about her is fake.

I like her 'cause she's pretty
And has great hair
Sometimes she wears clothes
That I wouldn't dare!

Her songs make me happy
And want to dance
And that's what I do
When I get a chance.

Holly Hinson (9)

My Favourite Person?

My favourite person
Is really rather small
She has a waggling tail
And loves her favourite ball.

My favourite person
Is happy throughout the day
She's very, very friendly
And willing to obey.

My favourite person
Makes the sun shine
But when we tell her off
She often seems to whine.

My favourite person
Likes to run around
She enjoys going on walks
And I'm sure she hates the pound.

My favourite person
Can you guess yet?
One more clue is that
She happens to be my pet.

Lucy Goodyear (12)

My Best Friend

My very best friend is Holly,
She's just a bit older than me.
We do everything together; we'll have a friendship forever,
Just my best friend Holly and me.

My best friend Holly lives on a farm,
There's just so much to do and see.
We play in haystacks and follow animal tracks,
Just my best friend Holly and me.

When Holly comes over to my house,
We play under the sycamore tree.
Climbing and swinging, laughing and singing,
My best friend Holly and me.

Rosie Stacey (11)

My Best Friend

I love my cat,
She is very sweet
I love to stroke her
She's got really stinky feet.

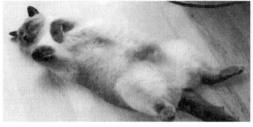

I love my cat
She jumps up and down like a rabbit
She lies on my lap
But rolling around is her most annoying habit.

I love my cat
She is very lazy
She sits on my lap, but watch out
When I play with her
She goes totally crazy!

Jemma Gilholm (11)

My Prince Pipkin

It's been a long night
A night full of princes and delights
They all had charm and wore white
But none were as good as my very own.

Mine is a gentle rabbit, who makes me feel at ease
Speckled, small and full of kindness
Large brown eyes, never in a stress.

Eats dandelions and listens to me attentively
I used to take him for granted,
But now I see how important having a friendly pet can be.

So to you Pipkin, I say
Thank you for being there for me every day
A curious and lovable character
Who never gets grumpy along the way
My Prince Charming through and through
Pipkin, if you were human, I would marry you!

Beth Cortese (13)

My Dad

My dad tells me jokes
And he makes me laugh
We play games
And go down to the beach ...
He's just great!

My dad reads me bedtime stories
And we go on cycling runs
He lets me help wash the car
And water the plants ...
He's just great!

My dad takes me on long walks
Especially out the braes
We go and explore the caves
And other things there ...
He's just great!

My dad soaks me when
We are having a water fight
On holiday he plays footie with me
He kicks it out of sight
Up into the sky ...
He's just great!

My dad plays the PlayStation with me
He races me but he usually wins!
He makes toy sailing models
And lets me paint them ...
He's just great cos he's my dad!

Claire Thomson (9)

Jasmine

I have a very special friend
Her name is Jasmine cat
She's really soft and cuddly
But she's very, very fat.

She likes it when I smooth her
She curls up on my lap
She snores and purrs happily
And has a little nap.

She sometimes brings me presents
A mouse or frog or rat
She drags them through the kitchen
And dumps them on the mat!

She used to be a thin cat
And could squeeze through any gap
But now she's often stuck because
She can't get through the cat flap.

She likes to think she's human
She eats crisps and Wotsits and cheese
And when we talk to each other
She never disagrees.

I'm very, very lucky
To have such a special pet
My lovely, furry, fatty cat
She's the best friend I could get.

Alexander Knight (9)

My Best Friend

My best friend goes *cluck, cluck, cluck*,
Her ancestor is in a book.
She has three lovely, feathery friends,
All living with her in their five star pen.
She lays an egg most days for me,
Which I can eat for lunch or tea.
When at night I go outside,
She's always waiting with bright, beady eyes.
In my arms she'll sit or lay,
And listen to all I have to say.
She pecks up grain from around her pen,
Because my friend is *Brownie the hen*.

Joseph Barton (10)

My Best Friend

She's my best friend ever,
I know her from school,
We've been friends for three years,
She is so cool,
You can always trust her,
She'll never lie,
You can always talk to her,
You can always try,
She's funny and amusing,
She's friendly and fun,
She's my best out of everyone!

Claire Aitken (10)

My Favourite Person

A poem to tell you
I love you so
Just isn't enough
For you to really know

I could talk forever
Tell you how I feel
Show you how, when we're together
I have never felt so real

You were there to catch me
When I madly fell for you
You opened my heart with your key
And whispered three words so true

You catch my tears
Every time they fall
You're the only one who cares
Every time I call

You treat me like your princess
A beautiful doll
You give me the best
And will never let me fall

So thanks for being
The person you are
You're the sweetest person I know
You'll always be my shining star!

Priya Kanabar (16)

Magical Mrinalini

Mrinalini is great,
She's my number one mate,
She's good at maths,
And music and learning facts.

Mrinalini is as good as gold,
And always does what she is told,
She loves to eat chicken roast,
And never cheats and never boasts.

Mrinalini is a great sister,
And when she was on holiday, I really missed her,
This poem has now come to an end,
Mrinalini's the best sister ever and a really good friend!

Malini Dey (10)

The Hedge-Orilla

Daring, but silly,
Adventurous, but hairy,
Dad, just Dad.

He smells like an unwashed chimp,
He looks like a hedgehog,
With the hair of a gorilla too,
I call him
The Hedge-orilla!

For him I would:
Fight an evil dragon,
Climb to the top of the Eiffel Tower, using a bit of string,
Eat a volcano or even stew,
Because he's my dad and I love him,
(Even if he's a hedge-orilla!).

William Davies (8)

Moaning Mum

My mum is always moaning
And wants gravy with her dinner
She's not grateful for the dinner
But just keeps on moaning

She always cares for me
And thinks what's right is right
She takes me here and takes me there
Oh what a lovely sight

But what I really want to say
Is that I love her
But only when and only then
When she has stopped her moaning!

Karl Phillips (10)

A Recipe For The Perfect Brother

Pre-heat the oven to 180ºC,
Put 2 cups of love into a mixing bowl
And add a tablespoon of friendship,
Pour 20ml of coolness and stir in a drop of laughter,
Put in a pinch of annoyance and mix thoroughly.
Last, but not least, add a dash of fun and slide in the oven for 12-15 minutes.
Enjoy, treasure, love him!

Larischa de Wet (11)

Always There

Always there
A shoulder to cry on
A best friend

Always there
When in need of a cuddle
When in need of advice

Always there
When I'm cold and alone
When my friends fall out

Always there
When we share shopping advice
When I need a new outfit

Always there
When we share make-up tips
Or go to a party

That's my mum!

Sarah Guise (11)

Gwen Stefani

Gwen Stefani is an idol to me
Her songs fill me with glee
I think her songs are great
I started to like her when I was eight
'What are you waiting for?'
Gets me shouting for more
'Rich Girl'
Gets me to swirl
'Hollaback Girl'
Makes me think I am a pearl
Her smile makes me glow
I wish she had a TV show!

Pippa McCollom (9)

My Favourite Person

My favourite person is my school
Because it's the one thing that will always rule!
Person I know it is not
But I like it a whole lot.
School days, school days
Dear, old, golden rule days.
Reading and writing and 'rithmatic
They say we'll soon get the hang of it.
If you give cheek or messed about
You would be sure to get a clout.
Still they're the best days without a doubt
When we were a couple of kids!

Courtney Wallbank (10)

My Favourite Person

When I first met her, she was nice to me;
That's when I realised she would be a good friend.

She was one of the people who cared;
Always honest and trustworthy.

Never late, always on time;
Never missed a day being together,
Shared our secrets and always kept them;

Because that's what friends are for ...
My best friend, April Davies.

Ami Slater (11)

Ambriya

Ambriya, funny, kind and clever,
We always hung around together,
I will miss her at my new school,
But plan to meet up at the swimming pool,
Reaching eleven can be fun,
But, for me, I'll miss someone.

Helena Bonallie (10)

My Best Friend

Sam is such a brilliant friend,
Hope our friendship will never end.

Whenever we play, we play together,
Sunny or wet, in any weather.

I will miss him at my new school,
Hope his teacher isn't too cruel,

When we play, it's so exciting,
Never teasing or any fighting.

If there are sweets, he'll share them out,
Even humbugs, without a doubt.

Sport and Tig, he likes those games,
But nothing nasty like calling names.

At new high schools miles away,
This is our final summer holiday.

Michael Bonallie (10)

My Favourite Person ...

My favourite person let me see
It is my dad, it has to be
He works for a company, oh, so big
And to relax, the garden he will dig

He loves his garden quite a lot
And plenty of plants he has got
He likes to play football with my brother
And ran the marathon, cheered by me and my mother!

I am so glad, that he is my dad
He really isn't all that bad!
You know that I can always see
What is in him, and in me.

Lucy McInally (10)

My Hero

With his striking red suit, he is so very cute.
He likes to swing on webs and has very sticky legs.

His webs are very spindly and he doesn't mind it being windy
He triumphs over evil and never is deceitful.

He is a very good glider and acts just like a spider
My hero, Spiderman.

John Cooknell (8)

My Favourite Person

My big sister is so nice
She doesn't like Mom's rice.
She always makes a funny face,
Even before she's had a taste.

My big sister doesn't like jelly,
But she likes watching the telly.
She doesn't like to fight,
But she likes to stay up late at night.

My big sister is called Sarai,
She's so tall she nearly touches the sky.
She looks so pretty when she has her hair done,
My big sister is my favourite person.

Eden Johnson (7)

My Mum

I love my mum 'cause she tucks me up in bed,
She loves me all the time and makes sure I'm fed.

She cares for my brothers and my little sister too,
She's always very busy, with the housework to do.

I love my mum; she cares for me a lot
And although it's hard for her, I'm never forgot.

Melanie Cooknell (9)

Who Is She?

She is so funny,
Even when it isn't so sunny.
She is an amazing mate,
And is never ever late.
She is my fave cousin,
The best out of ten dozen.
She is a party girl,
Who loves to twist and twirl.
She is nearly six,
And loves magic tricks.
She is so great,
Definitely a best mate.
She is so cool,
Even sometimes acts like a fool.
She is so lean,
And will never be mean.
She is so ace,
Her name is Grace.

Lucy Crawshaw (13)

My Sister

My sister is the best on Earth,
She's kind, loving and sweet,
I love her being my sister,
It really is a treat.
My sister is as soft as a cushion,
She'd never hurt a fly,
I love her being my sister,
I hope she'll never die.
My sister is a nine-year-old girl,
She loves playing with her bits and bobs,
I love her being my sister,
She often helps me do jobs.
My sister is sometimes annoying,
But that happens with all,
I love her being my sister,
And think she's kind of cool!

Laura Dowling (11)

My Dog

My dog is so great
She feels no hate
I love her so much
When she sits in her hutch
Then she falls asleep
To leap
In her dreams
Of football teams.

Sarah Oliver (10)

Black Prince

Unique is what I call my dog,
Not a cat, not a frog
Strong and brave, wild and free
Best of all my dog loves me

He's fun and crazy,
Sometimes lazy
He's scatty and fun
And my number one

Fuzzy and cute
Him and I suit
With him I'll play
Every day

Sometimes I think my dog can talk
Maybe even write with chalk
What if he had magic powers?
We'd have fun for hours and hours

When the day is done and through
He'll just snuggle up to you,
My dog loves me very much
I think he has a magic touch.

Danielle Winter (11)

My Favourite Friend, Raku

My favourite friend is Raku, my cat
She is not thin and she is not fat.
She spreads her litter tray all over the floor
And then she strokes me with her paw.
She is six months old and when she is bigger
We can hire her out as a building site digger.
She tries to kill my mice
She is covered in cat lice.
She chases my rabbit - a very bad habit.
She stares at my fish which is very foolish.
She wants to catch birds
Well, have you ever heard of a naughtier favourite friend?

P.S. 'Miaow!' says Raku. 'This house is a zoo!'

Joshua Betton (9)

My Dad

My dad's rebuilding a Land Rover
He's dropping bits all over,
He'll weld a bit on here,
He'll weld a bit on there,
He'll weld lots of bits on everywhere,
He's even got a bit of Mum's garden chair
I think he's a bit of a clown,
As he's welded it all upside down.
Now it's got four wheels,
New gaskets and some seals,
Will it stop and will it go?
We really do not know.
Now it's done we'll have some fun,
Greenlaning in the sun.
We'll take it out, scream and shout,
'My dad's finished his Land Rover!'

Kelly Huby (9)

My Favourite Person

Thierry Henry, Thierry Henry
He is the best for me
His football is clean
He is not mean
He runs so fast
A goal is a must
He hardly has a smile
If the ball goes a mile
A man of few words
Known all around the world
Thierry Henry is the man
Who helps his gang

Thierry Henry, Thierry Henry
He is the best for me
The fastest runner
Got to be the best Gunner
He is simply the best
That's why he beats the rest
He gives the game respect
And that's what we children expect.

Andre Gondo (9)

Eleanor

Eleanor is a beautiful name
She is my best friend
At school she draws me pictures
I draw her pictures too
She comes to my house
I go to her parties
She is pretty, kind and sweet
I wish she lived down my street.

Paige Brown (9)

Like ...

Like the stars that shine in the skies above,
A mother shines brighter in her child's heart.
Filling it with hope, love and care
From the moment it's born, from the very start.

Like a candle melting in the dark,
Enlightening the paths of her beloved ones.
Through sacrifice, tiredness and hard work
That is how a mother's life runs.

Like all the fruitful trees in the meadows,
Giving off fruits for no wealth.
A mother gives off her life,
Without asking for time for herself.

Like the mighty sun that floats in the sky,
Extending its warmth to the people on Earth.
Spreading comfort is what a mother does,
Without anyone knowing what she is truly worth.

Elias Khattar (15)

Remembering You

I remember the fun times we used to have,
Me, you, Nan, Mum and Dad,
I remember the cap you used to wear,
To cover the lack of golden hair,
I remember that special knock you had,
I used it to get your attention when I was sad,
I remember the caravan you used to tow,
Here, there, to and fro,
These are some of my memories of my special grandad,
Your memories will be with me always.
Love now and always.

Shannon Firth (11)

My Favourite Person

Giving up all your spare time
You always help me when I'm stuck
Making up my new routines
Now at last I've got my tuck!
Always cheerful with a smile
She's the one who makes gym great
Teaching us all she knows
In the gym she is the best
Careful now, she needs a rest!
So, can you guess who is the best?
My gymnastics coach!

Lauren Stonehouse (9)

My Favourite Person

In the morning when I rise
My favourite person is by my side
When the day is broken and I feel bad
My favourite person is there to make me feel glad
When the night coats the sky black and I'm frightened
My favourite person comforts me and the stars and moon brightens
My favourite person is always by my side helping me and guiding me,
She will provide, when I need her she will come
Cos my favourite person is my mum.

Marcelle Johnson (13)

My Favourite Family!

Three of my grandparents on the family tree,
Always love to spoil me!
When I visit them they give me a kiss,
This is a moment that I'm not allowed to miss!

Two of my aunties on the family tree,
Bring my cousins along to play with me!
We play all day and play all night
Of course my aunties are there in case we have a fight!

My one little sister on the family tree,
Seems to enjoy bothering me!
Although if she wasn't here I'd be really sad,
She still manages to drive me mad!

My two parents on the family tree,
Have never stopped being there for me!
I've always loved them, that's for sure,
Instead of giving me less they give me more!

My few pets on the family tree,
Love to take leftover food from me!
Every day they make me laugh,
From being silly and very daft!

Bethany Hirons (11)

225

The Silent Hero

As the hours of darkness slowly disappear,
And the diamond awakening for calls,
All but one is silent - the whisper of all rises,
The silent hero is at work - from sun-up to sun-down,
The silent hero is at work - from sun-up to sun-down.

Pure love will shine throughout the air,
And will never leave the land of peace,
Although through the peace, guilt lies in the unexpected
Even though the nations will approve and share beauty
Even though the nations will approve and share beauty.

Through each nook and every cranny
There lies the silent hero,
Although she is a slave for me.
Although she is my mother for me,
Although she is my mother for me.

The smile that appears across my face,
When the silent hero arrives,
That smile will last forever on me and you,
For the silent hero is at work from sun-up to sun-down
For the silent hero is at work from sun-up to sun-down.

Jodie Rogers (11)

Family (n)

Meaning:
A family is the greatest person you could ever know
Provided it's your family with you in it so,
Even if they live a million miles away,
Or if you can pop in to see them every day,
They're the best people you've ever had
From the youngest cousin to the oldest grandad.

It's travelling for hours and hours over miles and miles
And still getting to Auntie's covered in smiles.
It's going over to Grandma's and staying for tea
Lying, 'It's lovely, thank you. No, more for me.'
They're the best people you've ever had
From the youngest cousin to the oldest grandad.

It's your mum saying to you on a sunny Saturday,
'Homework, young lady - you can't go out today.'
It's fighting your siblings for the remote for the TV
And never getting to watch what you want to see.
Even so they're the best people you've ever had
From the youngest cousin to the oldest grandad.

Melissa Gardner (12)

My Favourite Person Is ...

My favourite person is my mum,
Because she's got a brilliant bum.
When she goes shopping she acts so dumb,
Then we sit down and have a juicy plum.

At last we go home and sit down
Now she puts on her crown.
Luckily it is time to go to bed
Oh now she is hugging her ted.

At last she gets out of her bed
While holding onto Ted.
Then she gets dressed in her gown
Whee, we are going to town.

Taylor Egan (10)

My Grandad Far ... Far Away

When his wrinkled face was finely seen, far away
I thought I was caught in the deepest dream, far away

I saw my grandad in his pyjamas
Wearing a white T-shirt and blue trousers, far away

Standing on the other side of the blazing fire
The precious person who I most admire, far away

Staring at his two blue glowing eyes
Seeing how his love magnifies, far away

Ogling at his warm cheeks behind the fierce flames, which appeared to be pale
Knowing that his pure heart remains one of nightingale, far away

Gazing at his ravishing smile
Imaging if it was possible to be seen from a mile, far away

Trembling like a leaf on the opposite side
He nodded at me, making it clear that he is my guide, far away

Taking a step back
I felt as if he gave me a pat on my back, far away

I turned round and glanced at him
But he had already vanished in the dim, far away

Knowing I was caught in the deepest dream, far away
Suddenly everything becomes unseen, far away.

Zaynah Sayed Ackbar (13)

Sophie

Her beautiful sweet
Roses dragging along
In her hair
Always knowing when
She is there
She always knows
What to wear
Along with her beautiful
Dresses she wears everywhere
The party starts
When she is there.

Emma Dawson (8)

My Hamster Avril

A lways there to cuddle and stroke.
V ery soft fur and that's no joke
R eally sweet face with two black eyes
I mpossible to see in the midnight skies
L ittle darling hamster, Avril she's mine.

Sophie Dawson (11)

My Poem To Dixie

I love a horse called Dixie; he's my path to light,
He kept me going through hospital, shining nice and bright!

Irish Draught, cross thoroughbred, he's a magnificent horse,
Show jumping, cross-country you name it, he'll do the course!

Born on the 26th May, sixteen years old,
Sixteen-foot one in height, so I've been told!

His mum was called Pixie Lugs; his dad was called the Squire,
I love his bright red ginger coat, similar to fire!

Feeding him some mollychop, carrots and hay,
He lifts his head and sighs, beginning a gentle neigh.

His head is soft, his feet are hard,
He's my angel and my guard!

As soon as I saw him, I felt butterflies,
I had a twinkle in my eyes!

Robyn Maddison (11)

My Favourite Dog ... Tilly

My favourite dog is Tilly,
She's black from head to paw,
She has some lines of grey,
But that doesn't matter at all,
When I take her for a walk,
She gets in such a mess,
My favourite dog is Tilly,
Oh yes, oh yes, oh yes.

My favourite dog is Tilly,
She is only three years old,
She's small and sweet and fluffy,
But doesn't always do as she's told,
When I put her in her bed,
She stays there more or less,
My favourite dog is Tilly,
Oh yes, oh yes, oh yes.

Sian Townshend (7)

My Favourite Team

Steven Gerrard is the best
He will beat all the rest

Millan Barass is so fast
He goes by the rules, will always pass

Jerzy Dudek saves every shot
He gives it everything he's got

Luis Garcia is never offside
He scores lots of goals and never dives

Jamie Carriger in defence is good
Look out for him you should

Djibril Cisse may be old
But he can still score great goals.

Joe Brace (10)

231

My Family

First there's Dad
Who's very, very mad

Then there's Mum
Whose now lost her tum

Dan is the first of us four
He knocks on his friend's door

Then there's Kate
Who has lots of mates

Then there's Joe
Who lets his imagination flow

Last of all there's me
The youngest of the family.

Anastasia Brace (8)

My Favourite Person

My favourite person
Calls me every day.
My favourite person
Comes out to play.
My favourite person
Is my best friend.
My favourite person's
Friendship never ends.
My favourite person
Loves the zoo.
My favourite person
Has animals too.
My favourite person
Is here and there.
My favourite person
Is everywhere.

Sarah Woodward (9)

Untitled

I'd like to tell you a little rhyme,
It won't take me a very long time,
It's about my favourite thing in the land,
To look after him, I need a strong hand.

He goes to the park to have a good run,
I love playing with him, it's lots of fun,
My favourite thing, if you haven't guessed,
Is my dog Bailey, he is the best!

Dominic Oatley (8)

My Brother

His name is Michael
And he's only six
He is good fun
To play and mix.

His eyes are brown
And his hair is blond
He supports Arsenal
And he is very strong.

He loves his fruit
Grapes the most
But he rarely eats
A piece of toast.

He is good at maths
Probably the best
I hope he has done
Well in his test.

He plays football
For our local club
He is a midfielder
And rarely a sub.

He is my best friend
And he's always been
I am proud of him
You know what I mean!

Phillip Dearman (9)

My Favourite Person

Daddy is funny
Clever and kind
When he tells me off
I don't really mind

He takes me out
To buy comics and sweets
Brand new trainers
To put on my feet

I don't sleep at night
Because I have bad dreams
My daddy calms me down
And tells me it's not as bad as it seems

When I am ill
He is my best friend
He looks after me
Until I am on the mend

I love him most
So thank you Dad
For being there
When I am good and I am bad.

Sammy Scane (6)

My Nanny

I love my nanny,
She always makes me laugh
And plays with me in the bath.
She likes to see a clean plate
And doesn't care if my room is a state!

I love my nanny,
She always gives me treats,
Usually they are sweets,
My nanny is always kind,
A nicer nanny you'd never find.

I love my nanny
She's gentle and doesn't shout
And she often takes us out and about.
We stay up late when she's here,
So we have nothing to fear.
I love my nanny!

Sophie Luckett (8)

I Don't Have A Friend, I've Got Two Of Them

One of my friends loves sports.
He also loves martial arts.
He's the greatest at maths
And he's crazy about art and DT.
Plus he's the fastest in the class,
That's why this guy's my favourite person.

Another one of my friends comes from a big family.
He's the toughest in the class, let alone the strongest.
He's the best at science
And he's crazy about sports.
Plus he's a chocoholic,
That's why this guy's my favourite person.

Joel George (9)

My Dad

If I'm ever in the darkness with a hundred different paths
I'll know which one to choose because I know I've got my dad
If it is my birthday, I know what to expect
My dad will get me a plane or even a jet
Now I'm going much too far, I know he can't do that
But instead he might get me the prettiest purple mat
If I'm feeling sad and blue
My dad's the person to go too
I have got the dad that's better than the rest
I have got the dad that knows that he's the best.

Naomi Chadwick (10)

Someone Special

It was a very bright summer's day,
When an angel came to me.
She asked me a question,
Then gave me a key.

Her question was, 'Who is special?'
My reply was,
'Someone in my heart at the highest level.'

I wondered what the key was for,
It was gold and circle,
Then I saw a keyhole,
In a box that was purple.

My key fit just perfectly,
So I opened up the box,
Then I saw a package,
Tied up with knots.

I managed to open it,
And inside I saw,
Some very special people,
Who I adore.

When the angel came again,
She asked me happily,
'What is your reply?'
I answered, 'My family.'

Krystal Rodgers (11)

My Fave Person

My favourite person is God,
He made people, land and oceans.
He created my mum and my dad,
He made the golden sand.
He created school where we can learn,
He created jobs in which we earn.
He gave our souls lives
He gave lonely men wives.
He created creatures and bodies
He gave men the strength to build lobbies.
He created the wonderful wavy sea,
But the most important thing He's made, are you and me!

Amanda Grigor (11)

My Favourite Person

My favourite person is my dog
Who is very cute and sweet
She loves to play with smelly socks
And her favourite food is meat

My favourite person is my dog
Who has a fluffy tail
She is trained to do everything
Except fetch the mail

My favourite person is my dog
Who has four furry paws
Which hurt if she scratches you
Because of her sharp claws

My favourite person is my dog
Whose nose is black and wet
But although she is a real pain
She is my favourite pet.

Jade Brothers (9)

239

My Mom

She makes me smile in times when I am feeling sad,
She makes me feel good when I am feeling bad.
In times when I have no one to talk to, she's always there,
Offering her love, protection and care.
The Black Country is where she is from,
Have you guessed who it is?
It's my mom.

Lauren Garbett (10)

My Family

My family is so special to me,
They're as special as special can be.
They make me happy whenever they smile,
They make me feel I can run a mile!
They make me feel so very tall,
Even though I'm kind of small.
They make me warm when they give me a hug,
As cosy as a bug in a rug.
They can make me feel I'm actually fab,
When I'm nothing but really sad.
I'm sorry when I act so bad,
Forgive me, forgive me or I'll be really sad.
My family is just great,
So I don't need to hesitate to say ...
I love them with all my heart!

Lily Wu (10)

Mum

It's a shame I take for granted
What she does for me.
But I'm not joking,
You really need to see ...

That she runs around the house,
Every single day,
Doing things for others,
So I'd really like to say ...

'Thank you'
For all she helps me with,
My homework and the dishes,
What she does is no myth.

It's amazing!
How she gets me to school,
And does so many other jobs
How does she keep her cool?

Rebecca Morton (10)

Guiding Angel

Tears strolled down my face,
My footsteps leaving no trace.
No one could follow behind.
No one to keep me in line.
I had left that life a long time ago,
And now I wander around all alone.

But through the mist and fog he waited.
'I am your guiding angel,' he stated.
He took my hand as he wiped my tears
With a wave, he dismissed my fears.
He told me I was better than that
I could make it no matter what.

He promised he would always be there for me,
And I saw no need to disagree.
He is my best friend, but most importantly, my brother,
It is because of him I refuse to surrender.
So no wonder he is my favourite person in the world and he completes me,
Because without him I wouldn't have a reason to breath you see.

Chorin Kawa (15)

Vita The Great

Vita the Great is my best, best mate
We play together but we're never ever late
One day we got lost at a certain rate
We were playing about on the streets of Dartmouth
When we just found out
That we felt quite bad
And then Vita decided to tell someone else
That we felt quite sad
And then it just happened
That we felt quite mad
But it was such a relief
When we met our mum and dad
Boy we felt glad!

Catherine Byrne (8)

My Favourite Person

Shadow is my hamster
He is all black
But not a gangster
Because he doesn't slack

I didn't want to call him Jack or Zack
Because he didn't step on a tack
That is why I named him Shadow
My true black friend.

Alex Clark

My Mum

When we are naughty ...

My mum is as loud as a bomb
Her shouts rattle off walls
My mum is as scary as lightning
My mum is as fierce as a lion.

When we are good ...

My mum is as calm as summer sea
Her words are like a soothing breeze
My mum is like the sun sparkling on water
My mum is like a cuddly teddy bear.

That's my mum!

Emma Bond (9)

Mum's The Best

Every day I see her in the morning
Mum is careful and always gives me warning.

Mum is my best friend
She will be there till the end.

She's there for me when I am ill
And always by my side still.

She's fun and kind
She's always in my mind.

She's my best friend
And always will
Be to the end.

Meghan Browett (9)

My Nan

When I was small we played with toys
As I am big we talk about boys
My fabulous nan is the best
She is so good we make her rest

My favourite person is my nan
If we can't do it she sure can
Her deep blue eyes shining bright
I smile whenever she's in sight

Her gleaming smile is so great
She is the one I could not hate
Her thin fingers oh so long
She is always humming a song

This is why I love my nan
If I can love her we all can!

Katie Heap (11)

My Favourite Person - My Auntie Nic

This is for my auntie,
My auntie the one I love.
The sharing, caring, kind of girl.
An angel, sent from above.
Amazing she is,
My auntie is amazing.
Although she has,
A wrapping paper craving.
All the people, around the world
They don't know my aunt, all that well.
But if they did, they would love her to bits.
Kiss her, then marry her,
My nan would be in fits.
Great, I could be a bridesmaid,
I'd only be 55!
We'd celebrate together,
Then eventually do the jive,
But she's not married yet,
And I'm not 55.
So let's look at the time we have
I love you loads, my big sis
Or in other words,
I love you loads my auntie Nic.

Aimee Cole (13)

My Grandma

(Dedicated to Irene McConville who passed away peacefully on July 5th 2005)

I love my grandma   she's a gentle carer,
And a fantastic love   and hug sharer!
Also my grandma can cook   delicious cake and food,
My grandma is the best that is   why she is never in a mood,
Grandma is always careful at the food shops with what she buys,
I sometimes give my lovely grandma a huge welcoming surprise,
Go to my great grandma for a snugly warm and happy cuddle,
When I go to see my grandma she's never been in a muddle,
In my grandma's wardrobe she has got black shoes,
When I see them I know which ones to choose,
She plays Uno with me and we have fun,
She plays with Dad and also with Mum,
She has lots to do at her church,
And her favourite tree is birch,
Grandma is great and fun,
She can cook great buns,
Grandma is the best,
And loves guests.
She is my
Gran!

Emily McConville (11)

My Favourite Person, Who Is It?

Likes to smile, likes to grin,
Has a very knobbly chin,
Very old and very wrinkly,
Very forgetful and even crinkly,
I love her very much and she's my friend,
Our love for each other will never end,
Who is it?
My grandmother!

Adam Jarvis (11)

Sister

You are embarrassing,
And though we have our rows
We make up in the end
And we are still friends now.

When I am bored
We always have fun
And even though you work a lot
At the end it's always done.

Sometimes I wish you were younger
But now I am thankful to you,
Because I know older sisters are cooler
And they always think things through.

You give me a shoulder to cry on
When I have had enough
And you are a comfort
You never cry, you are tough.

Sister, I am thankful
For having you there all the time,
Though sometimes you can be sweet
And other times as sour as a lime.

Suraiya Jagot (13)

My Mother

Oh sweet mother, sweet mother, sweet mother of mine
You're ever so loving and ever so kind
You've been there for me through good times and bad
You bring a smile to my face whenever I'm sad
You're a gift from God, one of a kind
You're precious like gold; I can never leave you behind
Loyal and understanding, confiding and forgiving
You are so special, I'm so glad you're mine.

Ayesha Adam (12)

My Brother

Silently and swiftly I pass by you
I slide my fingers through your mahogany hair
I see those eyes, they never hold lies
Your beautiful hazel eyes can hypnotise
I'm lucky you're related to me
A brother, a friend
What more could I ask you to be
You're generous and bubbly, kind and caring
You hold my tears, secrets and joy
You always keep me smiling not in puddles of tears
You're not too tall or not too short
 A package just right.

Maria Anwar (13)

My Favourite Person

I glance up, I see him as tall as a giraffe,
Smiling down on me like a ray of sun.
Lustrous, brunette, gelled hair,
Which reminds me of a pineapple
Sitting in a grocer's waiting to be picked.
Not just a brother but like a parent
Who cares and shares my hopes and dreams.
A friend who I can turn to,
Someone to reveal secrets and adventures to.
Always there with a shoulder at my disposal
To help when I'm feeling miserable.
He always sticks up for me even if it's something wrong,
Explains everything with great clarity
Making me understand and appreciate the rarity of such a beautiful bond.

Veena Patel (13)

My Grandma

You may be seventy-three but you're no less special to me.
You're there for me when I need somebody
And whenever I need you, your shoulder I turn to,
Because I look up to you Grandma and I love you very much
I don't know how it would be without your caring touch.

Ashish Raja (13)

My Dad

My dad, my dad, the best dad in the world,
He is a star, shines day and night.
He was always there, he was aware,
Because he would care, all his life he would try to share,
With his jokes I would be happy,
Because I knew he would smile for me,
He was not too tall, not too short, but a gift perfect.
He was my dad and also a best friend,
If I was upset or problems met,
I knew he was the one person I could turn too,
Before I would really regret.
He was ever so funny, gentle and kind,
His jet-black hair, chocolate almond eyes and
Generosity will always stay in my mind.
He was a dad, ever so trustworthy, special and sweet,
Ever so soft, polite and neat.
Whenever I was sad, because of the day I had,
He would stop me from feeling so bad.

Huda Jaffer (13)

Untitled

My mum is like a rose
Beautiful and sweet
She always looks after me
And gives me lots of treats

My mum is like a star
Sparkling in the sky
She has dark hair
And a twinkle in her eye

My mum is like a friend
Who cheers me when I'm blue
My mum loves me very much
And I love her too

So now I've told you about my mum
And I know you'll all agree
That my mum is perfect
And she belongs to me.

Govind Singh (13)

My Nans

Nans, well, what can I say?
They are there for you come what may.
They know what's best for you
And know what to say.
You can talk to them about anything
And they always know what to say.
They always make your troubles go away.
Well, what more can I say?
They always show you love and care
No matter what time of day.
Nans are very special people and play such a big part
I know my nans have a very special place in my heart!

Faye McGee (11)

My Favourite Person!

My favourite person is someone that I play with every day.
This person is a small person.
This person lives with me.
This person is special to me
Because he always has a smile on his face
And when this person has a smile on his face
It makes me have a smile on my face.
This special person is my little brother Menelik.

Jelani Agu-Lionel (11)

My Favourite Person

My favourite person is tall and pretty
I like her a lot
She is funny and happy
And she never gets snappy
She is my teacher of course
She is helpful and nice and kind to everyone
She is the best teacher of course.

Holly Henderson (10)

My Great Teacher

She's a load of fun
She's as bright as the sun
She writes on the board
Like she's been given an award
Her patience is great
She's never late
She teaches maths
Like it's a bundle of laughs
Her appearance is grand
With being quite tanned
She can be happy and sad
As well as crazy and mad
She's the best teacher in the UK
Of every week and every day
She's as sweet as a bird
And her name's Miss Heard.

Jessica Wood (11)

Alan

Alan Shearer the Newcastle king,
He can make that ball do amazing things,
He hits it with incredible power,
Is always a gentleman but never a fouler.

He was captain of the England team,
Some say he's the best they've ever seen,
He once came out playing in the Blackburn shirt,
But Newcastle was the team that he preferred.

He is a Geordie through and through,
The Newcastle's manager's job is his dream come true,
So I will keep practising my football skills,
To be like Alan who gives great season thrills.

Zac Rigby (10)

My Favourite Person Is My Grandad

I think my grandad is a hippy
He likes to travel around in his camper van,
Listening to his favourite band, The Rolling Stones
He parks up in the campsite,
Reading his book for the night.

The sizzle of sausage and bacon
The swishing of his tea mug, can be heard all around
As my grandad cooks his breakfast
And then he travels and stops wherever to rest
My grandad is the best.

Mikey Johnson (10)

My Dad

I love my dad because he never goes wrong,
He's got great big muscles and he's very strong,
He plays with my brother; he likes to play fight,
He puts us to bed and says, 'Goodnight.'

Suzanne Neville (11)

Special People

I have so many people for me to love,
Happiness flying through the air like a dove.
School friends, teachers, family too,
I love them all, believe me it's true.

Friends are great to have around
They pick you up whenever you're down.
My friends are great, loving and kind,
Without them I'd lose my mind.

My family are great even when they're strict,
I love them all, that feeling will stick.
No one can take away the love we share,
Even if I don't, they definitely care.

I have two cats both pretty and sweet
My friends all drool when my cats they meet.
My gorgeous cats, one tabby, one black
Are wonderful creatures, everyone knows that.

Amber Lilley (11)

My Favourite Person

My favourite person is mam
My mam is better than anything in the world.
She can make me laugh and wiggle
She is kind as a bee and sweet as a flower
And she is still lovely to me.

Danika Wheatley (11)

My Favourite Person

My favourite person is Lucy
She is six just like me.
I love her very much
And she sometimes comes for tea.
We play together every day
With Gabriella, Miranda, Carmella, Molly and Michael.
We play stuck in the mud and tig and races.
Michael's in a wheelchair and sometimes we get to push him round
He can't walk so we care for him.

Jessica Westwood (6)

My Puppy Bow

My puppy Bow barks with all his might,
He's my best friend that sweet little mite.

My puppy Bow is always there for me,
He likes being fussed, he's very friendly.

My puppy Bow will play with me,
He nips my nose and jumps on my knee.

My puppy Bow loves chewing pots,
If I treat him kind he will love me lots.

My puppy Bow is fun to play with,
He is the best puppy ever.

Bradley Tabberer-Mills (7)

My Mum

My mum is good.
My mum is great.
My mum is never late.
My mum drives me everywhere.
My mum is always there.

My mum is like a flower.
My mum is blooming too.
I love my mum so very much,
If you met her you would too!

Zoe Hickey (10)

My Favourite Person Is Emma From GT

E   mma is cool!
M   ore styles created by her.
M   any people read her pages in 'Girl Talk'.
A   hat, a scarf - she can make them look good on anyone!

G   o Emma!
T   ips on how to look fab and cool.

Hannah Beattie (10)

Poem

My brother is the best
Because he cracks at jokes and makes everyone happy.
My brother is the best
He can beat the rest in every test that he might have in his future.
My brother is the best
I am so lucky to have a brother like this.
When you see my brother on a beach
You may be wondering why he is wearing the colour peach.
My brother is the best because he always is so bright
When he's playing his kite.
My brother is the best
When he gets to mess around he thinks, *when will I get my crown?*
My brother is the best
And he really beats the rest.

Amardeep Singh (13)

The Best Sister

There is a girl
Who wears pearls
Inside her heart
Is a cart
Of love and care
She shares
Only with the best cuddly bear
Who? Me of course
Her best and only brother
She is the best
Out of the rest
Of all sisters
I think she is so cool
She rules
At pool
She likes chocolate biscuits
And all rock music
I love her so
I think she knows
That her bro
Shall miss her so
When she leaves for uni
But when she comes back for a visit
I don't want to miss it
Cos if I do
I will shout, 'Boo hoo!'
But then again
I will shout, 'Woohoo'
When I get a big hug!

Dharmesh Patel (14)

My Mate

My mate is great at football,
My mate is tremendous at basketball,
He knows all the tricks,
Down to the last bricks,
My mate is great at volleyball,
My mate is awesome at baseball,
That's my mate,
All in all he is great.

Mohammed Aqueeb Patel

My Sister

Haseena my beautiful sis
Always gives me a kiss
Spins round and round
Too fast, not often, falls on the ground

Haseena my joyful sis
Spins around like a dish
Haseena you have the best smile
You even swim half a mile

Haseena my bright sis
With a beautiful face like I had wished
Haseena your eyes twinkle like the shining stars
You always sit in the golden cars

Haseena you have gold hair like golden honey
Sometimes you act so funny
Haseena you are as brainy as a calculator
But not as hungry as an alligator.

Haleema Raja (12)

261

My Mum

My Mum, my friend,
Advice she's ready to lend,
Understanding and helpful,
Lovingly cheerful,
I love my mum.

Humble and kind,
Sweet too you will find,
Vibrant and fun,
Brighter than the sun.
I love my mum.

Beautiful, intelligent and of course extremely smart,
Always has my best interests at heart
When I'm encircled by the dark
She'll brighten my day with shimmering sparks.
I love my mum.

Without her I am no one
Thanks to her I am someone.

Shazia Kazi (12)

My Favourite Person

His eyes are round and coloured brown,
He is as happy as a clown!

His hair is black as coal,
He scurries round like a mole!

He's very cheeky just like a monkey,
He thinks he's cool and very funky!

And although he's only four,
He's the one that I adore!

Mariam Adam

My Favourite Person!

Face round like the shining sun
Soft as a chocolate bun

Fair skin the colour of an inside of a coconut
Hair the colour of chocolate

Sweet as honey
And very funny

Eyes twinkling like stars
Likes playing with toy cars

Beautiful as a rose
Cute, tiny, small toes.

Hina Goraniya

My Favourite Person

My mum is like a friend.
My mum is like a star.
My mum is the best, just like Amir Khan.

My mum is nice.
My mum is fine.
She makes people giggle.
She makes people smile.

My mum can be angry.
She can be mad.
She only gets angry when people make her mad.

My mum can sing.
She can dance.
She loves to smell roses because roses are red like her heart.

Tasneem Musa (11)

My Favourite Person

My best friend Aneesha
As lovely as a fuchsia
Intelligent and angelic
Her hair so static

Aneesha has a bubbly character
She is full of laughter
Her hair sways in the breeze
She loves eating cheese

She is bright as a star
But she can never go far
Her eyes glitter like a sparkling sea
She is busy like a bee.

Palvinder Kaur (12)

My Mum

When I am sad she will share my sorrows,
When I am happy her joy will be mine.

A shoulder to cry on,
A hand to hold,
Someone to talk to,
My mother, my world.

My past,
My present,
My future,
She moulds.

She lifts me up whenever I fall,
Always there to show me the road.

God bless my mother for being my world.

Ebrahim Sidat (13)

My Mum

My mum ... loves me greatly
Taking all the hard grief lately
Giving me all her support
She likes everything I do, like sport.
But what makes her the best
That you can tell her anything
Just get everything off my chest.
Another thing that makes her great
Is ... how we communicate.
She makes me leave with a smile
Quotes me on my style!
And it makes me so lucky to
Say ... that's my mum!

Sanish Prasad (8)

My Favourite Person

I know poems about mums are boring
But this one is alluring
I know she's the best
Because I have put her through a lot of tests
Scrapping and fighting
And then reuniting
She helps when I am mad
And even when I am sad
She is also delightful
And even wonderful
She is also very sweet
As sweet as juicy sweets.

Stefan Hallam (7)

My Favourite Person

To have a person like you
To stop me from feeling blue
Always there to guide me
Someone loyal and true
You are, only you
So sweet, so loving, so caring
You make me smile when I am down
Help me, when I am stuck
You bring me so much good luck
You're my guardian, you're my angel
You are my best friend
Together we can fix anything
When I need a friend it's always you to comfort me
You are, only you
Now, forever and forever
I will be by your side
Be your best friend
Stand next to you with pride
My sweet, loving, caring
Best friend Sadiyya!

Hoor Daud (13)

My Shining Star

Hazel eyes with a tint of blue,
Fudge-coloured curls looking shiny and brand new.
A shoulder to cry on, you're truly the best
With all the amazing talents you possess.
When I'm feeling down and lonely
You always comfort and console me.
I wouldn't be here without you
You're the one who's got me through.
A life of hurt, a life of pain,
Without you I'd go insane.
You are like a jewel precious and dear,
You're my everything, I'm so glad you are here.
A friend, a mother and ever better than a candy bar
You are my world, my mother, my shining star.

Asiyah Jassat

My Mum

My favourite person is my mum
She's more than a currant bun
She's the best
Leave the rest
My favourite person is my mum
I love my mum
She lies in the sun
Not all day long
That would be wrong
My favourite person is my mum
She works very hard for us
She doesn't go on the bus
Or make a fuss
My favourite person is my mum.

Yasmin Powell (9)

My Only Little Brother

Adam is my little brother,
My favourite person,
My forever friend.

Adam is the reason I dream,
When I have needed a friend,
The reason I understand,
When no one else does.

He can make me feel better,
When I am feeling bad,
He can make me positive,
At the most negative time of my life.

Adam is a light that brightens up my life,
A friend when no one else is speaking to me,
He is there for me,
When I most need someone to talk to.

He is my only little brother,
My only guiding star,
My only shining light,
My only Adam!

Zoe Beattie (11)

My Best Friend

My best friend will make me happy when I am sad.
Do you have a friend like this?
My best friend will trust me when others do not.
Do you have a friend like this?
My best friend will sit with me at lunch when others don't want to.
Do you have a friend like this?
My best friend is kind to me when others are not.
Do you have a friend like this?

Stephanie Powell (11)

My Poem

My scrummy yummy mummy
My lazy stinky daddy
My bossy wossy big sister
My naughty little sister
My hard-working grandad
My clothes buying grandma
All my family love me and all my family support me
And we all live happily.

Davan Rayat (10)

My Great Mum

My mum is a brilliant cook
She gets her ideas from a recipe book.
Cakes and cookies, pasta and rice
Whatever it is it usually turns out nice.

She works really hard all through the day,
But she always finds time to play.
This is not all completely true,
But I do love my mum from hat to shoe.

Bethany Penford (10)

My Gran Is ...

Happy as a bunny,
She's very, very funny,
Looks like Heaven,
As now I've grown from eleven,
My love to her,
Stays the same but,
Grows more each night,
As I love her with delight,
Her smile is ever so lovely,
As she is such a cutie,
All I want to tell you Gran,
Is that, I love you!

Batool Alsafar (12)

I Like My Dog

I like my dog because he's fluffy and poofy
And does what a dog's supposed to do.
He is playful and always begs for foods, that's why he is so fat.
He always wags his tail and we always have to give him his daily belly rub.
He has long fluffy ears and red eyes and is very fat.
He is the greatest dog mankind can ever have.

Lavelle Bedward (9)

You Are The Greatest

You are the best, can't you see?
And you are great, looking after me.
Getting ready for school is a bad thing
I like to be a nuisance like watching Kerching.
I love you lots to the moon and the sun
And I know you like it when your chores are done.
Then you can sit down and have a rest
And make sure I'm not being a pest.

Alex Blumire (10)

My Family

Mel, my sister is so great
She has lots of mates
When her money comes in
She has no sin
It will just go to waste.

Mum, my mum's the boss of the house
She can treat us like we're a little mouse
She likes to shop
And she likes to dance
Going round, prance, prance, prance!

Dad, my dad's the one, the man, the fixer
He can fix it in a flash
He's the loudmouth of us all
But he's still really, really cool
He's the king and he rules!

Cherry, she's the prancer not the prey
She's cute and likes to play
If she wanted to scratch
She would do it behind our backs
She's my baby called Cherry.

Lucy, she's a fluffy ball, she's so cute
She's a Skye terrier and she can fit in our big boot.
She loves our cat
And she won't hit her back
She's our lovely Lucy.

Jessica Brown (11)

You Make Me Feel

You make me feel like a tasty chocolate bar.
You make me feel like a shimmering star.
You make me feel like ice cream in a cone.
You make me feel like the Queen on her throne.
You make me feel like the deep blue sea.
You make me feel like a buzzing bee.
You make me feel like a pot of gold.
You make me feel like a diamond ring on a hand you hold.
You make me feel like the shining sun.
You make me feel like that because you're my mum.

Harriet Dean (10)

Untitled

I have lots of favourite people,
But I'm going to write about my grandad
He is kind and caring
And always gives you blocks of chocolate and a river full of pop.
My grandad is always up for a game and a hug.
He lets you watch movies and never really shouts.
My grandad always gives you blocks of chocolate
And a river full of pop.
There is one last thing I want to say,
You will never find anyone as kind as my grandad.

Maddy Hart (10)

My Gran

My gran is as kind as an angel.
Her hair is like a bunch of roses.
Her eyes are like the green grass in spring.
Her face is like sheep's wool.
When she walks she is like a happy little girl.
When she sits she is like a cuddly panda.
When she laughs it sounds like little bells ringing.
But the best thing about my gran is she loves me.

Jessica Rodinson (9)

My Favourite Person

My cuddly sister nice and warm
Cuddles me till day is dawn
She makes my face light up with glee
Her face glows as she runs to me
Most sisters argue and fight
But me and Carla are sisters bright
With love we share our secrets at night
I love my sister as she guides me through darkness and brings me light.

Chloe Waplington (12)

275

This Person

This person is the cutest in the world.
This person is softer than a teddy to me.
This person is small like a baby bunny.
And when he gets excited, he's just so funny.
He likes to listen to my music
And bounces around like Tigger
And do you know what?
Every day he just gets bigger and bigger and bigger.
This person I will look after,
Protect and love and honour,
Because this special person is my baby brother Konnor.

Corey Graham (11)

My Grandma

I love my grandma very much
She makes me tasty soup for lunch.
She has toy cars and lets me play
Until the end of every day
She acts in such a pleasant way.

I cannot wait to see her face
Her house is such a lovely place.
It's clean and fresh and fragrant too
And every word she speaks is true
She gives me chewy sweets to chew.

She takes me to the park for walks
And all we do is talk, talk, talk.
We smell the flowers on the grass
And watch the birds fly swiftly past.
I want these memories to last.
And when the sun is out of sight,
My grandma gives me a kiss goodnight.

Zofia Bungay (10)

My Favourite Person Of The Year

I have a friend who is shy,
She loves to buy,
She is always in a fashion,
With a little bit of passion,
She loves singing mad songs
And she loves singing sad songs,
She is always in a good mood,
When she eats her favourite food
Who can my friend be?
She is always with me.

Marin Thomas (10)

Best Friends

My favourite person is Kristin she likes to jump up high
She can't wait to see me we didn't say goodbye.

We couldn't wait to meet up
I miss her every day.

We could have a sleepover
Every Friday.

Evie Belgrove (7)

My Gran

Gran, you're great, you can really make a cake.
You're very cool, I tell people in my school.
We have good ideas you and me
And do them together before we have tea,
We are interested in nature, like dogs, birds and fish
And you always try to help me get my wish.
Sometimes we have a hug and a cuddle
Especially when I have been in a muddle.
I love you Gran, you've passed the test
That's why I think you are the best.

Daniel Gratton (9)

My Big Brother

B rothers are nice
R eady to play
O ne good brother
T rying to make me happy
H aving time
E asy going
R ight today.

David Byers (7)

My Baby Brother

I have a baby brother,
And his name is James,
But if you've met a baby,
They are nowhere near the same.

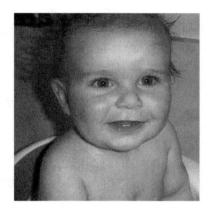

James is funny,
James is cute,
He hops like a bunny,
And if you care to look,
His eyes are blue,
And his hair is blond,
He has a button nose,
And he gets most things wrong,
James is still teething,
So his mouth is very sore,
But he is still my baby brother,
And I love him more and more.

I have a baby brother,
And his name is James
But if you've met a baby
You have *not* met James.

Eleanor Trott (10)

279

My School Friend

My school friend can be very cool,
But on the other hand, a very big fool.

This person loves his food
Especially when it's warm
But it's not very nice
When it's been cooled.

He's a very good speller
Gets along with the teachers
And can't wait to get his first job.

When it comes to playtime, he will play very well
But can be a tiny bit rude.

This boy likes the ancient world
And has good games that he enjoys too.

He's a good friend to have and you can trust him with secrets
And he will be there for you when you need him most.

He's always happy, loyal
And almost never sad.

We have a good relationship and we help each other.
So, overall, we are good friends to each other
And this person is, Thomas Lidington.

Matthew Zelmanowicz (10)

My Mum

My favourite person in the whole world
Would of course be my mum.

She cheers me up when I'm feeing glum
And always gives me the right advice.

She's always there when I need her most
And never lets me down,
She does her best to make me happy
But sometimes I forget that.

She can be angry and wired sometimes but
She never pretends to be someone she's not.

She loves to dance, listen to jokes
And laughs herself to the full.
She's kind and generous
And always makes the best out of anything.
Every Christmas she gives me
More than one present, including a DVD!

It's always nice to have her around
And she makes a good impression.
She has once or twice embarrassed me
But I can live with that.

She speaks her mind in a nice way
And does not make people feel unwanted.
She encourages me to do my best
And every time I do a test
She tells me to think before I ink.

No matter what people say about her
Whether they say she's nice or horrible
She will be my favourite person in the whole world.
My mum!

Jessica Quimpo (10)

My Favourite Person

My favourite person would have to be Kat
Because she's my girlfriend
And everyone knows that.
She's beautiful I think
While her voice sounds like
The beautiful singing of birds
When you wake up in the morning.
Her hair is like a shiny brown sensation
When I go to bed I think of her
With lots of expectation.
When I kiss her, it's like a dream
After I've done that
I feel supreme.
Her bluey green eyes
Are as beautiful as the skies
Except they haven't got a single cloud
And that's what makes me want to shout her name out loud.

Kieran Magee (10)

My Poem About My Brother Craig

Without my brother I wouldn't be able to play
Like I do each and every day.
I wouldn't be able to laugh all day
If my brother ran away.
My brother is a home to me
I hope you can clearly, clearly see.
I will never forget my brother in a while
Because he has a wonderful smile.
My brother is a wonderful boy
And he gives me so much joy.
I love my brother and he loves me
We will always be a family.

Darryl Wearn (10)

My Pet Narla

M y dog Narla is cute and sweet
Y ou and me begging at my mum's feet.

P laying and messing all the day
E very day friends join in our play
T elling her off when she is bad.

N arla goes crazy, Narla goes mad!
A fter days, many ways
R ipping toys for her play
L oving walks every day
A nd we go on walks at the bay.

My pet Narla please don't pass away
My pet Narla, I love you all the day.

Ben Udy (10)

I Love My Mum

I'll love you until the moon turns blue,
Because you are you and I am I
You've raised me well for the world to see
So keep it up!

Without you I am only half of who I am
Without you I am a fish with no lips
Without you I am a forest without trees
Without you I couldn't sail round the seven seas.
Without you I am like a teacher without chalk
Without you I am like a dog that can't walk
Without you I am like a panda without any black
Without you I am like a cat without its tail, it wouldn't sleep and would go crazy.
Like I would if you went away
I wouldn't be able to play any day.

Aliesha Lasisi (10)

I Love My Mum

I love my mum so much it makes me sad
I love my mum, I never get mad
When I am mad, she calms me down
But does not let me pull a frown.
I love my mum
I love my mum so much
I love my mum so it hurts my heart
My mum and me will never be apart.

Jon Styles (9)

My Dog Alfie

My dog makes me happy when I am down
I smile at him when I see him and when I play with him.

He gets the ball when I throw it
He also tries to get the guinea pig as well!

I love my dog, I hope he loves me
I give him his dinner and he takes mine, but I still love him.

My dog has lots of other friends apart from me
Like the guinea pig, the fish and my family.

I love my dog, so does my family
But I don't think the guinea pig does because he tries to eat him.

My dog loves to pull up plants in the garden
But my dad hates putting them back in so he gets cross.

My dog loves walks as well as me
We all go together, me, my dog and my family.

I love my dog because he's funny
And he makes me laugh!

Sarah Vince (10)

Amber

My favourite person is Amber
She really makes me smile
And when I have to feed her
I feel it is worthwhile.

She dribbles and she laughs
She plays peekaboo
And when you say your name
She will always point at you.

She is very intelligent,
Her crawling is just fine
She likes to play with washing
And she pulls it off the line.

She barely goes to sleep
And when she does you see
It is when want to go to school
Or have started to watch TV.

I push her in her pushchair
On the way to school
I take her to the shops
Which I think is really cool!

This is why I like her,
And why she's special to me
And when I take her out
We are always in time for tea.

Charlie Walker (10)

Ronaldinho

Ronaldinho, what a man
Can he score, yes he can!
He streaks up the wing
He is the free kick king
Skills and tricks
He knocks it through the metal sticks
Brazil four - Argentina one.

Nathan Silverthorn (12)

My Sister Eirwen

My sister is very annoying,
But also very funny,
Her favourite pets are hamsters
But she never lets them go.

She always prank calls her boyfriend
Because she thinks he's two-timing,
So she hates him very much
She is going to dump him soon.

I love her so much
When I'm in school I am lonely
Without my precious sister
She doesn't love me as much
I love her more
I still think she's annoying and funny.

Hywel Riley (11)

287

Guardian

I hear you in the wind.
I see you in the sky.
I drink you in the water.
I feel you by my side.
I know you're always near me
Though I cannot see your spirit
Shadow drifting, keeping close to me.

Ruth Singleton (17)

My Family

Plants will die
The moon will sail away
But you're the people
I think of every day.

In my heart
Your names will always be kept
From my soul
They will never be swept

The names of my family
Are forever in my heart
You truly can never
Tear us apart.

I really, really love my family
They are my heart
And my soul
They mean everything to me

When I'm with my lovely family
You can't tear us apart
Because you never ever can
Rub names off people's hearts.

Sabiha Khan (11)

Ellie-May

Ellie-May is a cat
She always sleeps on her favourite mat.
Ellie-May, she is the best,
She is better than the rest.
Ellie-May has beautiful blue eyes,
Ellie-May has a small black nose.

Ellie-May, I love her so much,
Ellie-May, she makes me smile,
Ellie-May, she is the best
Everyone thinks she is a pest,
Ellie-May, she is very cute,
She hides under the sofa and never comes out.

She is sometimes a pest but I think
She is better than the rest.

She cuddles up on my lap,
And she is not allowed through the cat flap.

Ellie-May, she is the best,
She is better than the rest,
But she is sometimes a pest!

Amy Lipyeart (10)

My Best Friend

My best friend is Colm
He is just the best
When I am playing with him
I never need to rest.
He has a house in Cambridge
I've visited once or twice
His bedroom is a huge one
And his ensuite is really nice.
I now like Risborough
But we still chat on the phone
He sends me funny emails
Saying, 'Homework, what a moan!'
He once came round to my house
We went to Hell Fire caves
It was dark and spooky
Really quite like a maze.
He supports Chelsea
And so do I
When they score
We both shout, 'Yes!' to the sky.
His parents are Liz and Kevin
Mine are Pat and Jo
They get on really well together
To each other they hardly say, 'No!'
Colm is my best friend and I am his
I'm really glad we met each other
Even when we have an argument
We are not in much of a bother.

Conor Walker (10)

My Dad

My poem is all about my dad
He loves and cares for me a lot
And in the evening when he comes home, I'm glad
And so is my family

My dad plays sport with me and my brother
He plays football, tennis, golf and more
And when we're finished, I love it so much I ask for another,
And so does my brother

My dad cooks my weekend meals for my family
He cooks potatoes, parsnips, chicken and more
And he serves it so happily
That me and my family ask for more

My dad helps me with lots of things
He helps me understand questions I ask
And he answers all the questions with joy
So I do not hesitate to ask more

My dad buys me all I need
He provides me with bed and food and more
And he lets me read
So that is why I love my dad!

George Moran (10)

My Favourite Person

I really like my grandma,
But she lives quite far away,
She thinks I'm really funny,
I'd love to see her every day.
We do see her quite a lot,
She has this really big house,
The only thing that would scare her,
Is if she sees a mouse.
She has this large garden,
Where she lets us do as we please,
Next door there live some sheep,
So I just feed them leaves.
My gran is a brilliant cook,
She makes the food really yummy,
I eat it every time
It always satisfies my tummy.
My grandma is the best,
She really is quite fine,
I really love my grandma
I'd choose her every time!

Emily Brundrett (10)

My Dog Daisy

My dog Daisy
She really is the best
She likes to bark
And round you up.

She once fell in the river
Thinking it was grass
She doggy-paddled out again
And shook all of the water off.

We've had her since before I was born
She's two years older than me
For her birthday we normally give her a chew stick
She always knows it's for her.

Once when we were on holiday, she got fleas
We got a man to get rid of it, but it didn't help
We had to go early
And in the car I could not sleep.

Once, she climbed on the table
My mum and dad got into a rage
She knocked over the glasses
Luckily we had some spare.

Overall I have to say
Sometimes she is a pest
The barking is loud
But I'm telling you, she is the best!

James Myerson (10)

My Dog Biscuit

My dog Biscuit, I love her
Because of her soft fur
She hates cats when they purr
And every time she's the boss
I always have to say, 'Sir.'

When I am at home,
I am never alone,
Because of my dog Biscuit,
That always moans
But then she stops, when she gets her bone.

When we go out for walks,
She always finds white chalks,
And when we go for dinner, we get our folks,
In the pub garden she has a sniff
And every time she gets a whiff.

When I am at home in my bed,
I am thinking of her in my dreams,
And when I do that, she always gleams,
But if you think she is a pest,
Well, I think she is the best.

Charlotte Rice (10)

Dominic, My Baby Brother

Dominic, my baby brother, is the best
He's fun and cheeky
His beakers are all leaky
He never wants any rest
At dinner time he's messy and sticky
He's covered with chips and peas
And other sludge, which might be cheese
Because he's so sticky, my dad takes the mickey
In the garden he tramples on plants
My mum goes nuts
Says, she'll turn us into rats
While Dominic shouts, you can't
When in the bathroom he splashes about
Puts rubber ducks in the bath
Makes the flannel into a raft
And shouts and shouts and shouts
Bedtime will never be forgotten
When lights are out, he screams
Instead of dreaming sweet dreams
So Dad comes up and has to pat his bottom
Early morning when we are all asleep
He wakes everyone up
Demands Mum's drinking cup
Then he gets tired again and weeps
It's two days till he is two
He will still be small
And not very tall
Though he will boss me around and tell me what to do!

Rosie Raven (10)

Dominic

My Mum

I have a special friend,
She's my mum.

She's firm but fair
A joy to have around
She's my mum.

She's hard-working
And you know you can trust her
She's my mum.

She can be shy or loud, happy or sad
Or she can nag, nag and nag
She's my mum.

She's forever outgoing
Careful and glowing
She's my mum.

Her enthusiasm's great
And she's always in shape
She's my mum.

She likes her shopping
And never is stopping
She's my mum.

Jamie Brooker (10)

My Grandad

I'll remember my grandad
He took us riding on our bikes
We went to a great big park
We stayed a lot over night.
He made us pizza with a bite
He likes cooking quite a lot.
But Nana makes the best jam tarts
Grandad sprayed us with a hose
But we got him with water bombs
Christmas with him is really fun
But now our time is nearly done
Because my grandad is really ill
And I shall miss him when he's gone.

Suzie Galvin (8)

George The Cat

She runs around the house as if she is saying,
'Don't stop me now because I am playing.'
She butts around her little toy mouse
She annoys everyone all over the house.
She's always acting as if she is hyper
Whenever she has a accident she might need a diaper.
After running around, she falls on the floor
We all stop worrying when we hear her snore.
She is crazy and wacky for hours on end
That is why she's my best furry friend!

Adam Williams (11)

My Best Friend, Luke

Luke is kind, very, very kind
Luke has a massive mind.
Luke supports Pompey and Man U
Just like I do too.
Luke is very bright
Because he likes to read and write.
Luke and I have a sister
When we go on school trips we really miss her.
He is my friend, so I like him the most
And when we play football he usually hits the post.
Me and Luke like to play every game
And I am nearly the same.
Me, Ross and my friend Luke
He has got to be the Duke.
Me and Luke are best friends
And we'll be best friends forever.

Ross Ellcome (8)

My Fabulous Friend

Her eyes are as blue as the Atlantic Ocean.
Her hair is as blonde as the summer sun.
She is as kind as a guardian angel.
She is as cute as a puppy.
She is as beautiful as a princess.
She is as funny as a clown.
As friendly as a dolphin.
She is as bright as the star on the Xmas tree.
She is as clever as a calculator.
She is as light as a feather.
She dances like a disco diva.
She is as sweet as sugar.
But most of all I like her and she likes me.

Hayleigh Redfern (9)

My Guinea Pig

My guinea pig is fluffy,
Her name is Salty Nut.
She mostly stays in her cage,
A little wooden hut.
She runs through wire,
She runs quite fast,
If there was a race,
She wouldn't be last.
She's fluffy,
She's jumpy,
She's cuddly,
She squeals,
She's the family guinea pig
Her name is Miss Salty Nut!

Emma Hartley (8)

My Mum

My mum's funny and amazing,
Love is just divine,
When I look into her eyes I see hearts,
But I sometimes see red wine.

She is that little twinkle in my eye,
And the someone that makes me smile
She is wonderful in every way
And for her I'd run a mile.

She is the best thing that's happened to me,
She has won my heart.
I love her with a deepest love,
I hope never to be apart.

Hollie Jones (10)

My Auntie's Dog Buster

My auntie's dog Buster has long dark hair,
He's like my auntie's baby and he's always there.
He loves to jump about and play,
But I think he likes it when my grandma has him the rest of the day.
He loves going for a walk, he explores and runs about,
But when he is by the road he trots along sticking out his snout.
So this is Buster, how cute is that?
He deserves a great big pat!

Shannon Davies (11)

Babies

Babies are small, babies are cute,
But remember one thing that they can't play the flute.

If you ever have a baby,
Remember it's not one bit crazy.

Babies always muck around,
Always squirming on the ground.

My baby sister cries a lot
So I cuddle her right on the spot.

Babies are small, babies are cute
But remember one thing, that they can't play the flute!

Jade Hipkiss (10)

My Favourite Friend

My favourite friend has to be
The one who shouts out with glee.

My best friend is Alex Yeo
And he makes the funny show.

Alex, yes, is my best friend
Until the end.

Louie Wilson-Richards (8)

Edward, My Brother

My brother's name is Ed
He's got a very big head
He's really cool
And he kind of likes school
For his nickname we call him Ted
He's really kind
And he's got a great mind
He's like an elephant, stomping around
All over the ground
And he can really climb.

George Wright (8)

My Favourite Person

My favourite person has to be
My mum that loves me.

She is cute
She plays the flute.

My mum buys me sweets
And she washes the sheets.

Grace Green (7)

Friends

I don't have one special friend,
But when in need of a boost friends are there.
When I'm upset or lonely
They comfort me slowly and that's why I'm glad that they're there.
When down in the dumps they're there.
When down and in need they are there.
When sleepovers come we play with our hair
And that's why I'm glad that they're there.
Days go on you see your friends, one, two, three maybe four
Even in the holidays you go through a phase,
You have to see a friend soon.
That's when you try to make new ones,
But that doesn't work in the end
So you go back to school and for hours on end you say and say
'I'm glad you're my friend,'
You say and say, 'I'm glad you're my friend.'

Rebecca Green (11)

My Uncle Matthew

Uncle Matthew, why did you move?
Uncle Matthew, I love you.
I like it when I visit,
Uncle Matthew, I miss you.
I know you're in America, but I hope you see this poem,
Now we're all one big family English and American
My sister misses Alec and Jaclynne and we all do too.

Jamie Buggy (10)

My Favourite Person

My favourite person is my mum
She's kind, generous and nice,
And the food she cooks is really yum
She's also special to me,
And that's never going to change until the death of thee.

Dominic Simon (10)

My Family

My brother is cool.
My sister is small.

My mum likes swimming
In the swimming pool.

My dad is tall.
My uncle likes pool.

My sister Zoë acts like a fool.

Danielle Hickey (10)

My Big Sister

My big sister always makes me smile,
Her hair is long and brown,
And she dresses with hippy style!
When we come home from school
We play silly games,
But sometimes she calls me horrid names!
However, we always make up and be nice sisters
And one last thing,
She always looks after me
When I've got blisters!

Maria Webb (8)

About James

James is my big brother
Sometimes he is quite a bother
He plays with me nearly all the time
Sometimes he tells me a rhyme
He buys lots of shoes
He can count up in twos.
I love him very much!

Sophie Chorlton (8)

Eliza Is My Favourite Friend

I am fond of her the most,
She never boasts.
Eliza is my best friend
She makes all of my sadness end.
When she comes round my house
We have so much fun.
She never stops playing with me
Eliza and me are still best friends
Because our friendship never ends!

Jade Rodriguez (9)

My Nan

M y nan is the best in the world.
Y ou will be sad not to meet her.

N ot everyone's seen her but ...
A nan is not always seen
N an is the best person on Earth.

Sadie Bridger (10)

Thierry Henry And Me

I like Thierry Henry,
Because he's the opposite of me.
He scores loads of goals,
While I fall into holes.
With a ball he can head,
While I lie in bed.
He dribbles and shoots,
While I clean my boots.
He does a fantastic volley,
While I struggle with a trolley.
While he scores the winner,
I'm eating my dinner.
He's my all time hero,
Even though I score zero.

Ryan Parker (11)

My Friend Syma

I have a great friend called Syma,
She's a laugh and she is cool
But I am really going to miss her
Cos I'm off to secondary school.

Syma's been in my class
From Year Three until Year Six
I can still remember when
We used to play with sticks.

Syma's off to the grammar school,
I know she'll enjoy it there
Even though I'll miss her
We can still meet up somewhere!

I will definitely not forget Syma
And she won't forget me
Cos she still will be able to
Come round my house for tea!

Molly Nevitt (11)

Joe

As I look at the sky
No matter how far I walk towards it
I can never touch it
But, I know it's there.

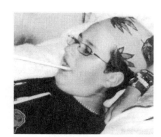

So as with my brother I can no longer touch him
But I still remember him
As I can remember a red sky
My brother, my friend
Forever in my mind, forever there
Always changing, always different
Unable to talk and to feel
But I close my eyes
And I can hear and see him
I remember and it makes me
Smile!

Mark Owen (10)

Charlotte

My best mate Charlotte,
Forever we've been friends
And we're gong to be together
Right until the end.

She has long dark hair,
And she's very tall
And by the way
She thinks I'm very small.

One day we had an argument
All because of a clown
I thought I had him first
Then Charlotte had the crown.

Of course we're still best friends
I'm being very careful
We're always together
And she's being very helpful.

Eve Durand (9)

Anya, Keiron And Joseph

A lways around
N ever good
Y oung at heart
A ngel in my eyes

K eeping his room tidy
E veryone's friend
I nto everything
R ushing around
O n the ball
N ever on time

J ust the best
O n and on at me
S lipping about
E veryone's friend
P laying with me
H appy little face.

Lily Francis Reece (11)

Harvey - My Special Friend

Harvey is a good friend, he's very, very kind
Wherever I am with him, he just rocks my mind.

He has lots of talents, football is his best
When he's on the football pitch, he always beats the rest.

When I think I'm lonely and no one else is there
Harvey always comes and shows he'll always care.

So now I'm never lonely, I'm happy everyday
This will carry on until Harvey moves away.

Bethany Marsh (11)

My Mum

My favourite person is my mum,
She helps me feel better when I am glum.
When I am naughty,
She isn't very bossy.
And that's why I love my mum.

My favourite person is my mum,
She really is my best chum.
She always takes me somewhere fun,
Sometimes she buys me a big cream bun.
And that is why I love my mum.

My favourite person is my mum,
Sometimes she wishes she could smack my bum.
But deep inside I know she loves me,
And settles down and makes me a cup of tea.
And that's why I love my mum.

Hannah McClure (9)

Untitled

My mum is my best friend till the end
She is like a fluffy cloud
My mum is quiet, she doesn't make a sound
My mum is very kind
She is lovely and she's got a brilliant mind
She is like a lovely calm sea
My mum is pretty, she's a good friend to me
My mum is like a white sheep
She is a pot of treasure that you can keep forever
I always want my mum to be with me
My mum is as cute as can be.

Lori Carr

My Best Friend Megan

My really very best friend is Megan,
She makes me feel like I am in Heaven.
She really likes to ride a horse,
You should know that by now of course.
She really, really likes the colour blue,
She also likes to stick with sticky glue.
She has two sisters both are small,
And her dad, he is very tall.
She has neat writing,
She doesn't like fighting.
That's all from me,
She's my best friend,
Go away cos that's the end.

Molly Grace Robson (8)

My Dad Is Special

My dad is special because he loves,
My dad is special because he cares,
My dad is special because he shares,
My dad is the best,
He can complete with all the rest,
I know he can go mad and lose his key,
But I love him because he will always stick up for me.

My dad is special because he rocks,
My dad is special because he's cool,
My dad is special because he's my working tool,
Nobody gets better than my dad,
Because if they do I'll go crazy and mad.

Michael Hales

Emily

Emily is great,
Emily is sweet,
Emily is pretty,
But you should smell her feet.

She is funny,
She is smart,
She is fantastic,
A work of art!

I'm glad that she's my cousin,
She makes me laugh you see,
Although she lives quite far away,
She's always there for me.

Harry Card (8)

Mrs G!

Mrs G is my teacher,
and no one will ever beat her.
She has always got a smile on her face,
unlike an alien from out of space.
She always makes jokes for the class,
about centimetres, numbers and mass.
She wants us to join the Beano club,
but sometimes we think she gets drunk at the pub.
She gives us lots of homework each day,
but we don't care anyway.
I'll miss her when I go,
but I'll remember her even though.

Charity Cornforth (11)

My Favourite Person

My cousin's name is Salma
She is the most graceful
I love her to bits cos she's helpful
How can I miss her, she's so enjoyable

When I look at her she's so marvellous
When she's there she's generous
Her heart is not full with jealousy
Though she's full of humorousy

When I am with her she is so bubbly
She's so full of trustworthy
I love her cos of her so-called friendly!

Aneesha Sidat (12)

My Favourite Person

My favourite person is like a golden sun setting,
My favourite person is like sulky sea water,
My favourite person is like the moon piercing the dark, starry night,
When I see that person I know everything's all right,
I'd hold on tight
For that special person I'd jump a great height,
My favourite person is me!

Sabrina Carroll (10)

My Friend Scratchy

My friend Scratchy
is the best,
He once bit me
but he's better than the rest.

He's a little bit furry
but I don't mind,
He really likes me
even though he's blind.

My friend Scratchy
has four paws,
All his friends like him
though he breaks the laws.

He's got a small tail
and has two pouches,
Oh, that gave it away
but he always slouches.

My friend Scratchy
his cage gets cramped,
But can you guess?
He's a hamster!

Alex Montgomery (9)

Eric The Cat

My favourite person has to be
the cat who loves me.

He's black and white and really fine,
he's cool and mine.

He's my number one,
he's lots of fun.

I love him so much,
I like to play touch.

He is supreme,
his favourite colour is green.

Millie Bassett (8)

Digital Dad

He's a digital dad,
but he's driving us mad.
Keeps hogging the screen,
you know what we mean?
Every time is the same,
he takes over our game.
And we can't make a fuss,
he's much better than us.

Bethany Ford (9)

My Favourite Person

My favourite person has to be
my mum that plays with me.

She has got a boyfriend Lee
and he can really see.

She really loves me
and she really loves peas.

Amanda Bassett (8)

linda

My Special Friend

My special friend is my nan,
She always does the best she can,
She listens, she cares, she understands me,
She smiles when she sees me,
Her garden is full of flowers in bloom,
Smells so fresh of lovely perfume,
She's trying and learning new ways of today,
She's going back to school for fun, learning and play,
She's seventy years old, and she loves to be with me,
Together we are so happy,
My special friend is my nan you see,
Evelyn May Comerford and me.

Amanda Lee Coughlan (11)

My Playscheme Teacher - Mark

He is a good teacher
We have lots of fun
We play skipping, run shows
Make things and play games
He makes my long school holiday enjoyable.

William Penny (5)

My Favourite Person

My favourite person has to be
The magnificent Miss B.

She is very kind
And has a wonderful mind.

Miss B is the best
She is better than the rest.

She plans things out very well
All of the things never fail.

She has to be my teacher!

Katie Welsman (8)

Robson Dobson

Robson Dobson is so good
He could beat the best person
He could beat the best footballer in the world
So great everyone likes him
Robson Dobson is so brilliant at recorders
The best one ever
Robson Dobson.

Gabriel Seatter (7)

My Mum

My mum is very pretty,
She's got blonde long shiny hair,
Dark blue eyes,
Nice brown skin,
Lovely personality,
That's my mum.

My mum is very caring,
She drives me places,
Spends time with me,
Always there for me
That's my mum.

My mum loves having fun,
Loves looking after children,
She loves the way they act,
The way they do things,
She is always looking after them,
That's my mum.

My mum is always up for a dance,
She loves cuddles and kisses,
Always ready for a party,
Making birthdays great,
Always organised
She is very special to me,
That's my mum, *the best!*

Jessiamée Richardson (9)

Antonia

Antonia is a helium filled balloon
That will keep on trying and will never go down,
A magnet that is always stuck to her friends,
An everlasting gobstopper, sweet and stays as long as you want.

Antonia is a flowing stream of words
Chattering away to all of her friends,
A bright firework sending off energy and light all around her,
A gazelle swiftly bounding across the meadows.

Antonia is loyal golden retriever,
Playful, and *Man's Best Friend,*
A thousand colours mixed together in a sparkling gem,
The eye of the world looking down on everyone, checking we're OK.

Antonia is a unique diamond from an angel's pocket!

Cecilia Herbert (11)

My Best Friend

My pet dog is called Brucey,
If he had been a girl we would have called him Lucy.
He is seventeen years old and hates the cold,
In the day he loves to play,
And at night he goes to sleep on the floor, and begins to dream and snore.
Brucey is very sweet
When he jumps on his feet,
He barks out loud when he is in a crowd.
Brucey's colour is shiny and black
And his best friend is Poppy the next-door's cat.
My dog loves his food
And if he cannot get enough he gets in a mood.
When he gets bored he tries to talk
To tell us all to get his lead and go for a walk.
He sits in the sun all day long
And listens to the birds in the trees singing a merry song.
I kiss and hug him, with all my might,
My favourite person, Brucey, is my favourite sight.

Laura Kemp (11)

Our Headmaster

Our headmaster he's so cool
he likes to laugh and play the fool

Guitar, piano at any old bar
He'll get a tune out of a big jam jar

Now he's leaving, it's so sad
the whole school might go completely mad

He doesn't like to shout
but he doesn't like to mess about

We'd like to say
thank you for our pay

See you soon, have a good rest
we will always remember you as the best!

Georgia Pangratiou (10)

323

My Favourite Person

C razy as a lunatic
H appy as a clown
R ich as a TV star
I mportant as a policeman
S uper as a superman.

E xciting as a circus
N oisy as a bomb exploding
G roovy as a disco diva
L ightfooted as a ninja
A mazing as a magician
N aughty as a naughty monkey
D ull as a brush.

But he's the best thing in the world.

Joseph Evans (8)

Catherine Wilson

Catherine Wilson is my best friend,
She keeps me laughing through the day,
When I see her,
I make a smile,
That stays on my face all year.

After school it's very sad,
In the morning it turns around,
That's because I miss her at night,
Then in the morning,
I see her at kids club.

Now that she has moved away,
I'm not as happy as I used to be,
She's in Aberdeen,
I'm in Dunblane,
It's just not the same.

Johanna Martin (10)

My Best Friend

My best friend is Jordan Scott.
She is the best out of the lot.
She is cool, she is clever.
But her mood depends on the weather.

Jordan is a great singer.
She calls me a little springer.
She is funny, she is great.
And she is a fabulous mate.

Jordan used to have a horse
And she has an outstanding force.
She is perfect, she is mad,
And she says her dogs are bad.

Jordan's room is sexy pink,
And she makes a tasty drink.
She is cool, she is clever,
But most of all she is the best friend ever.

Kayley Ann Burnett (10)

Pat And Cricket

My favourite person is Pat
Who likes to play cricket,
Every time he bowls a ball
He hits a wicket.
He hits the ball far and wide
All the way to the other side,
He runs between the wickets
Just like Jimmy Cricket.
He scores lots of runs
Because it's so much fun,
He got voted 'man of the match'
Because of his great catch.
He's my best friend,
From Matthew.

Matthew Martin (11)

My Favourite Person

My favourite person is always there.
She always helps me when I'm down or upset.
I don't often see her, but in my heart she is always around.
My favourite person is my best friend.
She always has been and always will be.
My best friend is called Ellie Childs.

Teagan Jelly (9)

Amazing Abbie

I have a niece, she's my amazing niece,
And when I'm with her I am at peace.

My amazing niece, she has blonde hair,
She's eight years old and loves to share.

She comes from London, which isn't very near,
She's good at maths, but her writing isn't clear!

I love her dearly and she loves me clearly!
That's why we're best friends!

Becky Rotherham (10)

My Very Special Friend!

I have a very special friend
Who is great.
She doesn't look different to you and me
But my friend is disabled.
And uses a wheelchair.
Many people stop and stare.

My very special friend is as bright as the sun
And always has lots of fun.
She can do most things like you and me
But some people treat her differently.

My friend is great.
Her name is Helen
Helen is my very special friend.

Lauren Scrivens (10)

My Special Friend

I have a favourite person
Nobody can see but me
It's a very special person
Because it belongs to me
It helps me when I'm feeling glum
It tells me what I have to do
So I am always happy
Wherever I may be.

Lindsay Horner (8)

My Friend Abena

My friend Abena is the best friend
We've been together always till the end
We always go swimming and have lots of fun
Although we play always we get work done
We always have sleepovers and have lots of sweets,
We always play dares and go off to sleep
We always tell secrets and swear not to tell
And even if we do we end up again together
For always me and my best friend!

Comfort Adekunle (10)

My Dad

He laughs, he giggles and always tickles!
He's always about and never shouts.
We sit on the log by the fire,
With me playing my flute and Dad beside me singing sweetly.
I don't know what I would do without my fab dad!

Sometimes he's happy or feeling blue
But he always says, 'It's not me, it's you.'
Sometimes I don't understand what he says.
He's funny and even bought me a bunny! With money!

Most days he wants to relax or play his drum.
My dad is not like yours, he's cheerful and fun.
My dad works in a school
And is a teacher for you and me!
He also owns a car!

I love him so much! I cuddle him!
We laugh and scream and always buy ice cream!
I love him, he loves me, we love each other,
He laughs and giggles and always tickles just for me!

Shanara Phillips (9)

My Favourite Person

My favourite person is Mum,
She always makes things fun for me.
She knits and she cooks,
She always reads books,
My favourite person is Mum.

My favourite person is Dad,
He is always glad,
He never gets mad,
My favourite person is Dad.

My favourite person is my sister,
She likes the ice cream Twister,
She likes dogs, she likes cats,
She likes all kinds of pets.

Which is my favourite person?

Marina Shurakova (10)

My Friend

You pick me up when I'm down,
You dry my tears all the time.

You're the eagle that soars with me,
Far and high, away from Earth.

You're my torch through the dark tunnel of life,
You're my listener, and penpal, and healer, and helper.

The amazing person is a friend, teacher and parent,
He is ... *the Lord!*

Rebekah Burgess (13)

Ellen MacArthur

King fisher
Well wisher,
Sea sailor
No failer,
World record-breaker
Good navigator,
Weather nice
And cold as ice,
Up the mast
Hold on fast,
Off today
On my way,
No mishap
Back ASAP.

Ruth Pollard (9)

My Friend

My friend is funny, fast and fearless,
My friend is full of laughter and kindness,
My friend is someone I would not replace,
My friend is powerful,
My friend looks happy all the time,
My friend is good at sport,
My friend is the best!

Beatrice Moreira-Watkins (9)

My Sister

My sister's name is Sarah
She's whom this poem is about.
Now that I have started
I surely can't be out.
Her favourite food is rice,
With lots and lots of spice.
Her favourite dessert is ice cream
And Chelsea is her football team,
She likes to go swimming
But she doesn't know how
She's going to get lessons
But later, not now
Although she is eight
She is really great
I wanted a sister, not two, but one
And on March 16th my wish was done
On TV she likes to watch 'Hi Hi Puffy Ami Yummy'.
Her favourite ice cream flavour is toffee
And she also likes chicken roast
She likes to look at the bright moon
Whilst eating something with a spoon.

Maha Ali (9)

Alfie

My dog is cute
He really smiles
He has a cheeky grin!
Alfie is his name
Alfie, that's him
I love him so much
He cheers me up when I'm down
He makes me smile and takes away the frown!

Ellie Thomas (10)

My Wonderful Dad

My dad is a brilliant man
And me, I'm his number one fan
He's caring, loving and kind
A better dad would be hard to find
He helps with homework, then we play
Tennis in the garden at the end of my day
He makes me happy, he makes me glad
I'm lucky to have him as my dad.

Caitlin Maynard (9)

An Ode To Georgia Nicolson

This girl has spark,
This girl has style,
Don't underestimate her,
She can always make me smile.
This girl is not a mate,
This girl is not a friend,
She's a character in a book,
One I hope will never end.
Loves trapping boys,
And having fun,
This is my ode,
To Georgia Nicolson.
She says 'groovy bananas,'
And 'Tres, tres bon.'
Georgia was created,
By Louise Rennison.
Her best friend is Jas,
Who has a boyfriend called Tom,
Georgia loves her Ace Gang,
To her, they're never wrong.
She lives with Mutti and Vati,
Who drive her up the wall,
So do Angus and little Libby,
But they don't care at all!
Georgia loves going to gigs,
And dancing around madly,
If I could ever meet her,
I would do it gladly!

Emma Buckee (11)

My Nan

My nan is my best friend,
If I hurt myself, she helps me mend,
When I sleep at hers, I get lots of cuddles,
When it rains, we jump in muddy puddles.
My nan is old and has lots of grey hair,
To me, she is young, my cuddly bear.
Whenever I'm sad and start to cry,
She sits me down and asks me why.
We go on bike rides and long walks,
And sit in the park and have long talks.
Everyone says their nan is the best,
But no, my nan is better than all the rest.

Georgina Abbott (9)

My Favourite Person

Kelly Holmes has won medals for running,
That is because she is so cunning.

She does a lot of training work,
Even through all the dust and murk.

I like Kelly Holmes because,
She is so brave and would save anyone.

Natasha Davis (10)

Jenny, My Sister

My sister and I never used to get on when I was young,
We'd argue and fight all day long,
But now we've aged and changed,
We get on and spend more time together.

We go out to eat and catch up on each other's gossip,
To talk about our problems, to help one another out.
I love it when we go to the movies, she buys the tickets,
I buy the sweets.
We are both great film critics,
My sister is full of knowledge,
She doesn't mind helping me when I have homework trouble.
I definitely look up to her,
We still have our disagreements,
But it's all fun and we hardly ever really fall out.

Jenny is my big sister,
She's brilliant.

Sarah George (17)

My Love For You

(Dedicated to Danielle Brown my baby sister)

My love for you is stronger than me,
My love for you is stronger than my bike
My love for you is stronger than a brick,
My love for you is stronger than concrete
My love for you is stronger than life,
My love for you is stronger than this world.

Because you are my guardian angel
You make me smile when I need it,
You are in my heart wherever I go
And that is why I love you.

Andre Straker Brown (10)

My Kitten

My kitten Twiglet
Is as naughty as can be
Climbs up the curtains
Sits on the TV
He chases the birds and eats the flies
And looks at us with appealing eyes
We can't help but love him.
Though he makes us cross
Sixteen weeks old and already the boss.

Cara Sawyer (8)

Nipper

Nipper is a charming boy,
He stands so still he is like a little toy.
The colour of his coat is a lovely brown,
The colour is like the houses' roofs in the town.

He loves to be ridden among the trees,
When he's on his own he hates the fleas.
His best friend Crystal is lovely and white,
And when they're both together it is a lovely sight.

After a ride, he likes a brush,
And after that he rolls in the mush,
Nipper likes a little treat,
But we still try to keep him nice and neat.

He eats a lot of grass in one day,
But in the summer we have to watch out he doesn't get hay,
In the winter he needs more care,
And soon he will grow his winter hair.

I love him and he loves me back,
And I think he really enjoys the tack,
Nipper also likes Mum and Dad,
And when we say goodbye he looks really sad.

Jennifer McNicoll (10)

There's One Special Girl In My Life

There's one girl in my life,
Who I see almost every day,
She's one of a kind,
Special in every way.

She's caring,
She's smart,
She's pretty,
And pure at heart.

She'll never let me down,
She really rocks my world,
She'll always be there for me,
Even when we're old.

There's one girl in my life,
Too great for words to say,
She's my favourite person ever,
And I wouldn't change her in any way!

Wendy Bold (12)

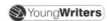

Obi-Wan

Obi-Wan has brown hair like the crispy leaves in autumn,
He has a beard like the bark on the tree
His clothes are as brown as a bear, soft and cuddly,
Obi-Wan's lightsaber is as blue as the clear blue sky.
He is as fast as a lion,
He is as strong as the world's strongest man.
Obi-Wan's powers are like the gods of Greece
He is as tall as a horse, galloping in the breeze,
He is as bright as the sun,
Obi-Wan is as skilled as a football player dribbling with the ball,
He hates the droids they can be a pest
But Obi-Wan you're the best!

Joshua Eardley (9)

My Mami

She wanders round the house,
As quiet as a mouse.
Doing all the cleaning and cooking
As well as the shopping.
That's my mum,
She is the kind and friendly one.
My mum is very caring,
And always helping.
Her name is Enfys, which is Welsh for rainbow,
And she cheers everybody up when they're feeling low.
Is there a better mum? No such!
Because I love her very much.

Angharad Lewis (11)

My Tiny Friend

Tiny is my little dog
She's not much bigger than a frog
She loves me to rub her tummy
She likes to eat my bread and honey.

Tiny and I like to play
Rolling around in the hay
Tiny has a squeaky ball
And we play out in the hall.

Tiny is a very old dog
She's always getting lost in the fog
Tiny is my very best friend
I hope you like her too.

Angharad Kate Mathew-Blake (7)

Family

F irstly, I don't have a favourite person
A nd I am not about to choose
M ainly because all my family is favourite
I never will decide that in my life
L ove makes it hard to choose
Y ou couldn't decide, could you?

Rebecca Prince (11)

Who Is My Favourite Person?

When I come home she comes and comforts me.
When I go away she says she will miss me.
When I get angry at her she always cuddles me.
When I want something she always gives it to me.
I am always right and the others are wrong.
When I can't go to sleep at night she sings me a song.
She says she loves me more than anything in this world.
Gold, salt, plastic or silver, she will even give me a throne.
If she could walk she would always run with me.
If she could reach the stove she would cook anything for me.

I love this person very much and hope she will never die,
Otherwise I'd cry and cry and cry.
Until she comes back to me,
Yeap you have guessed it, it's my beloved gran,
Who will always love me!

Nida Shah (11)

My Favourite Person

My best friend may be dumb, not!
But she is also quite numb.
Like a bear being stung.
She thinks I'm clever,
But really I'm just like leather.
My best friend Florence is as lucky as Heather!
I'm glad I met her because she is quite funny as ever.
She has never, ever, ever put me down.
But we do sometimes get a frown.
If I am ever upset she would come to me and pretend she's the funniest clown of all!
All best friends do is just smile into a pile,
Once they've sorted out their problems!

Teresa Fan (10)

Sooty

Sooty, my cat,
Is very fat!
He's fluffy and furry.
Always in a hurry.
And loves wearing a hat.
Miaow!

Chelsea Lewis (9)

My Dog Tilly

My best friend is Emily
My best friend is imaginary they said
It was going around my head!
Then I said to Fred,
'My best friend cannot speak
And she has no feet.'
I wanted to tell them more and more
So I said she has four paws,
She's not polite like you or me.
And she has disgusting tea!
When I wake up she's always there
Giving me that loveable stare.
I bet you will never get what she is
Because she's a dog, that's what she is.

Emma Dracup (9)

Daniel, My Brother

When I first knew my mom was having a baby,
I looked straight to the bad points.
I never realised, it wouldn't be like that!
And he would be the best brother ever.
He may not give great advice;
As his vocabulary is rather limited
But he is a great listener,
His adoring smile and giggle,
Reassures me, and I know he understands
I can't wait till the future;
When he takes his first steps
And says, 'Siobhan.'
And starts his first day at school
But I love him the way he is;
And I'm proud to be his sister.

Siobhan Harris (13)

My Mam

She is so funny,
She hops like a bunny.

She loves texting on her mobile,
She's got a very punky style.

She loves cats,
She dislikes rats.

She always looks after me,
And makes me a lovely tea.

Helping is her favourite thing,
Unfortunately she cannot sing.

Nicole Keeton (9)

My Favourite Person

Friends are people who are always there,
Friends are people who always care.
Whoever you are, your friends accept you,
To yourself and your friends, you must be true.

I used to have three best friends in a group,
But they weren't who they seemed, and they gave me the boot.
Ever since the time, I've had no real friends,
Except for one person, upon whom I can depend.

This person is very special to me,
In times of need, she's the one I can see.
She's helping me to get over the loss of my mates,
She knows if I want to talk, and if I don't she'll wait.

This person knows when I need to cry,
I know to me she'd never lie.
She's always been there, even through the bad,
She'll stick up for me whether I'm happy or sad.

She's my best friend; it's plain to see,
We are very close because she understands me.
She doesn't spread rumours behind my back,
She's not two-faced, that's a fact!

She's known me since I was born,
I know our friendship will never get worn.
Friends like her are hard to find,
She's so wonderfully nice and she's always kind.

You may be wondering who my best friend might be,
She's the only person who knows the real me.
With my friend I have so much fun,
My best friend is my mum.

Tabatha Leggett (14)

My Best Friend

My favourite person is my best friend,
I bet you cannot guess her name,
She is the sort of friend I need,
Making me smile and laugh.

In literacy and maths if there is something that I need,
That something my best friend can lend,
If you have not guessed her name
My best friend's name is Ruth.

Tanya Stubbs (10)

My Friend Sam

I was born one day, came home and saw,
A dog named Sam, that followed me round.
He was better than toys, never a bore,
When my nap time came he never made a sound.

When I turned three a surprise came to me,
My brother was born, oh yes indeed!
He came home from hospital and watched me eat tea,
Sam and me still played without a lead.

It seemed like minutes until I was six,
Running about with Sam still close by.
But we've no problems to fix,
But soon I'd be ready to have a good cry.

I turned seven way too quick,
For soon he was a dead doggy without a coffin.
I felt very sick,
For my best friend had just gone to Heaven.

Rachel Biott (10)

Tony Pratt

Tony Pratt is a very special person,
And also very rare,
Even though he has got grey hair,
He is one in a million,
He's worth a billion,
He takes me out places,
And pulls funny faces,
He drives a motorbike,
And takes me on his trike,
And we also like catching pike,
He has a cosy flat,
And he's lazy like a doormat,
Although he's very old,
He doesn't like to be told,
We've had lots of good memories,
And had lots of tears,
And we've also caught some deers,
And I love this dear person like an uncle,
Even though he's got a little flat,
I will always love this Tony Pratt.

Sean Ewen (14)

Karate Kid

I am the karate kid,
On my bike I do some skids.
My friend is next door,
He spat, I had to clean the floor.

I like karate because it's fun,
My instructor said not to eat bun.
You shouldn't eat too much food,
You will feel sick and be in a mood.

I am on purple belt,
When I grade it's a softer felt.
I think it's nice,
Go buy food at Sugar Spice.

Shanice Bailey (10)

Best Friends

We are best friends till the end,
Even when I move away,
I'll write letters and then send.

Me, Alex, Sian and Alanah,
We're all crackers and bananas,
We love to jump about,
We chitter and chitter and shout.

Now you know who we are,
We are all special stars.

Ailish Taylor (11)

Lost Little Boy

Wherever I go things seem to flow,
It feels like I'm on an ongoing show,
If I had known,
That I'd feel blue,
By seeing a child,
In the wild,
It hurts to think that,
Nobody cares,
Where he is at and what he wears.
A lost little boy
Without his toy,
With no one to help him
Cos the world's so dim
Open your eyes
And share the prize
'Cause this little boy deserves a life!

Sophie Lawrence (17)

David Beckham

D is for dribbling the ball
A is for autographs
V is for Victoria his wife
I is for idol
D is for defender

B is for Brooklyn his first born son
E is for excellent goals
C is for circling the ball
K is for kicking the ball
H is for hairstyles
A is for athlete
M is for mad riot.

Grant Jennings (10)

My Dad

My dad is always a happy jolly man,
Who is an avid Man United fan,
He may be short,
With a shiny bald head,
And sometimes can't get out of bed,
My dad is

D omesticated
A nd a
D reamer

He dreams of buying fast cars,
Always saying that he could go far,
But for now I'll keep him as he is
Because he's my dad and I love him to bits.

Becci Byrne (10)

My Dad

My dad is like the sun
So fun to play with
And so joyful with me
We go to Lowestoft and splash in the sea.

We play and go swimming
And go to kick-boxing and Cub Scouts
He walks me to school
And then we play out.

We go to the park
And I play on the swings
I love my dad,
Because we do all these things.

Joshua Beach (8)

About Olivia

Olivia is my sister
A great one too.
She's really sweet,
And loves a hip hop beat.
Everyone loves her
Especially me.
Olivia's great to hang around
She will always be found.
I hope you'll see her
And see how sweet she is.

Becky Slatter (11)

My Mum

I wake her up when morning comes
When she rises she brightens up the sun.
She opens the curtains
And starts to clean
All the while she looks at me
She starts to cook and get dressed
And I know my mum's the best!

Ciara Ford (11)

Archie

Archie is my favourite person
Archie likes loads of sweets
Archie never cheats
Archie is very funny
Archie pretends to be a bunny
Archie is never bad
Archie is never sad
That's why Archie is my favourite person.

Shauna-Mae Burnett (8)

Mum

My mum's great, there's nothing else I need,
Not a billion pound mansion, just a hug and a squeeze.

My mum's great, she's like a Christmas pudding - nice,
Not over the top and most of all, good looking.

My mum's great, she can be lots of fun,
Except when she's being boring like sitting on a deckchair in the sweltering sun.

My mum's great, not only because
She'll take me shopping to Toys 'R' Us!

Bryn Pryse-Jones (11)

Snap

I've got a friend called Snap
He's the best cat
He's ginger with a drop of white
He twinkles in the starlight

I've got a friend called Lish
He's the best fish
He's orange with a hint of red
He has a very small head

I've got a friend called Hog
He's the best dog
He's brown with a bit of black
That's my friend called Hog.

Lindsay Birch (9)

My Sister

My sister is the best
She's better than the rest
She loves secondary school
I love her 'cause she's cool.

She hangs out with her friends
Their talking never ends
Always on the phone
Guaranteed to moan!
They put the world to rights
Without starting fights.

Boys! Boys! Boys!
She forgets to play with her toys
Big sisters are a pain
Because they are so vain
I love mine a lot
Even if she's lost the plot!

Robyn Smith (10)

My Big Brother

My big brother, he's the best
He is better than the rest.

He's the biggest, he's really tall
He loves to play basketball.

He's a really good artist
In school he's the smartest.

He has a big appetite
But you don't want to see him in a fight.

He's my big brother
And I look up to him
And his name is Timi.

Oluwagbeminiyi Tinubu (11)

My Favourite Pet

My favourite pet is a cat,
It goes by the name of Pat,
He's black and white,
And he doesn't bite
My favourite pet is a cat.

Pat is small and very thin,
He likes to eat his food from the tin,
He likes to play,
In the bales of hay,
My favourite pet is a cat.

Pat the cat once was a stray,
He used to visit us twice a day,
Now he will stay,
All through the day,
Pat *'our'* cat!

Katie Cummings (10)

Mum

Mum, Mum, she is the best
All her recipes would put you to the test
Mum, Mum, she's really, really cool
On a hot summer's day she'd jump inside a pool
If we fall in a puddle of rain
She'd be there to take away the pain
At the end of the day she'd tell you a joke
That would make you laugh forever
My mum is really clever.

Caitlin Stewart (9)

My Dad My Hero

My dad's my hero because he is the best in the whole wide world.
My dad plays golf and he takes me too.
My dad loves me even when I'm bad.
My dad is my friend and I am glad he's my hero.

Harry Law (8)

A Mam In A Million

She's a mam in a million,
And does everything for me,
I love her to pieces,
She's the best, can't you see.

She cooks and she cleans,
She cleans and she cooks,
Everything always gleams,
And she buys me poem books.

Her name is Kay,
She hardly ever goes out,
She's in the house all day,
She truly is a mam in a million.

Kaysha Smith (11)

My Mum

My favourite person is my mum,
She's been there for me since I sucked my thumb.
Giving birth to me in 1995 then still caring until 2005.
She *always* thinks of others
Even though I have no brothers.
When my sister is being lazy
Mum goes a bit crazy.
Mum does the cooking, cleaning, and booking tables for restaurants.
My mum is super cool,
And wishes we had a swimming pool.
My mum likes rock 'n' roll
Backwards, forwards, to and fro,
Dancing away and here we go,
My favourite person is my mum,
She's been there since I sucked my thumb!

Charlotte Woolley (10)

Francesca

I have a best friend
I drive her round the bend
She's mad, but never sad.
She's pretty, but witty,
Her name is Cess
She likes fancy dress ...

Megan Turner (8)

My Big Brother

He's really good at football, so he's basically like me,
Need advice about homework?
He's your man, you'll see.
He's great fun to have around and jokes a lot.
He never lies and when asked to help, he is sure to do.
He's very good at tennis, athletics is a breeze.
Sometimes he jokes too much and can be a tease,
His name is Conor and a better brother I would never find.
My really big brother, all in all; is clever, funny and kind.

Aedan Barrett Nnochiri (9)

Paddy And The Back Of The Net

My favourite person is Paddy,
And every time he kicks a football
He makes the players cry, 'Daddy!'
Even though he is not very tall,
He plays like a professional.
He never stops running around the football pitch,
Even when he gets a stitch,
He kicks a ball into a net,
Faster then you can say, 'Jet'
He plays in the blazing sun,
All for the cause of fun.

Perry Saunders (11)

My Brother

My brother is a scary monster,
He can even be a dinosaur.
He bites me when he gets mad,
Sometimes he can be very bad.

My brother can turn on the cooker,
When he eats spaghetti he gets very messy.
He pesters me when I'm doing my homework,
And he can sometimes make even more housework.
My mom gets very angry when he makes a total mess,
But sometimes he can make less.

When he's naughty he can be a pest,
Sometimes he wears a vest.
He even does his very best,
But I'll let you into a little secret, only at school.

He is my little brother
So don't try messing with him!

Rachael Pestridge (9)

My Anaconda

He slithers
He smells
He goes to mum and tells.

He's smart
He's a good piece of art
He's like a fast little dart.

He's hairy
He's lairy
He's really very scary.

Sam Coates (10)

My Little Furry Friend

I have a cat named Thomas
He's a fluffy little thing.
He plays and plays and plays all day
And once fell in the bin.

He always plays with my slippers
And *never* lets me be.
I hate it when he chews my things
They always get ruined.

He's a greedy little monster
He eats out of the pan.
He even eats Scotch pancakes
And Mum's Cheerios when he can.

But nothing can change the love
Between him and me,
Or we would never be.

Selene Antonas (8)

My Favourite Person

This has to be,
Either my cousin Bee!
My brother
Or my mother.

Or maybe even my father too,
For sorting out the bullies that go moo!
I think I will choose.
Bee, but this doesn't mean that the others lose.

Even though we fight,
Or may even bite,
She still loves me,
And I love her, can't you see?

She is more of a friend
All the clothes we lend,
Than any cousin,
In any dozen.

Rebecca Cheong (13)

My Favourite Person

M y favourite person is ...
Y   oung person

M arvellous at cooking
U nderstands everything
M erry and happy
M arried to my daddy
Y   awns a lot!

Who is it?
It's my *mummy!*

Emily Beswick (8)

Friendship, Happiness And Love

My favourite person is so funny yet so rare,
She is like the stars, the moon, and life itself.

When you're down, just to see her face
And hear her tender voice
Would put a smile on your face.

My nan is my favourite person
The person with a heart of gold
And one day,
One day I will see her *again,*
My loving nan
Dedicated to you with all my love.

Eileen Reynolds (13)

My Favourite Person

I had a hamster named Cuddles
I liked him very much
He was so cute
But I had to give him away when I moved
He ate nuts and other seeds
I wish I still had him.

Emily Clark (9)

Toni My Sister

My name is Billie, and sisters I have three,
I didn't think it possible to choose a best one for me.
Then all of a sudden, one was taken away.
Now that changed my mind, after that dreadful day.
My sister's name was Toni, the oldest one of us lot.
She was bossy, she was funny, and yes she said she was hot.
Memories are all I have left, but they are really good.
We laugh, we cry, we think about her, just like we should.
I have lots of brothers and sisters, and I love them all the same.
But I just can't help thinking, *she's my favourite.*
When I hear Toni's name.

Billie Stevens (9)

My Dog Mouse

M y dog Mouse
O ut in the garden
U nder the apple tree
S leeping in the shade
E arly in the morning.

Hayley Burrows (10)

Krystal

K rystal is a Labrador,
R eally cute when she scratches at the door.
Y et she snores when she sleeps,
S he will yap when something beeps.
T hrough the day she is playful,
A t night she is a handful.
L ovely, cute, soft and cuddly ...

That's what Krystal is!

Emma Nesham (9)

Misty Is My Favourite Pony

M isty is my favourite pony.
I ntelligent and bright
Alway S on the look out for
T rouble and delight.
Mist Y is my favourite pony

Rebecca Blenkiron (10)

Furry Friend!

Cuddly and cute,
With a wet nose,
Where there's a bone,
That's where she goes,
Wagging her tail happily,
That is my Razzle,
Cute as can be!

Racing around,
With little sharp claws,
On her bone,
That's where she gnaws,
Never barking angrily,
That is my Razzle,
Cute as can be!

Kate Bernard (9)

My Hamsters Peppermint And Fudge

Peppermint is round, fluffy and cute
Her white and black pattern gives her a suit
Escaping from her cage is her favourite game
Her best hiding place is always the same.

Fudge is agile, without potential lacks
With a golden stripe down his elegant back
He is amused by swinging on bars
And also likes roaming around in mini cars.

Peppermint and Fudge are the same at times
And both commit what we call hamster crimes
Peppermint is round but Fudge is bony and rigid
Both have differences as you can see
But the pair are very close to me.

Ellen Kingston (10)

My Cat

She is brown, black and white
I love her very much
She's been in the family for years
And I'm glad she's mine.

She is a bundle of joy
I stroke her a lot,
She is very cute and her name is Puggles.

On her small pink nose
She has two patches
One black, one brown
It may be her birthmark.

She has a silver collar
Which we change every year
She is always there when you're sad.

She is the oldest cat I've ever known.
I love her to bits.

Tia Coles (7)

My Favourite Person

My favourite person could be someone unknown.
My favourite person could be someone all alone.
But to me it doesn't matter who they are
Because there's nothing special about just one person.
Everyone in the world is my favourite person.

Amber Temple (14)

The Coolest Dad Around

I have a dad and his name is Brad
I like to spend time with him
Because he is a cool lad.

He helps me with my projects
And does not leave me out.

My dad is a cool cat!
He even does my hair in a big plait.

He is the coolest dad around
That no one can match

He smothers me in gifts
And sprays me with the hose!

There is a lot more about my dad
But I surely can't fit it in.

So there you have it
A little bit of *my dad.*

Cha-Lee Hall (10)

369

My Pet Manson

My dog is a Border terrier
Or a Border terrorist
When I'm with him I'm a lot merrier
When we play games I'm sure he's the happiest.

My poem may not rhyme
I've tried my hardest though
I took my time
And watched my furry friend grow.

There's not much more to say
He's called Manson
I watch him every day
I think he's special in every way
My poem is now done.

Carrie Bancroft (10)

My Favourite person

My favourite person has to be
My caring Mum who loves me.

She loves to paint white mugs
But she also loves big hugs.

She's loving and caring and very nice
But she hates wild mice.

She likes to have a lovely bath
She's the greatest Mum I could have.

Jack Saunders (8)

best mum

My Favourite Person

My favourite person has to be
A favourite teacher that's nice to me
This favourite teacher is Miss B
She does a lovely beat
Miss B is nice she likes mice
Miss B is fab
She's like a lab.

Deeka Abdirizak (8)

Rabbits

Rabbits are cute
Rabbits are cuddly
Rabbits nibbling at their food

Rabbits could be black
Rabbits could be white
Rabbits could be grey
Or even brown

Rabbits leap out of their cages
Rabbits hop out of your arms
Rabbits bounce round and round
Rabbits spring here and there
Rabbits spring from you to me

Rabbits here
Rabbits there
Rabbits, rabbits everywhere

We love rabbits, you love rabbits
Everybody loves rabbits.

Rachel Gascoigne (9)

My Best Friend Rachel

She laughs, giggles, gossips, shares.
She plays, smiles, jokes and cares.
Rachel is a pretty,
Smart, creative best friend,
And if I sent something to Mars
She'd be what I would send.

This is because I think they'd see,
What wonderful people on Earth there can be.

Molly Watters (10)

Charles

My friend Charles
Has ginger hair,
We play together everywhere
I see him every day at school
My friend Charles is really cool
He likes hockey and I do too
He likes horses and makes me laugh
We'll be friends forever.

Christopher Dawson (7)

A Special Friend

There were once two girls that had met,
That time I could never forget.
Her name is Radha, she's the *best!*
Together we will beat the rest.
She is so lovely, nice and kind,
Together we will hunt and find,
An ever everlasting love,
She is the rainbow and the dove,
Good friends that we will always be,
Which will make her special to me
I hope we are friends forever,
Because I can never forget her.

Kelsea Young (11)

My Grandma

I love my grandma
She's a sewing star
Although she's clever
She doesn't drive the car.

Whenever I need her
She is always there
With a kiss and a hug
And I know she'll care.

She gives me sweets
When I come out of school
And when that happens
I think it's cool.

We both go home
For cake and tea
She is my grandma
And she loves me.

Aimee Charman (10)

Tigger The Tiger

My favourite person is my cat
And she wears a little hat.

Even though she scratches and bites
We hope it's windy to play with my kite.

She sometimes holds onto the tail,
When she realises it's going up she lets go again.

When she's got nothing to do she sleeps all day,
Sometimes when I try to stroke her she runs away.

She likes to play with bits of string,
But looks up immediately when the phone begins to ring.

I think she should be in the circus as she does backflips,
The best thing about her is she kisses you on the lips

Hollie Clements (11)

Two Best Friends

N is for Nya who is always there.
Y is for she's in my year.
A is for argue but still friends.

&

S is for a name called Safiya.
A is for we may have accidents.
F is for best friends.
I is for we are interested to learn.
Y is for sharing yummy food.
A is for a ... great day.

Hadiya Modeste (9)

My Favourite Person

He makes me laugh, he is kind and gentle
He's funny, silly and some say he is a bit mental.

I follow him around like a little dog,
I even wait outside for him to come out of the bog.

He looks like an actor off the telly,
You know, that funny guy called Jim Carey!

We usually meet around our nan's home,
When he is around I never feel alone.

I'm glad to have the chance to allow me,
To introduce my favourite person, my cousin Lee!

Simone Liotti (9)

Mum And Me

My favourite person is my mum
Because she is kind
And she looks after me
I love my mum
She helps me out and supports me.
My mum lets me have friends round for dinner
When I get stuck on my homework
Who is there to help me?
My mum!
My mum is the best!
My mum gives me food and buys me presents.
My mum takes me on holidays
And lets me go round friends' houses!
My mum is the best!
My mum gives me things that I want,
My mum takes me places I want to go.
My mum lets me play out with my friends.
My mum takes me shopping
My mum lets me have pets
I love my mum!
My mum is the best!

Bekki Carson (10)

My Poem About Rachael

Her name is Rachael.

She is very nice,
Like exotic spice,
She is my number one,
Around my house she'll come.

We'll play until we are worn out,
But then will scream and shout,
I like her the best,
She's seen a bird in a nest.

Now I'm having a rest.

Chantal Da Silva (9)

My Favourite Person

My mum is so cool
She makes all the boys drool
Her hair is red like fire
She's certainly a live wire.

Maddie Clark (10)

My Sister - Charly

My sis is great sometimes,
She can be really cool,
Sometimes I do not like her,
But she still totally rules.

And when we start to argue,
She thinks she's always right,
But when I prove her wrong,
I always win the fight.

Even though I dislike her,
She's really special too,
And if I ever lost her,
I wouldn't know what to do.

Jennifer Peach (9)

My Rabbit

My rabbit is so funny
He is such a little honey
He loves to play all day
And he loves to eat his hay.

He likes to go for a long, long run,
He finds it a lot of fun, fun, fun,
Until it's time for him to rest his head
Then little rabbit goes to bed!

In the mornings when it's sunny,
He lies down showing his big fluffy tummy,
This makes me want to pick him up
And give him one great big hug!

That's my rabbit he really rocks
And his cute little name is Sox!

Lydia Ventre (9)

Bruno

Wet nose
Brown eyes
Whiskers that tickle
Ears as soft as velvet
Paws as big as dinner plates
Tail like a fox brush
A loyal friend that gives unconditional love
That is our Bruno.

Belinda Massmann-Oakley (12)

My Teacher

Tells me good advice,
Always gives me a hand,
Making sure I understand,
And always ready to land.
How grand!
She's now the teacher of the year,
And who'll just appear,
I'm getting old,
It'll be foretold,
Even though she's got a fear,
Of balloons popping.
That's my teacher!

Fauzia Jabeen (11)

My Favourite Person

My granny has a poorly heart,
Sometimes I really worry,
'Cause she can't run or dance or skip.
Or do anything in a hurry.
She'll always be my best friend,
'Cause she's always there for me,
I love looking after my granny,
And making her a nice cup of tea.

Lyndsey McCormick (9)

My Friend Freya

Every time you say goodbye
It always brings tears to my eyes
Your face is soft
Your eyes are bright
Your heart is full of the light
You are always there for me
To support me on to my destiny
Your games are full of magic
You are fun, full of jokes
You are the best, as well as your folks
You are the best friend I could have
You live in Wales
You're so far away
But our friendship bond will always stay.

Gurleen Dhillon (11)

Dad

My dad's a slightly greying dad
A love of reading
History and BBQs sort of dad
Sailing is his favourite hobby
It makes him smile and glow
When I give him a hug
And tell him he's my sort of dad
A real softie.
He has a phobia of rats and snakes
He wants us to be happy
Whatever it takes
He wears the same old jeans every weekend
The old tradition he'd never bend,
He is the greatest dad anyone could ever be
But that's tough because he belongs to me!

Isabella Letty (11)

My Dog Benji

My dog Benji is lazy like me,
He would sleep away the day,
But only wakes for his food,
I take him for a walk so he can have a wee,
But we always make it back for tea,
But when night comes he will soon be
Asleep in his bed until six-thirty,
I love my lazy dog Benji ...

Chloé Gulliver (9)

My Brother Harvey

My brother Harvey is great,
He makes a really good mate,
He plays with lots of toys,
Or makes a really loud noise,
He likes to play outside,
And really loves to hide!
Harvey is my mate.
He really is so great.

Alice Scales (10)

Oh Diamond

Oh Diamond,
Those innocent eyes make me laugh when I come back
To the messy kitchen after cleaning it up a minute ago.
Oh Diamond
I can always count on your floppy ears and slobbery mouth
To keep my deepest, darkest secrets.
Oh Diamond
You are full of mystery - I mean, how did you manage
To get some of your dinner on the top of your head?
Oh Diamond,
You are a one of a kind dog, and can give what *no* human can,
Oh yeah ...
Oh Diamond,
Thanks for *'eating'* my homework.

Sarah Sperber (11)

My Favourite Person

My favourite person,
Was my bestest friend.
She always made me smile and giggle,
And never once did we split or have much trouble.
She was the world's most beautiful blossom.
Once upon a time she made my dreams come true.
She was warm and soft like a bird's feather,
All her charming qualities made us stay together.
When I was hurt yesterday and the day before,
It was her to my rescue.
Saving me from the bitter, sour sadness.
I moved on to discover that she was God's gift,
And she meant it all from her heart.
A phrase I always uttered to her was,
'I love you truly and dearly.'
Happiness was all I loved.
My favourite person made me happy.
Loneliness was what I disliked and
My favourite person avoided this for me.
Ice cream was what I loved eating and
My favourite person brought sweetness to my life.
I'll always keep her in my heart, mind and dreams,
I'll even keep her in my inner soul.
Never in my life did I forget her,
She was my biggest present I ever received.
My favourite present, my priceless gift,
And my bestest friend!
A dear friend leads to a never end!

Amnah Rehman (12)

385

My Favourite Person

My favourite person has curly black hair,
She has taught us how to care and share.
My favourite person has teeth as white as snow.
She gives me milk to make me grow.
My favourite person has twinkling brown eyes.
When we come back from school, she gives us French fries.
My favourite person has a lovely hum
But whatever may happen, I'll always love my mum!

Anam Ijaaz (9)

Stevie G

Stevie G, Stevie G, where have you been?
I hope not to London, you know what I mean.
Old José Mourinho is all talk and show,
If you left Liverpool, there'd be one way we'd go.
One night in May, AC came to call,
We were 3-0 down, but drew three all.
Shevchenko we feared,
But Crespo scored two.
Maldini the captain, he scored first
Four minutes in, Liverpool were burst.
The blows came from Crespo, he was looking for more
To add to that growing AC score.
Half-time came and Rafa was positive
To win the game, for the boys to get on with
Gerrard said, 'Let's go out and win.'
And Liverpool really started to spin.
Out of the tunnel Liverpool came
Football faces in full flame
Gerrard kicked off with an awesome header
Most people called it the Liverpool shredder
In the shoot-out, Liverpool won
It all turned out to be a bit of fun
Jerzy shaking and putting them off
But AC they took it serious enough
Gerrard lifted that beautiful cup
Taking his team all the way up.

Alex Rowe (10)

Time, Place And Situation

Exciting Christmas Eve,
With Santa in the wings.
Tearful toothache,
Dentist *(Oh no!)*

Scorching hot day,
Mr Whippy cools my tongue.
Double figure birthday,
Postman with a bulging bag.

Funky disco night,
Outrageous Green Day.
Past war times,
Winston Churchill our saviour.

If I were to choose,
My favourite person,
It would depend on,
The time, place and situation.

Daisy Minto (9)

My Mum

My mum is always there for me whether I am ill or well
She helps me with my homework and helps me learn to spell
Her eyes are blue, blue like the bright summer skies
As she moves her hips from side to side
My mum is very special and I love her so
She's funny, she's great
She's not only my mum, she's my best mate!

Sophie McNally (9)

My Favourite Person

Jacqueline Wilson may only be a human
But to some she is a heroine
To some she uses her time
Her and her imagination make a good team
Together they create things that are unique
Things such as books
Which are a big part of our lives
She owns a gift
A talent
Something nothing can replace
I would keep it forever
I'm sure she would too
It is a matter of opinion how well she does
Some say she is nothing
But I think she is something
Big
Bigger than the highest consolation
Or the deepest ocean
Her thoughts stretch for miles
And her future is bright
She is more than just a human.

Rhiannon Hutchings (10)

My Aunt

All she was doing was going for a drive,
Shot five times,
No more alive,
The car crashed,
The window smashed.

She had to wait,
Because the ambulance came late,
That was the date she died,
With her mate by her side.

Bianca Polizzi (11)

Rooney

Although you may get sent off,
Underneath you're really soft.
Now you play for Man United,
I honestly think you should be knighted.
If it's Everton v Man United,
We all get very excited.
You could now beat them fourteen-six,
Because you always score from free kicks.
If the keeper lets it in,
You will surely kick him in.
But Rooney, Rooney whatever you say,
I will like you every day.

Christopher Curtis (11)

My Grandfather

In his life he played many parts.
He was once a baby with a young heart,
Who was always full of love and joy.
He was spoilt rotten like a typical boy.
As he grew older a schoolboy he became,
Always teacher's pet, good grades were his aim.
Then he became interested in girls and became a lover,
Who read the sports and car magazines from cover to cover.
Going out on dates with the popular girls,
Bringing them gifts like flowers and pearls.
Then comes the soldier, young and strong,
Who writes letters to his girlfriend and a love song.
In the army he will stay and for our army he will fight.
Guns at hand, places took, there he battles with all his might.
Now he's home and home he will stay,
Bringing up a family and bills to pay.
As he gets older his children will move out,
He is left alone without a doubt.
A grandfather now who is wise and old,
And tells me off when I am bold.
Now he is even older and is getting ill,
He lives his life on a single pill.
We will miss him when he goes,
But when that day comes, nobody knows.

Venetia-Justine Polizzi (16)

391

My Mum ...

I love you with all my heart
Our love is strong that it will never die
We'll never be apart
Thank you for comforting while I began to cry.
We've shared the laughter and the tears
Whenever I worry, Mum would erase it from my mind
She would listen as I told her my darkest fears
Whenever I felt blue, Mum would show me how to have a good time.
Whenever I had a problem,
My mum would always do her best to sort it out
And she'd always help me out with my homework
Whenever I accomplished something,
Mum would always stand proud
And she's always out in our garden, planting,
She always has her hand out in the dirt.
She's done such lovely things for me
Mum I want you to know I care
If I ever thought I couldn't do something,
She'd always tell me to try it and to believe
Mum, whenever you need support I'll be there.
Mum, I love you with all my heart
Thank you for showing me so much love
I've always loved you right from the start
And most of for being my mum, thank you very much!

Katie Johnson (15)

My Favourite Poem

J umpy and joyful, always cheering me up.
U seful for fixing things for me.
L ovely and friendly girl.
I ntelligent and smart, always helping me when I'm stuck.
A crobatic, always playing with me.

W ise and clever, top in the class.
A musing and funny, making me giggle.
T alkative and chatty, always gossiping to me.
K ind and sweet, helping me when I am hurt.
I nstrumental, always playing her music for me.
N ever unkind, always generous.
S uper friend.
O bliging and considerate, always helpful.
N othing can tear us apart because we are best buddies.

Melissa Birkett (10)

My Fab Sister Fern

M y big sister Fern is the best,
Y et she lives so, so far west.

F ab, fab, fab that's what she's like,
A t times we have been so bad,
B ut still she's an angel to me,

S o I say let her be
I wish the world were like that
S till I don't wish that at times she is better then all that
T oday's a day we're apart
E ven though we can be the baddest part of life
R eally she is the best on Earth with the name Fern.

Anastasia Taylor (8)

Friendship Of My Sister

Lovely soft smelling strawberry lipgloss
Beautiful hair like golden threads gleaming in the sunlight
My sister is as soft as the feathers of a beautiful peacock
She sounds like birds singing on a Sunday morning
But on other days she sounds like a screeching parrot in a
Pet shop waiting to be bought,
Her eyes are like the shiniest jewel in a jewellery box
Sometimes I creep into my sister's bed when I have had a bad dream
Then she wakes up and we sneak under the covers and share
our secrets
All of these things make me think of my sister as a ballerina
Dancing gracefully like a boat waiting to be sailed through the
pages of a book
I love my sister.

Bethany Ferguson (8)

My Mom

My mom, my mom is like a mouse,
Always running around the house,
Always scurrying
And a-hurrying,
To get the cleaning done,
My mom,
My mom,
My mom.

Molly Ashfield-Hayes (8)

My Best Friend

As a person she is so full of life
Every path she takes alive and new,
Everywhere she travels she continues to strive
And glistens like the morning dew.

She contributes to everything, especially sport
A classic game of hockey, her pride,
A unique sportswoman of the sort
Everything she has tried.

She has a sensational character
Helping others find their way,
Improvement is her main endeavour
Succeeding each and every day.

A unique character she does possess
Always speaking in a caring manner,
And constantly helping those with less
She is my best friend, Hannah.

Ramandeep Kaur (17)

Like A Star

(In memory of my uncle Ali Shinta)

In the darkness of life I needed a friend,
Someone who would comfort me to the very end.
A friend who would make my troubles seep away,
And from pain and misery I would fray.

If I am lost with no hope of direction,
All he'd do is smile and he'd set me free of frustration.
He would be my star that would pierce through the embedding dark,
And as a light he'd stay and make his mark.
Blinding me of all that's bad in this world,
As if making me feel happy and loved was his only concern.

Yet what came to follow was a torturous path,
Where I knelt beseeching to unleash his enamoured laugh.
For he was ill and was deafened to the tear's hope,
Even though I knelt by his end and let him a rope.

I wish I could have been by his side when it was near,
Yet the fact that death would come struck me with fear.
I felt that his warm light was painfully fading,
As he fought to stay alive, all muscles straining.

It was a battle of justice in the palace of life,
As waning hope gave into a municipal strife.
The kneeling of his soul in defeat,
I couldn't take it, I wish it were me.

This pain has been witnessed every minute,
Whether it is starvation, cancer or even evil committed.
People leave this world to live in their 'real' home,
That which is the immortal cup, where life is the slowly
vanishing liquid that roams.

Yet I used to question why happiness still loitered
in my heart,
I then realised it was that my uncle was here and
we will never be apart.
I remember once someone asked me to think of
my special place,
I thought of my uncle and his smiling face.

I still weep in the arms of my dreams,
For that's the only place left where his love is sealed ...

He has left to live in a better place,
Where his imagination can roam in a world of empty space.
And he will prevail in the mysteries of my very soul,
I miss his smile - it will never fade - I will never feel alone.

Hassanin Yousif (15)

Sarah

My older cousin Sarah
Might just seem to be
A girl who makes me smile
And gets along with me
But if that's what you thought
I might just eat my hat
So let me warn you now
Sarah's so much more than that
For starters on her gap year
She flew off to the east
To no other place than Japan
And had sushi as her first feast
Yet instead of spending all her time
Just having plain fun
She wrote me many long letters
On where she'd been and done
Now I definitely think so
And I'm sure that you'll agree
It's a very kind gesture
To write a special letter to me
Now one of my memories
And I was only six, mind you
Was Sarah giving me a bobble
And I've still got it too
It's things like this which make her
So special, such a carer
By now you should understand
Why I did this poem on Sarah!

Alice McCartney (10)

Europa

Europa, my fantastic rabbit
Is an incomparable friend.
We've had adventures together
From the beginning to the end.

One golden, jubilant day, we went to the beach
Europa kept munching her carrot,
I read my book, 'James and the Giant Peach'.

We had fantastic fun,
We ran and played and swam.
About being let to run, she went bonkers.

We crunched a lot, packed our possessions.
Conversely, unexpectantly
We had to go back.

I shared with you my greatest adventure
From beginning to end.
With Europa, my best friend.

I can remember how she ran with me
By warming my hands
She made me happy.

Pratik Bikkannavar (10)

My Special Grandma

My grandma is very special
In every kind of way
And every time I see her
She brightens up my day
She always has the time to spare
And always has a smile
But to teach her anything technical
Now that could take a while.
First she has a mobile phone
So we can ring when she's not home,
But oh we find it very hard
She hasn't got the right sim card!
She says that now she can turn it on
And tries to select a different song,
But all she gets is how much credit
The amount of time she must of read it.
And so we give up on the phone
And head towards another zone,
Of course she'll never be as good as me
When she turns on her PC
'Is it right click here, or left click there?'
She's sure to drive us to despair,
'Is it copy? Is it paste?'
Don't press print, look at the ink you'll waste.
What comes next? Oh the Internet
Connect, download, oh what the heck
Trojans, worms and viruses
I hope it's not contagious
And so it's simple I'm sure you'll see
She isn't one for technology,
But when it comes to being number one
She isn't just anyone
She's my *grandma.*

Kenndrah Warren (9)

Me And My Best Friend

My best friend is called Ann-Marie
And she is the best friend for me
We play with each other every day
When we give each other presents, we say - hooray.

I might be older than her,
So what!
It's about the friendship that we have.

When we have our arguments,
We feel bad
We feel rotten and sad
We go up to each other and say sorry
Then the rest of our friends get worried
We say - it's OK we are friends again.

Ann-Marie is always fun
And she is my number one.

Mary Anifowose (10)

Best Friends

Best friends are kind
They are people *(for silly things)* who don't mind

Best friends are very good
They are people who can share food

Your best friends can fight
But will come back to sight

A best friend is a person you like
They are so kind that they can give you a ride on their bike

You have to be kind to them as well,
So that they become fair.

And my best friend is Ruth
Because she always tells the truth.

Anushua Teresa Grace (10)

My Favourite Person

There once was a man from France,
Who plays football and has lots of fans,
He kicks a ball,
When playing for Arsenal,
The keeper tries to save it but Henry has other plans.

His name is Thierry Henry,
He's a brilliant player to me,
I've supported Arsenal,
Since I first saw football,
Just watch him play and you'll see.

Ryan Phillips (10)

Best Friends Poem

My best friend is called Septic
He is a little hectic,
He's a rabbit,
And he's developed a bad habit,
For a rabbit,
He nibbles everything in sight,
He nibbles with a very strong bite,
He's still very light,
He likes the sun,
We've got another rabbit and she weighs a ton!

Jacob Hampshire (11)

401

My Favourite Person

Liverpool leader
Cup winner
Paced runner
Clever thinker
Powerful shooter
English midfielder
Hard tackler
Liverpudlian legend
Toughest captain
Goal creator

Hint: *Liverpool FC football player*

Who is it? Steven Gerrard.

Craig Phillipps (11)

My Favourite Person

She was the first person I saw,
And she loved me most,
But can be a big bore,
And loves the coast

She is always there for me when I am down,
Even when she's not around,
And will always be my clown,
And will be there when I am outward bound.

My mum!

Kenza Thompson-Hewitt (11)

My Favourite Dog

My dog is ...

A loud barker
A sea swimmer
A fast eater
A water dripper,

A good runner
A playful cuddler
A hairy monster
A tail wagger,

A food snatcher
A dirty digger
A posh stander
A lazy sitter,

My dog is the best dog in the world.

Vicky Cook (11)

My Favourite Person

Lettuce chomper,
Woolly jumper,
Carrot nibbler,
Nose twiddler,
Neat burrower,
Never a worrier,
Always playful,
Rarely wasteful,
Grass digger,
Jumps like Tigger.

Who could it be?
Lucky the rabbit.

Laura Barr (11)

405

My Favourite Person

Seed muncher,
Treat cruncher,
Skilled climber,
Never a whiner,
Often squeaker,
Sometimes meeker,
Avid gnawer,
Excellent clawer,
Nose twitcher,
Lovely picture.

My gerbil.

Abigail Barber (11)

My Favourite Person

My favourite person is my dad,
Because he helps me when I'm sad.
When I was little I used to cry,
And introduce me to friends when I was shy.

When I was scared I used to hide,
But he said there was no reason to hide.
When I screamed on fast rides,
He said, 'We'll go on slow rides'.

When I was sick or whining
He always found a way to entertain me.
Instead of farting quiet
You'll be surprised how far they are from quiet.

Richard Poole (10)

My Best Friend

Carly's my bestest friend
She's chatty, funny and kind,
She can be very naughty,
But she still has a generous mind.

Her eyes are hazel,
And hair is brown,
Her worst hobby is shopping
Even though she loves to go down town.

In school she's jumpy and giggly,
And sometimes gets in a row!
We always play together
Like we're doing now.

Carly's a girl,
That I know I can trust
She can keep secrets,
That's why she's the best.

Angharad Roberts (11)

My Best Friend

Carly is my best friend,
She is nice, kind and cool,
She is lazy in the mornings,
But fun in the afternoons,
She is funny, mad and sporty,
And can be very naughty.

She has long, dark brown hair,
And it is very wavy,
She is tall and thin,
And has got hazel-green eyes,
She is pretty and friendly,
And very helpful,
And it is Carly.

She has long blonde hair,
She has small brown eyes,
She is small but thin,
And is really kind,
She is pretty and chatty,
And very friendly.

She loves her sport,
And especially netball,
And the reason she is so small,
Is because she only eats pork,
And I write about Sophie.

Carla Richards (11)

My Favourite Person (My Sister)

Thunder may roar,
And enclose me in a cage,
My shadow sore,
From being trampled on with rage,
It appears that I have no hope,
And I could never grin,
I have no choice but to grope,
I can never win.

But then the sun comes forth,
On a lush and distant hill,
And this light is not to morph,
And I possess free will,
However this light is not a star,
Or supernatural at all,
And even though it can be far,
She'll catch me if I fall.

And even though she may have flaws,
And tell of untrue things,
She'll always open up the doors,
She'll always give me wings,
This girl will always make me laugh,
She'll make me see the world,
She'll lead me down a righteous path,
And the bent will uncurl.
And even though her height is small,
I'll look for her in the skies,
She'll always answer when I call,
This girl rarely defies,
I love my sister, of whom I write,
And I always will,
She's the sun that I sight,
Upon that distant hill.

Nikhila Patel (12)

My Mum

My mum
Is the best mum in the world,
She always helps me,
Even with my boring homework,
When I am sad
My mum
Cheers me up,
My mum is thirty-two
But she looks as if she's twenty,
My mum has bright blue eyes
Like the sky,
She has long hair
With highlights just like mine,
Except mine is short,
I really love my mum.

Scott Davies (11)

408

My Favourite Person Is My Dog

My favourite person is my dog,
He runs with me when I go for a jog,
I always forget his name is Todd
But I remember it rhymes with cod and odd,
Sometimes he is shy,
And then he goes to cry
When he's sad
Or when he's bad
I cheer him up
He's my mum's favourite pup.

Jame Perriam (11)

The One Girl

Bethany's the one girl
That belongs in my heart,
She has long brown hair
And brown chocolate eyes.

She has long, lean legs,
That's the girl I love,
But I've one problem,
She does not like me!

Aled Miles-Pengilly (11)

My Favourite Person Ellie

Ellie is my best friend
She has a large mouth
Which is very loud,
She has large blue eyes
And very thin blonde hair
She's a very, very lively girl
That's my favourite person.

Nia Thomas (11)

My Uncle's Dog Bouncer

Bouncer is cool,
Bouncer is good,
He likes to lie down,
He likes to eat lots of food.

He is gold,
He was really old,
It's a pity he died,
I liked the way he smiled.

Owen Harris (11)

My Favourite Film Star

I have a favourite film star,
His name's Orlando Bloom,
But in some magazines I read,
He's called Orlando Swoon,
It's true!

All I know about his past,
Is that he always did his best,
Well, at least I think he did,
In every single, solitary test,
Maybe?

He's played a part in so many things,
Like 'Midsummer Murder', and 'Ned Kelly',
'Kingdom of Heaven' and 'The Calcium Kid'
They're all 12s, PGs, and 15s
Almost all of them I've seen.

Ever since I first saw him,
And when I found out who he was,
I then began collecting posters,
And now know exactly what he does,
And want to do it to,
Wouldn't you?

Saeran Rowland (11)

Paddy

My favourite person is my dog Paddy,
His master is my daddy
His favourite place is at the sea
Because he likes to chase the seagulls.

He can run for miles and miles
But when he comes home
He's all wound up
Knocking things over with his wagging tail.

He's really fussy with his food,
All he likes is Frolic and bones
He likes to cuddle and play with me
He is the best dog anyone can have!

Sophie James (11)

My Brother Rhodri

My big brother Rod
Thinks he is a god
He is very kind
And has a sharp mind.

His brown curly hair
Makes him very fair
He's strong and tall
In rugby he likes to maul his enemies to the ground.

Strong, smart and silly
He's allergic to lilies
He has a lot of friends
And he sends - *emails* to the group.

In the middle of his GCSE
He still had time to play with me
My brother Rhodri.

Rhys Jenkins (10)

Mum

I love my mum
She's as sweet as gum
I love my mum
But she has a big bum.

My mum is the best
Better than all the rest
My mum is the best
She's like a secret treasure chest.

She's there for me
When I'm sad,
But shouts at me
When I'm bad.

But you know what?
It's not so bad
Even when the way
Is barred.

Because I know
The way is clear
Every time she
Holds me near.

Kathryn Pritchard Warwick (11)

Bridie

Bridie's very cute
She loves to eat fruit
Bridie is a bit of an alcoholic
She likes Strongbow the best like me
She is the boss
And sometimes she gets lost
But she is my dog and I love her to bits.

Jessica Hoey (10)

My Favourite Person

Can you guess who my favourite person is?
Well, my favourite person is my sister, Ellie
I know what you're thinking.
Who could ever choose someone like that?
Well, I can, and this is why.

Sometimes your brother or sister
Can be very annoying, but sometimes
You feel you can't help smiling.

My sister's only seven
But acts like she's from Heaven
The real truth is,
She can be a bit bossy
And also very naughty
But I still love her anyway!

Olivia Coles (10)

Thominah

She's cool, she's fine!
She's hot, she's mine!
Not mine! The boys;
To her they're like toys.

She's fun, she's sweet
She hasn't got a lot of meat!
She's caring, nice,
But afraid of mice!

She's great, you'll love her!
You can't get enough of her!
She's the most perfect girl,
In the world!

Salima Azad (12)

Surya

Surya is my favourite person in this world,
She's a great footballer and her hair is in curls.

She's my best friend in the whole universe,
No matter what, she always comes first.

Our memories are in a great big chest,
Trust me, Surya is the best.

Amarah Harris-St Aubyn (11)

A Friend

A friend I can talk to,
A friend I can whisper to,
A friend I can shout to,
A friend I can go to.

She's got that special smile,
That always cheers me up,
And we all say this sometimes but ...
I do have to say *shut up!*

She's really, really cool,
She isn't that tall,
But all in all ...
She's got it all!

Leah Rogers (9)

Untitled

My brother is so sweet,
He really likes to eat,
His favourite food is meat,
Yes that's what he likes to eat.

My brother is so cute,
He likes to ride his bike
His bike horn goes hoot,
Yes, he likes to ride his bike.

My brother is the best,
Harry my brother, oh yes,
But he can be a pest,
Oh yes, he is the *best!*

Jade Weller (10)

My Dog Bonnie

My dog Bonnie is as beautiful as a bird,
She charges like a bull in a raging herd.

Dances like a diva chasing her tail,
Over the hill in heavy hail,
Gracefully sleeping like a silent storm.

Bouncing all day,
Off the hill as we play,
No dog's better than Bonnie!
No dog's better than Bonnie!
In all ...
Everyone loves my dog Bonnie!

Carl Ford (10)

My Sister

My sister Bethany is really sweet
With tiny hands and tiny feet
She drinks from a bottle with a teat
Pink is her favourite colour I think.

Katie Addicott (9)

Willem Dafoe

Willem Dafoe is a friend not a foe
He stars in movies, films and TV shows
He normally plays the bad guys, but he is not really a foe
He comes and goes, does Willem Dafoe
He's the one that takes the blow.
Oh yes he does, does Willem Dafoe
I will be sad to see him go
Because the best man in the world is
Willem Dafoe.

Robert Manghan (10)

My Friend

T aylor is funny and she is so smart
A lso she is very good at art
Y ou will not believe how crazy she can be
L uckily she is as pretty as can be
O ften she cries when bees are dead
R eally she is the best, that's what I said.

Katie Boddington (9)

Mothers

M others are always princesses
O h like honey on a spoon
T eaching you right from wrong
H ere to stay in your heart
E ver gentle and calm
R eassures you when you're down
S o mothers' understanding can help you go along.

Kimali Brook (11)

I Love My Dad And Mum

I look into your eyes; they are deep and shallow,
Sometimes they are wide and narrow,
You look around the world; it's filled with empty spaces,
And then I look and see a smile upon your faces.

I will know you forever, I love you lots,
You're a great part of me; I'm a great part of you,
As long as we're together
You will always be my family.

Jahanna Genesis (8)

My Favourite Person

Mummy you light up my day
And give me hugs when skies are grey
I love you and you love me
And that is what makes us family.

I love you Mummy!
You're huggably and loveably kind
My name begins with Y
And I see you with my eye.

On my birthday you will say,
'Happy birthday and have a great day.'

Yasmin Ball (9)

My Best Brother

My brother is funny and he is the best of all.
He helps my mum but he's not dumb.
He's good at stuff, not bad at stuff.
He's the right person for me, not the wrong person for me.
He's not bad and he's not sad.
He is fast at running and he's not a loser.
He's good at football and he's good at tackling.

I love my brother, he's the best,
No one should say he's a pest.

Hayden Hyde (8)

Some Mums

Some mums are pests
Some mums are good
But mine is the best
And so she should.

She is pretty, she is fun
She is my number one
I love her lots
And she loves Jelly Tots!

Emmie Cason (9)

My Favourite Person

My favourite person in the world
Will always care
And always be there
She's my best friend
And it will never end!
She's my dog, *Matilda.*

Cherrise Woodrow (9)

421

Maria Carey

Maria Carey is the best,
She could pass any contest,
With that voice, it's unique,
You can't hear one tiny squeak,
Out of her mouth comes my favourite song,
'We belong together' I've liked it for so long,
She is my favourite celebrity,
She's so cute, like a little kitty,
She's so cool, I like her so much,
There is no such person,
That I would like more.
She's cool and trendy, I like her a lot,
I have never forgotten,
One single world from the song I'm completely in love with,
I will like her for as long as I live.

Layla Jackson (11)

My Mum

My mum is my favourite person because she looks after me and my
brother and sisters.
She cooks us our dinner and goes shopping for us
I like her because she's a lovely person
And I love her so much nobody would take her away from me.

But sometimes she can be a bit bossy.
I think she's the best person because she always makes me happy,
She always takes care of me no matter what happens.
She's got red hair, brown eyes and she is very nice.

I don't know how she manages to do all the stuff she does,
Because I watch her every day and I don't know how she even does it.
But she said to me, 'You'll be like it when you're older.'
So now you know who my favourite person is.

Danielle Rolfe (10)

Why Do I Like My Dad?

Why do I like my dad?
Because he's so cool
Wherever he goes
He doesn't act the fool.

Why do I like my dad?
Because he's good at art
For me
I'm a good start.

Why do I like my dad?
Because I like his chains
I look at his clothes
Not one or two stains.

Why do I like my dad?
Because he's a good athlete
When he runs
He keeps himself neat.

Malik Deacon (9)

My Best Friend Danielle

My best friend is called Danielle
My best friend nearly fell
She nearly fell loads of times
My best friend never whines.

I would never tell on Danielle

I play with her every day
I don't like you; I've never heard her say,
A perfect pair I think we make
Don't think I don't like her for goodness sake.

I would never tell on Danielle

She became my best friend in Year 2
And we stick to each other like glue
She has a great big garden
And I don't think her heart will ever harden.

I would never tell on Danielle

I told Danielle nearly all my secrets
Some of my biggest ones they were.
I know I can always trust her
And that is why Danielle is my favourite person.

Sarah Smart (10)

My Dad

I love my dad
Of that I am glad
My dad is the best
Better than all the rest
His organic herbs are superb
We went to the Royal Cornwall Show
The day went slow
I really, really love my dad
Because he is so fab.

Kristianne Stride (10)

My Auntie Annie

My favourite person is my auntie Annie
Sometimes it feels like she is a nanny,
She's sweet and helpful and very kind
She has a very thoughtful mind
Her real name is Alison, but I call her Annie
I would still love her even if she were a mannie
She's nice and cool and very funny
Her personality is very sunny
I love her as long as the longest path
She has a very, very noisy laugh
You can hear her laugh a mile away
She makes me giggle throughout every day
We have so much fun together
Through wind and rain and any weather
Her fake tan is quite uncanny
O' how I love my auntie Annie.

Emily Taylor (10)

My Mum

When I fall over
She puts a plaster on me
She's always nice and beautiful
She cooks food when I'm hungry

She plays games
When we have been good
She always cares for us

She tucks us in bed
And gives us a goodnight kiss
My favourite person is my mummy.

Iseboa Woollands (7)

My Favourite Pet

My guinea pig is very fine
She's so quiet and just mine.

We get up to lots of adventures together
She's going to be my friend forever.

I'm never going to leave her
She's going to be my friend forever.

Alex Yeo (8)

My Mum - Cinquain

My mum
My mum is great
She's a really good mate
She really, really loves to hum
My mum.

Jade Montagna-Malcolm (10)

426

My Mum

She gave me life
She gave me food
She gave me love from me to you
I'll always love you no matter what
Even when there's a new baby in my cot.
I'll love that baby as much as you
Even if she does a great big poo.
For all the love you gave to us
It's time for us to make a fuss of you.

Aemy Gilson (11)

Charlotte

C lowning around like a cheeky monkey
H opping and jumping up and down
A round and around till we fall down
R apping and dancing to the jungle sound
L eaping and laughing till the sun goes down
O nce the moon comes up
T hrough the night we continue to rock and roll
T o the morning bop
E veryone joins in with the fun.

Emma Sansom (10)

My Cat

Somebody's furry and kind like me,
Somebody's name begins with C
Somebody loves me and tiptoes around!
Who could it be? Could it be me?

Somebody makes only one noise,
And somebody has not even one toy,
Is it a boy or is it a girl?
Who could it be? Could it be me?

Oh no, I forgot, how could it be me?
I'm not furry not hairy as can be?
So that leaves only one person I'd never forget,
My beautiful cat,
Who always lies on my lap!

Chloe Slaney (11)

Scooby-Doo

Scooby-Doo is really cool
Scooby-Doo runs into walls
Scooby-Doo hates history
Scooby-Doo solves mysteries
Scooby-Doo hates ghosts
Scooby-Doo loves toast
Scooby-Doo needs a rest
Scooby-Doo is the best!

Reece Evans (8)

Don't Hang Tinsel On The Christmas Tree

Don't hang Tinsel on the Christmas tree
Spikes will go up her nose and between her toes.
Don't hang Tinsel on the Christmas tree
Her whiskers are always twitching, running round in the kitchen.
Don't hang Tinsel on the Christmas tree
She squeaks a lot and slips in little slots.
Don't hang Tinsel on the Christmas tree
She likes to eat and run and sleep in the sun
Don't hang Tinsel on the Christmas tree
Although her eyes are pink and bright, they are not a Christmas light.
Don't hang Tinsel on the Christmas tree
She's my guinea pig and she loves me!

Meg Young (9)

Annie

In the park she zooms in front of me
Her flapping ears shake rapidly
Her four paws barely hit the ground
As Annie runs around and around
And as it's obvious to see
Annie is a dog, but a friend to me.

Annie, when she's tired
Is as tired as can be
She lies down in her bed
Then stumbles up to me
And now it's obvious to see
Annie is a dog, but a friend to me.

Millie Cook (10)

Beautiful Beau

My faithful dog Beau
follows wherever I go.
She's there when I'm sad
She's there when I'm glad.

Her lovely black fur
is sleek and shiny.
She has soft brown eyes
and feet so tiny.

This dog of mine
is gentle and kind.
She loves to bury things
that we can never find.

There never was a dog so special
as my *beautiful Beau!*

Lauren Phipps (9)

My Grandparents

My grannie
My grannie loves to sail,
She's hardly ever here.
Her bags are ready the night before,
Packed full of all her useful gear.

My gran is a perfect gran,
She does have one small problem though.
She burps and farts and swears a lot,
She's always on the go!

My grannie loves to drink,
Her favourite's got to be gin.
My grandad likes to drink as well,
But don't let me get started on him!

My grandpa
My grandad is a laugh,
That's if he's here.
He's forever on his boat
And soon he disappears.

I watch him leave the harbour,
His Union Jack waving.
It really is exciting,
Seeing him go sailing!

You never know what words you'll hear,
Polite or best not heard.
They may be greetings, or, 'How are you?'
Or another word for turd!

But when he's home he's always there,
Playing tricks and joking.
It makes a change from on a ship,
But at least you're dry, not soaking!

Olivia Kennaway (11)

431

Mrs Buzzy

You are a very busy, buzzy bee,
No matter what, you've been there for me.
From Reception to Year 6
I had lots of problems
You could fix!
I worked with you for about a year,
When I needed to talk you were somewhere near.
And through the years I have known you,
You've picked me up when I was feeling blue.
And you made me wear a frilly dress,
It must have cost a pound or less!
Although I left Parnwell School,
I will never forget you,
Cos you're *cool!*

Hayley Lawrence (11)

My Mum

My mum hugs me to my death,
Then she sorts out what is left.

My mum gives me hugs when I'm sad,
Then she tickles me when I'm glad.

My mum helps me with my times table,
Then she tells me a little fable.

My mum helps me to do some art,
Then she teaches me to be very smart.

My mum is my best friend
And she loves me to the end.

Terri Merrett (8)

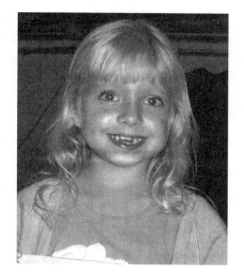

My Favourite Person

My favourite person is my pet.
She is very fluffy,
She hates the vet,
She likes to scratch and twitch her nose,
She eats the flowers,
My mother grows!

She likes to run and eat all day,
She's lots of fun,
She likes to play.
When holding her I stay alert,
To stop her nibbling at my shirt!

She has long ears
And a fluffy tail.
She likes to talk to garden snails.
This person has some funny habits.
This person is of course ...
My *rabbit!*

Amy Sargeant (10)

My Favourite Person, Mum

My mum is so lovely, she tidies up my clothes.
She kept me safe when I was little.
She feeds me when I'm hungry
And she breastfed me when I was a baby.
I hated vegetables
And my mum explained how healthy they were
And then I started eating them all up.
She cooks dinner for me
And makes breakfast before I go to school.
She helps me with my homework when I need her to,
And arranges my uniform before I go back to school.
That's why my mum is my favourite person.

Fatou Panzout (9)

My Mum

My mum ...
Hates it when I suck my thumb,
I'm her lamb,
Always give her a hand,
Her laugh reassures me when I'm down,
She never wears a frown.

Mum you care for me,
Your smile's filled with lots of glee.

She plays with me a lot,
Like an unmasked dragon ... *not!*

Yasmin Miller (7)

434

Like Winter Snow!

I love him so
Like winter snow
I love him more
Right from the core
It's his grin, it's his chin
My love for him will never dim
He makes me laugh, he makes me smile
He'll keep me thinking for a while
His tender touch
Means so much
His big blue eyes
To cloud nine I rise
My thoughts he is in
His cute, sexy chin
Like winter snow
I love him so!

Megan Fussell (13)

My Grandma

My grandma is cool,
She's fab and does not growl.
She cheers me up
When the weather is foul.

She teaches me things,
Like to knit or to sew,
Which without her help,
I would definitely not know.

With Grandma around,
Every day can be fun,
Especially if we
Are having a run.

So wonderful Grandma,
This poem is for you,
To say a big thanks,
For all the things you do.

Laura Scott (9)

The Answer To Our 'One Year'

Cold, sad days fill me with gloom,
I know you will come and save me soon,
Like a doctor you heal the sick,
I know I can depend on you to come quick.

Glorious things happen to me,
When I know you are there watching me,
Safe from harm, the love you give
Is an undersea search for water.

Do you remember when we slept outside?
All the creatures were around us.
You remind me of a busy bee,
A buzz that keeps on watching me.

'Will you still be my friend?' you ask,
But what you don't know is,
I love and forgive you for the past,
Isn't that what best friends are for?

The heavens greet us open armed,
Trees wave us to walk on by,
Together holding hands,
We walk through these open lands.

Elizabeth Hamlet (16)

My Hero

(A tribute to my grandad)

I remember my story-times,
eyes wide,
jaw dropped.
Tales from the sea, when ships were proud,
not from books but only in memory,
as alive in reciting as it was then.

Pirates! in stealth
in the far China seas
and machine gunfire on a dark, stormy night.
A great white finds his supper
in the friend you shared breakfast with,
lessons in love on a tropical shore.

The eyes now old but the memories intact,
a hero in slippers but one never the less.
He dozes after dinner and dreams of the sea
of oceans and sky, and memories for me.

Rhys William Last (13)

Rooney Number Nine

Rooney trains before every game,
Rooney always plays in the sun and rain.
Rooney's player number is nine,
Rooney is running down the wing line
As the ball slowly rolls.
Rooney kicks it in the goal
As the keeper misses the ball.
Rooney is the best of them all.
When Rooney holds the cup
They all cheer and hold it up.

Stacey Gair (10)

My Mum

My mum is …

Cute
Cuddly
Friendly
Kind
She takes me on a fairground ride
Cakes
Sweets
Chocolate
Wine
I give to her, to show she's divine.

That is my mum!

Lauren Thompson (9)

My Best Friend

S he is funny at all times.
T errific at every game and never gives up.
E xciting, fun to play with,
P erfect in every way,
H appy every day of the year.
A lways kind to other people.
N ever shouts if you upset her.
I n no trouble at any time.
E ntirely a true friend.

Laura Watts (10)

My Author

If you see me reading a book,
Then take another look.
I'll probably be reading a book by Pat Moon,
Or at least I will be very soon.

It seems to be
That it occurs to me
That there's an author I do love.

I like an author who likes
Everything and everyone.
I love an author who loves to have fun,
I like people who are real,
To know how they feel.
I also love cliffhangers,
Suspense and thrills,
I love to know who wins and who kills,
But if you're asking me
Who my favourite might be,
I'd have to confess ...
Pat Moon's the one for me.

Margot Goldman-Edwards (10)

For My Mother ...

The beauty within, the pulled-up chin.
The elegant walk, the high standard talk.
The mingled intelligence, the heart immense.
The hidden map, the thinking cap.
The talent demonstrated, the over frustrated.
The very funny, the cute honey.
The intense bravery, the lovely savoury.
The so cheerful, the shy tearful.
The always proud, the over loud.
The short temper, the canine distemper.
The tongue twister, the motive transister.
The fragile fingers, the perfume lingers.
The smooth hair, the great care.
The cherished eyes, the very wise.
The Nobel Prize, the no goodbyes.
The big sis, the secret kiss.
For my mum, the favourite one.
The great joker, the non-smoker.
The shrill laughs, the good-at-crafts.
The best dancer, the great answer is ...

My mum!

Kiren Rao-Nebab (13)

My Choice Of Person

I have a good choice of person to find
I like people who are kind.
Loving and caring every moment
I work and communicate with the person I like
And keep away from the people who I dislike.
People who are friendly with me
They make me smile
When I need a person to chat with
I can just dial.
When I need a person to tend when I am upset
They always sort it all out and mend.
In my choice of person
I'll always pick the good people
Who don't get me in trouble
And all good people who I like
We float like a bubble.

Aneela Aziz (12)

Mrs Radwell

M iss Harmsworth and Mrs Davison are her helpers.
R egularly kind to Class 3
S ometimes angry at a messy classroom.

R eads books to us if we have spare time.
A lways helps you with difficult work.
D oes neat handwriting
W ants a very quiet classroom,
E veryday she comes in jolly,
L ikes a relaxing holiday away from us.
L ikes quiet people in class.

Aisling Guerzoni (8)

My Dad

He's a DIY man
doing what he can
He fixes this
he fixes that
he knows exactly
what he's at
He does the garden
when he can
he's not really
a gardening man
He goes to work
in his DSL van
he's a very
handy man
He takes the dog
and has a jog
he goes to boat fayres
to get his wares
He likes to build up
motorbikes
we go to the sea
my dad and me
He really loves
his family
and that's how
a dad should be.

Natasha Buss (15)

Mum

My favourite person is kind,
My favourite person is cute,
My favourite person is not a brute,
My favourite person is full of love,
My favourite person comes from up above,
My favourite person is one of a kind and
My favourite person cannot be replaced.

My favourite person is my mum.

Laura Rann (12)

My Favourite Person

J ack is my favourite person in the whole wide world,
A nd he is also my favourite little brother,
C limbing trees in the breeze,
K nowing him I think he's the greatest.

A rt and design, Jack can top it,
N ever-ending sky's the limit,
T erminating baddies on the PS2,
H e is a natural born leader,
O ver everyone he is the best,
N ever fails to be kind to others,
Y es he is my favourite person.

C ourageous, willing, ready to go,
R ainy days don't stop us playing,
A ll people love to have Jack with them,
I n our imagination we fly to the moon,
G reat just to have Jack with me.

Paul Craig (10)

My Best Friend Georgia

My friend Georgia always plays with me,
we bumped into each other in the nursery.
We usually play tag and stuff,
but when the boys play it gets pretty rough.

We love to sing and dance and run,
that is how we have our fun.
When we have sleepovers she's the first one to nap,
while I play with my toys in my lap.

Georgia is eight, she's nearly nine,
but my birthday is in plenty of time.
Georgia is sweet, Georgia is kind,
but she loses things that she cannot find.

She likes to eat, so do I,
the only thing we hate is apple pie.
We do have arguments but that's hardly ever,
and the best thing is we are very clever.

Me and Georgia are best friends
and when we have fun it never ends.

Lauren Taylor (8)

My Favourite Person

I cannot choose like others can,
One person that I love best,
Mum, Dad, grans, grandads, aunts, uncles,
Cousins, sisters and my great gran!
Do not make me choose as others can!

Tegan Crocker (10)

My Mom's Adopted Son

Now I have a lot of favourite people,
This one came out of the blue.
What I describe may seem a funny type of evil,
And maybe a bit weird to you!

Cool but serious,
This person is.
Weird and mysterious,
This person is.

My mom's adopted son,
I call him my brother.
I've two before this one,
Great, here's another.

We fight all the time,
Although we're having fun.
He always loves to dance and jive,
In time to the musical rhythm.

His name is Segun and he's thirty years of age,
But if you want to know more, join in the rampage!

Athene-Nanette Idiabor-Moses (12)

My Favourite Person

My favourite person,
Who could it be?
Mum? Dad?
Let me see.
Auntie Sarah, Uncle Len,
Or maybe my big brother Ben.
It's hard to say,
It's hard to pick,
I think I'm starting to feel sick.
Decisions, decisions, who could it be?
Oh what the heck, I'll just pick me!

Megan Williams (11)

445

Mrs Gifford Is The Best

Mrs Gifford is the best
She never thinks I am a pest
Mrs Gifford is my LSA
She helps me with my work and play
Mrs Gifford is so kind
She helps me sort out my mind
Mrs Gifford has a special gift
And always gives me a lift
Mrs Gifford will give me a hug
When I am feeling down
Mrs Gifford is so fine
She always gives me some time
Mrs Gifford is like my mum
Always ready for some fun
If I miss my mum in school
I look at Mrs Gifford and all is cool
Kind and caring
Loving and sharing
Happy and smiling
Always ready to share
Ready to take on a dare
Always ready to help me
You see ... she is my favourite person
Mrs Gifford is the best.

Rebecca Blair (9)

My Brother

My favourite person is my brother Ross
We call him Ross the sauce
He is good at art
He dresses smart
He definitely likes jam tarts
He is cool
But he is not a fool
But
He thinks he is the boss
But he is not the boss
He sometimes makes me cross
He thinks he rules
But he does not rule

Even though he bugs me
I will always love thee
Because he is my
Brother Ross.

Zoe Donaldson (11)

My Lovely Mum

M others are lovely people loved by
Y ou and me.

L ove is their middle name,
O r it is kind, gentle or
V ery kind indeed.
E verybody
L oves their mum, except when they tell
Y ou off for not doing your homework.

M y mum really loves me
U nderneath the frowning I know she adores me
M y mum is my favourite person in Shepperton.

Esme Trice (9)

You'll Always Be My Bezzie (Best Mate)

My favourite person has been there from the start,
Our vow to each other was never to part,
From thick to thin, you've always been there,
For the past 11 years we've had stories to share,
You'll always be my bezzie.

All our adventures turn out to be great,
We've never properly argued so it must be fate,
I'm not gonna mention all the fun things we've done,
Cos I'd be here all day and it would spoil the fun,
You've always been my bezzie.

I'll give you some clues about the times we have shared,
We've laughed and cried but mostly cared,
We've had some frights from the dingy nights,
And had some laughs from the funny sights,
You've always been my bezzie.

You know more about me than anyone I know,
I'm certain all our secrets will stay down below,
When I've run straight into my own bit of trouble,
You've always been there for me on the double,
You've always been my bezzie.

But the day I'm never gonna forget, never ever,
Was when we were talking about our times together,
And you turned around to me and said I'm like your big sis,
That's the day I'm gonna forever miss,
You'll always be my bezzie.

Rachel Forrester (13)

The Perfect Pup For Me

I have a dog who started like a hamster,
tiny and beige in the palm of my hand.
So hairy and scary of all that's around her,
strange faces and noises and smells everywhere.

I have a dog who's fluffy and mad,
she jumps and rolls and never does what she's told.
She squeaks when she barks and loves going to the park,
strange puddles and messes and poos everywhere.

I have a dog who's nearly grown up,
she still bites and chews all my things.
I have a dog and I love her to bits -
cos she fits in so well with the family I have.

Tianna McCormack (8)

My Baby Cousin Aaron

He has luscious curly hair,
He loves his teddy bear.

I give him his milk,
His cheeks are like silk.

He does stuff in his nappy,
But he is always happy.

His teeth are coming through,
He is beginning to chew.

He is adorable and cute,
Especially in his best suit.

Frances Hosken (11)

My Best Friend

Every time I see my best friend,
I just can't help but smile.
She fills my heart with delight,
All and all the while.
She has long black hair,
The colour of midnight.
Her blue eyes are so bright,
She will give you a fright.

She's my best friend,
Yes, my best friend,
Christina, that's her name.

Amy Trott (10)

My Dad

My dad: brave, hairy, funny, friendly
Small, happy, helpful, kind
Busy, old, caring, good
Loves to watch TV
While reading the newspaper
My dad.

Matthew Stout (8)

My Favourite Person

My favourite person is three years old
I like to play with him in all kinds of weather
He looks at me with his little brown eyes
Just sat there staring like stars glittering from the sky
That shine with the light from the sun
His cute little face is the cutest face ever
And he has a little, black, wet nose
His cute, brown, floppy ears are very smooth and warm
My favourite person in the world is actually my dog.

Becky Appleton (11)

One In A Million

Cute, cuddly, as round as a ball
But unfortunately he's not very tall
We play our favourite games
Laughing all the time
Especially when I win the winning line
Sitting on his knee
He'd read funny books to me
We share our tea
And the last biscuit
He gives to me
But months ago
He was not there
And spent five long weeks
In a strange hospital bed
So I rushed home and gave him cuddly ted
He's better now I'm glad to say
And hopefully will be home to stay
Cuddly, cute, round as a ball
He's always glad to see me call
He's just one in a million
  My grampie.

Gabrielle Swales (10)

My Favourite Person

My favourite person is warm and cuddly just like a bunny
She loves me dearly and with her lovely smile
She warms and brightens my heart
When she cuddles me tight I feel so alive
And I know she will always be there
Through rain and shine I know she's mine
Ever since I was born she was my best friend
And she will be to the end.

Francesca Goodman (12)

My Best Friend (Chantelle)

She is funny, she is kind and is shy
She's always there for me
And she never lets me down
Any time I sit down if I'm lonely I see a girl's legs
And when I look up it's my friend Chantelle's
She's the best friend a girl could ever have
There are lots of Chantelles in the world
But she's the best.

Dupe Adeagbo (8)

My Mum

She's a smart organised table
She is as fun as a funfair
As smart as a hare who always takes care
As graceful as a dove
As bright as a pink blossom
The sound of chirping birds
As peaceful as the sunset on the horizon
As warm hearted as an angel with a calm voice
She is as light as a butterfly that always comforts me
When I'm sad and frightened
She's always there for me to make me feel better
She is as neat as a pin
As pretty as a flower
And as soft as a pillow
As sweet as honey, as smooth as fur
As bright as sunshine
And as strong as a wrestler.

Anesu Madamombe (11)

My Favourite Person Is My Nan

M e and my nan make a perfect team,
Y ippee, I'm going on holiday with my nan.

N ever has an attitude like she never cares,
A lways passing her love on to other people,
N ever looking down, always happy to be around.

Kelly White (11)

Oh, I Love My Mum So

Mum, you're so totally cool,
It's obvious that you rule.
Your wish is my command,
You must have been born with charm.

You always make me smile,
Even if it's just for a little while.
I love you because you're my favourite friend -
And I promise to love you right to the ... end.

Vienna Farnell

My Favourite Footie Player

My favourite player is Steven Gerrard,
He is better than all the rest.
When it comes to scoring goals,
He even makes holes in the goals.
He is a great player and not a complainer,
He's the one, that's Steven Gerrard.

Charlotte Bibby (10)

Polo

Polo is our school hamster,
he's not a bit like a gangster.
His little pink ears
and the way he peers
is really, really cute,
and his age is two
but we're never blue
when Polo's around.
His little red wheel
and his peanut peels,
his little clay bowl
and in his nest, a tiny hole.
He sits in our classroom
while we go boom, boom!
There's *never* a dull moment
when Polo's around.

Louise Ingham (11)

Dad!

You're a great and groovy golfer,
As great as great can be.
Even though you're not Tiger Woods,
You're good enough for me.

I love that you are polite and fair,
Even though you've got grey hair.

That's how cool you are Dad.

You are different and dependable,
And as cool as cucumber.
You're clever, calm and chilled,
As funny as funny can get.

That's why I'm glad you're my dad!

You're always right and relaxed,
As clever as clever can be.
You're brave, courageous and strong,
You're Eric and you're excellent.

That's why I love you Dad!

Ellie Bushell (12)

Two Special People

My special person is my mum
I love to see her gorgeous smile
She means everything to me
And I will love her for a while.

I have another special person
It is my very precious friend
We really think a lot of each other
And our friendship will never end.

Evelyn Johansen (8)

My Favourite Person Is My Mum

My mum does lots for me,
The best thing is she gives me cuddles.
When she gives me cuddles
It feels like I'm on a soft cushion.
I love Mum, she is the best.

Peter Fearne (9)

My Family

This is a poem about my family,
All that they do and what they mean to me.
I live with a fab father and brother,
A person that no word describes is my mother.

When you're cold or feeling blue,
Sat at home with terrible flu,
When you're being bullied at school,
Being intimidated to feel like a fool,
There is one person there, that is like no other,
Yes of course, it's my mother.

If you're feeling all alone and just want some fun,
Someone to talk to when your homework is done,
In need of someone loyal and on which you can depend,
Turn to a relative who at times can feel like your only friend.
There is one person there, that is like no other,
Yes of course, it's my wonderful brother.

If today your happiness is less,
If you need someone to turn to for some seriousness,
A person that you love and trust with anything,
The only person that doesn't laugh when you try to sing,
There is one person there, that is like no other,
Yes of course, it's my fabulous father.

This poem sums up my family rather well,
But most of all I want everyone to know,
I wouldn't swap them for a thing,
But money - that would be nice!

Katie Bailey (13)

Miss Cunningham

My favourite person is my teacher Miss Cunningham.
She is not at all glum,
She is full of fun,
And her smile is as warm as the sun.
I see her every day when I work and play,
She always has a lot to say,
At the beginning of the day,
And all the children must obey,
But she is nice and kind,
A better teacher you will not find.

Melissa Hill (10)

Sisters

S isters are annoying
I n the meantime they're boring
S ometimes they're fun and at
T imes they are
E very bit lovely
R eally lovely
S o lovely, sometimes my sister is the best sister
anyone could have.

Daisy-Mae Cole (10)

My Sister Poppy

458

Thierry Henry

T alented player
H overing runner
I nternational striker
E xcellent tackler
R oaring goal scorer
R apid thrower
Y ummy for the World Cup

H igh driver
E xcellent crosser
N ice passer
R aging corner taker
Y ellow card receiver.

Alex Dalrymple (9)

My Sister Lucie

M y big sister Lucie
Y ou are my sunshine

S he is always there
I love her in every way
S he smiles like the sunshine
T he maker of the day
E ven when she is far away
R unning out to meet her each and every day

L ucie for evermore
U nderground, over ground, Lucie is always around
C are and scare you are always there
I love you to the moon and back
E ither here or there, she is everywhere.

William Kingston (11)

Minnie Mouse

My special friend is Minnie Mouse
I even met her in her house
It was a very long flight though
It cost a lot of money, so
I also met Mickey Mouse and Donald Duck
I also met Friar Tuck
And now you know about my holiday
To see a friend far away.

Francesca Fisher (8)

My Friend Isobel

My friend Isobel is kind and always well
She has been my friend for six years
Whenever she walks past you always hear cheers
She's nice and truthful, she never lies
Anyway, she always tries
I like Isobel and Isobel likes me
We are best friends and always will be!

Rachel Jones (9)

Guess Who?

When I'm feeling down
I give a little frown,
Who's always there?
Is it my dad, nana, auntie,
Uncle, friends or cousins? ... No.

If I was to say how cool this person is,
I would have to say 10/10,
This person I am thinking of
Is really kind and funny.

This person cares for me
When I'm feeling ill,
This person heals my cuts
And my bruises.

I'm not ashamed to say it,
Yes, it is true,
This person I am thinking of,
Is of course my mum.

I love you.

Dani Flynn Mushett

The Girl In The Star

One night as I was under my bedcover,
I saw a star that stood out from all the others.
It made a bright glow,
That shone through my window.

It sparkled so high,
As it sat above in the dark night sky.
I saw a kind face in this star,
That smiled at me in the distance far.

I believed the star was a she,
Her happy face looked down on me.
I sat on my bed and looked at her,
I did not move, I did not stir.

That night I had a dream,
About the star that I had seen.
I believed this star was a special one,
It came back like it had done.

It came every night,
When it was dark and never light.
It was the best star I'd ever seen,
Every night it helps me to dream.

The star is my friend, my bestest friend,
My bestest friend Daisy, is the star.

Summer Coles (12)

My Mum

I'm so glad to have a mum like mine,
Cos she always tells me I'm on her mind.
She's stuck by me through the good and bad,
And I thank her for that all the time.

She'll go through anything to try and please me,
And believe me, that ain't easy.
I don't want to lose her cos she's precious to me,
I don't know what I'd do if she left me.

Whenever I'm melancholy she makes me smile,
When she puts her arms around me.
I feel the warmth and love that
I have never felt with anyone before.

No one can replace my mum,
Cos she's one in a million,
And I love her a billion.

Farah Choudhry (14)

My Mummy

I love my mummy
She is like chocolate in my tummy
She hugs me when I am ill
Says sorry when she hurts me
She's my mummy and always will be
Even when I'm eighty.

Miriam Simmons (9)

My Hero

At six I began to like football
so decided to call upon Dad
to ask who he had supported
when he was just a young lad.

Only one team will do he advised me
and that's Leeds United FC
so a Leeds fan I quickly became
to support them brought great joy to me.

But one player would always inspire me
a striker so talented and strong
who played with the heart of a lion
and in my eyes could never do wrong.

I decided to repaint my bedroom
in Leeds colours of yellow, white and blue
then stick up all my Leeds posters
of this blonde Yorkshire man loyal and true.

Then one day I turned on the TV
to see my hero playing in red
no longer a Leeds super striker
but a Man U player instead.

So if you have not guessed my hero
let me tell you his talent's no myth
he is fast, he is strong and courageous
and my hero is called *Alan Smith.*

Alexander Hill (10)

My Mum

M um you're like a monkey
U are the best
M aking me happy all the time

U seful in every way

A brilliant person
R eally, really nice
E veryone loves you

B rilliant Mum
R eally good at caring for me
I love you Mum
L ovely that's you
L ove you Mum!

Abbie Brough (10)

The Family Member

My favourite person
Is my thoughtful brother,
Who looks after me
Just like my mother.

He likes to do sports,
And his favourite is football,
And when he plays football,
He can sometimes fall.

His favourite subject at school
Is the magnificent geography,
And his favourite books are
Signed biographies.

So now I know
His special person is me,
Because we are one
And one we'll be.

Steven Tremeer (10)

The Best Sister I Could Ask For

Her name is Ellie Rose
She has a cute little pose
She may only be 16 months
But she cheers you up when you're down in the dumps
Her beautiful, blonde, wavy hair and her big blue eyes
That even light up when she cries
She likes the characters Piglet and Roo
Out of Disney's 'Winnie the Pooh'
Ellie Rose my little sister
When I'm at school I really miss her.

Nicolle Shaw (12)

Friends

I have lots of friends,
They treat me nice,
So I treat them nice,
I think friends are the most important thing in the world,
You'd be lost without them,
If you're upset you can always rely on ...
Friends.

Abbie Bratt (10)

466

Me And My Sister

My little sister
Is a sweet girl
She makes me laugh
She is my best pal

We enjoy playing together
It brings me good memories
We run and have fun
And end the day with fun stories.

Not everything is perfect
She does annoy me with her bites
But I love her a lot
No one is perfect, even roses have spikes.

Linda Azma (9)

My Favourite Person

Those wonderful days when you read to me,
Those days when you taught me to write,
How I loved those days that we spent together,
Till you went out of sight.

When I was still small you passed away,
You ended your great life,
But you will always have a place in my heart,
Until the day I die.

At night I still remember those days,
When you taught me to read and write,
I miss it now, how it used to be,
Inside my head someone's turned off the light.

I write this poem just for you,
Because I want to say,
That I really love you Grandad,
And it's always going to stay that way.

Sophia Oakes (12)

My Favourite Person

My favourite person is my mum
She's caring
She's daring
She's lots of fun

My favourite person is my mum
She's playful
She's cheerful
She's lots of fun

My favourite person is my mum
She's loveable
She's huggable
She's my mum.

Kezia Morgan (10)

My Favourite Person Is ...

He runs like a cheetah
He eats like a pig
He looks like my twin
And he's got a cheeky monkey grin.

He fights like a tiger
He cuddles me like a hamster
He also likes to catch a fish
Just to make a wish

My favourite person is
My brother!

Melissa Daniels (10)

My Mum

My favourite person is my mum,
She is kind and intelligent,
I love her to bits.
She does moan at me now and then,
We also argue a lot now that I'm almost a teenager.
I don't feel embarrassed around her,
Because I know I can talk to her about anything.
I love her so much,
And there are no words to explain how much I love her.

Rebecca Quinn (12)

My Mum!

My favourite person is my mum,
She helps me when I am feeling glum,
My favourite person is my mum.

My mum cooks and cleans,
Till everywhere is glowing.
She scrubs, she polishes,
And does all the mowing.

My favourite person is my mum,
She helps me when I need to add sums,
My favourite person is my mum.

She pays all the bills,
Buys us what we want.
She teaches us stuff,
Does things we can't.

My favourite person is my mum,
She cures me when I have a bad tum,
My favourite person is my mum.

She wakes us up,
To get us ready for school.
Works real hard,
Helps me with my homework too.

My favourite person is my mum,
She makes food that is yum-yum,
My favourite person is my mum.

Nkechi Uwaezuoke (10)

I Can't Choose!

Who is my favourite person? It's really hard to choose,
It feels like it's a competition that I don't want anyone to lose.
I love my mum 'cause she is great,
She's not just my mum, she's my little mate.
And I love my dad 'cause he is cool,
He likes to play with me and mostly we play ball.
I also love my uncle, we like to play cards,
If we don't play inside, we play in the backyard.
I also love all my aunties and they love me too,
But there's one in particular who lets me watch 'Doctor Who'.
I also love my nanny, she plays shops with me,
She likes the little kittens who chase bumblebees.
And last but not least I love all my friends,
We see each other at school but sadly it ends.

Ellie Marlow (9)

Chloe, My Best Friend

Chloe, she is very cute
She's got a good thing for fruit
She's very kind and sweet
And her handwriting's very neat
She's always silly at school
And she can't swim very well in the pool
She's always playing shops
Also she likes lollipops
Her favourite jewellery is silver
She's got lovely golden hair
And a very gluey chair
She sometimes wears dresses
And likes to play games of chess
She's got a very strange laugh
And likes to go to the cafe.

Louise Spence (8)

My Mum

My favourite person is the best
The prettiest and the best dressed
She's not my age
But is always there in times of need when I want care
Have you guessed yet?
I know you're not dumb
Yes of course, it is my mum.

Amber Harwood (12)

My Mum

The things I like about my mum
Is that she makes me smile when I am glum
She makes me laugh when we have fun
We laugh so much, it hurts my tum.

When she puts the kettle on to make a brew
She sometimes lets me have one too
She is the best, best, best, best
She is so much better than all the rest.

Elisha Jane Stott (11)

Mum And Dad

My mum and dad are just like honey,
Sticky, sweet and runny.
My dad he is a postman,
But doesn't drive a mail van.
I help my dad deliver post,
But he normally delivers most.
My mum she is the house's heart,
And she always plays the biggest part.
Cooking, cleaning, ironing too,
All these things she has to do.
Buying us food every day,
Makes us feel good and gay.
They buy me my school uniform,
And jumpers to keep me warm,
That's the way all parents should be.

Lauren Wood (11)

Lois Stephen - My Favourite Friend

My favourite person has to be
Lois Stephen as she is very special to me.
Josh is her brother, he is her twin,
She can be very loud or quiet, so you could hear a pin.

We catch the bus together every day,
I bet we're still friends when it comes to May.
We have every class together apart from DT
And I'm not in her form so we're not together in PSHE.

Lois is my special friend,
She'll be my best friend to the end.
We always eat dinner together,
I hope she'll be my best friend forever.

Roxanne Wain (11)

Untitled

My favourite person is Jade,
My friend is very tall,
Where as I am very small,
Jade is brave and not afraid.

Jade is my best friend,
She is extremely grand,
And she's always got an open mind,
And our friendship will never end.

Jade is like a sister,
Jade is my very best friend,
And always will be my friend,
She will even pop a blister.

Lois Stephen (11)

Super Clarets

Burnley, Burnley are so good
Burnley, Burnley are as hard as wood
Burnley, Burnley always score
Burnley, Burnley never bore
They will win the League
They really intrigue
Burnley, Burnley are the best
Burnley, Burnley could beat the rest.

Josh Broxup (11)

Man U, Man U Are The Best

Man U, Man U are the best,
They're better than all the rest,
If Man U took a test,
They'd probably pass it because they're the best.

If Man U are feeling down,
They shoot back up because they have the crown,
They love to play footie and when they're not they are down,
Sir Alex Ferguson runs the club, he's the best in town.

Man U's stadium is so big,
If you went out you'd have to dig because it's so big,
Burnley's stadium is a tin, it might as well be in the bin.

Man U, Man U always win,
They never lose, they always win,
People say Burnley are better than Man U,
But how are they the best,
If Man U and Burnley had a match they wouldn't draw
Because Man U's the best.

Man U have brilliant players like E Van der Sar,
Rooney, Ronaldo, Ruud van Nistelrooy and Rio are the fantastic four,
Thousands of fans go to each match
And when others are bad they are shown the door,
Man U, Man U are the best and have never played poor.

Man U, Man U are the best,
Better than all the rest.

Declan Lowry (11)

475

My Favourite Person

She is always there when I need her to be,
She washes my clothes and makes my tea.
She drives me miles to see my friends,
Even though sometimes she takes dead ends.
She can't sing to save her life,
But she keeps on trying till we all start crying.
She sometimes lets me stay up late,
Which I think is super great.
But doesn't tell my dad cos he will go mad,
And that would be bad and then we'd be sad.
She makes me smile and laugh all the while,
The crease in her head means it's time for bed.
She helps me with my homework without getting too stressed,
And that is why she is simply the best.
My favourite person as you may have guessed
Is my mum.

Joshua Gregory (11)

My Dad

My favourite person has to be my dad
He is the best of all the rest
He sends me love from far away
He makes me feel like I want to stay
He sometimes bugs me
But I say don't rush me
I really like him, my dad.

Megan Barnett (11)

My Favourite Person

My favourite person has a big belly,
he likes to snore in front of the telly.
Out of his nose grows long black hairs,
his chest reminds me of a grizzly bear.
We all call him werewolf feet,
they scare all the people that he meets.
He's nearly forty and getting old,
but please don't tell him he's going bald.
But don't be scared, don't be sad,
this is my mate, my pal, my dad.

Zachary Green (11)

My Favourite Person

My favourite person has to be
Well of course, Thierry Henry.
He's scored many goals,
The half-time bell calls,
The score is two-nil,
His best mate is called Phil.

My favourite person has to be
Well of course, Thierry Henry.
He's scored many goals,
The finishing bell goes.

Hooray!

Jodie Hunt (12)

477

My Mum

This poem is about my mum,
She is special and lots of fun.
My mum is so special to me,
Gave me life so I could be.
She's there for me when I'm ill,
She even pays the telephone bill.
When I'm alone or feeling blue,
My mum's the one to see me through.
Someone to trust and care for me,
We share the good times and the bad.
She's the best mum I could ever have.

Anthony Benson (11)

Angel Of Angels

My favourite person would have to be my dog,
She's so nice and cuddly not like a frog.
When I am lost she will come and find me,
She runs like a cheetah, she jumps like a frog.
Angel, she listens when I'm sad,
Angel, she listens when I am mad.
Angel, I love her she is the best,
And that was why I wrote this poem about her.

Georgia Cooke (9)

478

My Mum

My mum is funny and has a heart full of gold,
And she always says to me, 'You'll be driving me round when I'm old.'
She has a soft voice and doesn't like to shout,
And if I want her to she will take me out.
I love her for lots of reasons, that's not the end,
Even though we sometimes drive each other round the bend.

Kerry Louise Gaul (11)

My Mum

My mum's the best
She's better than the rest,
She's a good cook
And has a good look.
She has lovely blue eyes
And black hair,
She's never late to pick me up
Always there to run me everywhere.
To football, parties and days out with my family.
Thank you Mum for everything.

Sam William Jones (9)

She

She likes holidays, beaches and bingo,
She's a pigeon in a flock of flamingos.
Not that she's boring, she makes me proud,
She stands out from the crowd.

She helps me succeed in all I do,
In fact, there's not much she can't do.
She is there, every day,
Helping me, along the way.

She's sometimes annoying, I have to say,
But they're all like that really ... aren't they?
She's mostly kind though, loving and caring,
She's like a timid mouse though, not very daring.

I wouldn't change her for the world,
To me she's like Supergirl, brave and bold.
She's my mum, most important to me
And my mum is all I want her to be!

Joanna Samuel (11)

My Dog, He Is The Best

My dog he is the best,
Better than all the rest.

My dog he doesn't bite,
He cuddles me through the night.

I look at him, he looks at me.
That's the way it's meant to be.

My dog has big green eyes,
They look at me when he cries.

I love my dog, he is the best
Better than all the rest.

Aron Jones (13)

Monet

Monet is brilliant,
Monet is fab,
I really love Monet.
We have a good laugh,
We sometimes argue
But never for long.
No need to apologise,
We just give each other
A great big *hug*.

Nisha Patel (11)

My Favourite Person

Is a librarian
She works in my school library
She's called Mrs Sharpling and is the best
She helped me with my homework
She's really, really kind
I think she deserves
A chocolate
Because she's lovely.

Lauren Marie Harrison (12)

Missy

Missy my dog is my favourite thing
You might think that I am weird!

Fact is she is beautiful
And no one can change my mind,
Very sweet
Oh, I can't believe it.
Use that as an excuse,
Really small.
I'll never forget her
Timid and quiet
Extremely lovable.

People look at her and say she's cute
Every time I can't resist saying
Right, she is pretty, I know!
So I love her like a sister
On the Earth or far away
No one will say anything nasty.

Is she the one to love forever?
See I'm clever and I'll never forget her
Ever! Ever!

Catherine Richardson (12)

Smiler

My favourite person
A smile on her face
Greatest person
In the human race.

Singing, singing,
Sings the day away.

Bringing, bringing,
Love, every day.

When I'm feeling lonely,
Sad, scared or small,
I just remember them
And I'll grow ten feet tall.

Reading this poem,
Who it's about, you've not got a clue.
But if you just think
It could just be you.

Edele Watters (10)

My Favourite Person Is My Mum

My mum is very pretty,
she's also very witty.
Her eyes are like the ripest tree trunk,
and she's got that sparkling funk.
Her cheeks are like two beautiful roses,
wrapped with ribbons to make up posies.
My mum always tries to go to the gym,
she's always wanting to get more slim.
So that's my mum,
My mum's not dim
That's my mum,
Her name is Kim!

Samantha Telling (10)

Edward

My favourite person is not really a person,
Although he's a really good friend.
He gives me big hugs, he sits on my rug
And when I talk he listens.
I tell him my secrets
And talk to him when I'm sad,
And when I've had a horrid day
He stops me feeling bad.
He never answers me back,
And when I want to play, he's ready.
He really is the best of friends,
He is Edward, my teddy.

Jasmine Leigh Perry (10)

Madonna, How Can She?

How can she do it,
All that work
And still look so great?
How can she cope with all that fame?
I suppose it must be fate.

How can she live another life,
And raise a family?
How can she be a wonderful wife,
And still have time for me?

To me she truly is the best,
The greatest one of all,
She certainly beats the rest,
And makes me feel so small.

She is my hero!

Jennifer Wade (11)

My Mum Can Jump Over Mars!

My mum can jump over Mars,
Past all of the stars,
Past all of the planets as well,
She'll jump over the moon,
Leave in April and come back in June,
And far beyond Heaven and Hell,
She's as bright as a spark,
And as happy as can be,
And she'll always be there,
And she'll always love me,
My mum can do everything, it is true,
Well, not everything, I'll just tell you ...
She can't drink 1,000 gallons of water in only one gulp,
She can't eat a pink bar of slippery soap,
She can't milk a cow with not even one hand,
She can't tie up an elephant with an elastic band,
She can't pick up a porcupine with only one thumb,
But she's still my crazy, happy, lovely, pretty, giving mum!

Grace Cherry (9)

My Pet Rabbit, Lucy

She's my fluffy, furry friend.
It's my lop-eared rabbit, Lucy.
When she runs around the garden,
Her ears bob up and down,
When she runs down the garden path,
She kicks up her little legs.
Her big brown eyes watch
And follow you round the garden,
Every time I go in the garden,
She runs after me.
Begging me to stroke her.
At night I always put her in her hutch,
And make sure she is OK.
When it's her birthday,
I always get her a present.
I do the same at Christmas.
I love my three-year-old lop-eared rabbit, Lucy.
So that's all about me
And my fluffy, furry friend, Lucy.

Rachel Hurst (11)

My Favourite Person

My favourite person in the world,
Has to be my mum.
She makes every day,
So brilliant and fun.
I enjoy being with her,
Every single day.
My mum's my favourite person,
Is what I'd like to say!

Rachel Brunner (9)

My Grandma

Grandma, I love it when you cook,
Your chocolate cake is yummy,
The apple crumble is scrummy,
And you could write your own recipe book!

Grandma, I love it when you're funny,
Sitting in mud on holiday,
Joking the day away,
And hopping around like a bunny!

Grandma, I love it when you sing,
You sound like birds,
How do you know all those words?
And your voice has a sweet ring.

Grandma, I adore it when you say, 'I love you.'
You wrap your arms around me tight,
How you fill my life with delight,
'Grandma, I love you too!'

Hannah Redhead (11)

My Brother

My brother always has a big smile on his face,
When he takes me somewhere.
Richard and I are alike because we both have ginger hair.
Richard and I like to play swing ball
And we like to play with the diablo that he gave me
And we like to play football.
Richard and I like to take his dog for a walk down to the river.
And when I have to come home, I don't want to.
For my brother is the best brother in the world.

Margaret Palmer (10)

My Best Friend

My best friend is really fun
She likes to sunbathe in the sun
But then along comes her mum
And tells her off until the day is done.

The next day
I went over to stay
We went to the movies
Where we had to pay
After that we had a relaxing lay
Then we made a sculpture out of clay.

Now as you can see my friend is fun
And she does like to lay in the sun
But this time along comes her mum
And surprisingly they have fun.

Vishala Nadesan (10)

Mummy

Mother, Mummy, Mum, Mama
All meaning the one same beautiful thing
A special someone you treasure forever

Love for her is a very precious thing
We're born to her, strangers to the outside world
She holds our hand
And guides us through the rough
Which makes us tough

I love the way she holds me tight
And tucks me into bed at night
I love the way she kisses me goodnight
And sometimes, in laughter, she gives me a fright

My mother means the universe to me
Her child means the universe to her
She's there when I'm lonely
She's there when I'm lost
She's there when I'm angry
And I'm grateful for that a lot

My heart feels love for her like nothing else in the world
I love you Mummy, so much
You're everything a mummy should be
Love you always.

Amandeep Marway (14)

Katrina

... Went abroad when I was young,
We couldn't talk by word of tongue,
Thrice a year, or thereabouts,
We'd see each other
And scream
And shout
And then we would just dance and play,
Dance and play with glee all day
And then we'd stay up late at night.
But
Time was short and time was tight
And she or I would go back home
And thoroughly we then would comb,
Our houses
For some bits or scraps
Of paper so that just perhaps
We could send a note or line,
From my house to hers, or hers to mine
After our partings I would feel sad,
So sad, it almost drove me mad,
For Katrina is the best of friends,
Not intent on her own ends,
She always has a smile or wave,
The perfect friend,
The memory to save.

Flora de Falbe (9)

YoungWriters

My Favourite Person

Whether you see her at school,
Acting like a fool,
You know she's so great,
And a real groovy mate.

Molly is my bestie,
She can be a pestie,
But I really don't mind,
She's a girl that's kind.

She throws food at you,
But she's cool, it's true.
Molly's excited every day,
Even if she wants to work all day!

Victoria Ma (11)

Pip The Dog

My dog, Pip, is my bestest friend
We'll always be friends until the end.
He loves to play football, so do I,
Pip and me both love cherry pie!
We go for walks that go on for miles,
But Pip is rubbish at going over stiles!
We've been up Snowdon, well, ran most of the way
And were very tired at the end of the day.
Pip loves to play tug-o-war
And when he wants treats, he gives you his paw.
He's really clever, just like me!
We go on adventures, with Pip's other friend Fi Fi!
Once we found a cave
And inside was a bear called Dave.
We stopped for tea,
Me, Pip, the bear and also Fi Fi.
The bear cooked cakes,
But they tasted fake.
But we said thanks for a lovely tea,
Me and pip once got chased by a bee.
The bee was twice the size of me!
But Pip ate it up, that told that bee!
Once I fell in a pit, but Pip saved me
And that is why I love him more than Fi!
He really is very, very, very special to me.

Kate Louise Morris (12)

My Nan

My favourite person is my nan,
I can talk to her all the time.
Even if I think she isn't there,
Even if I can't see her,
Her presence is near.

A shoulder to cry on when I am down,
An ear listening to what I have to say,
The sun appearing on a cloudy day.
A rainbow high above the sky,
A bunch of flowers in spring.

A campfire keeping me warm on a cold and frosty night,
Eyes in Heaven, watching over me.
Even though she may not be around,
She is with me always and forever.

Magdalene Cassidy (12)

Little Kiera

Kiera is my little niece,
She never gives me any peace,
Full of fun and only one,
And walking life has just begun,

I like to take her for a walk,
She sees the cows and tries to talk,
Kiera just won't hold my hand,
She would rather play in the sand.

She is always happy, never sad,
I wonder if she knows she's bad,
She nips people, I know it's sore,
She just grins, and I love her more.

I play with her every day,
I try to teach her what to say,
She tries so hard, this I know,
This is why I love her so.

She really is a little pest,
I'll be glad to get a rest,
Even when I go to bed,
Her little grin is in my head.

Gail Kirkpatrick (10)

My Cat Cosmo

My cat Cosmo,
A little, pretty boy,
Has a bit of fluff,
That he calls a toy.

He rolls it in the morning,
Plays chase with it before,
It runs away so fast
And it rolls out the door.

He loves to play these games,
His favourite one is either,
But what he doesn't understand is,
His fluff's a seven-legged spider!

Hannah Street (10)

Henry The Cat

Henry the cat saw a rat,
And dragged it onto the mat.
Henry's got the most beautiful green eyes,
And he adores chicken pies.
Henry's got the most lovely white fur,
And I love his *purr!*
Henry knows when it's teatime,
And of course he has to whine.
Henry love to lie about like a lion,
And he hates the dreaded iron.
Now Henry's very poorly,
There must be a cure, surely.
He's got a tumour in his brain,
And if that wasn't a pain,
Henry's got a bad kidney,
And the vet who found out was called Sidney.
So that's the end of my poem about the ...
Glorious, brilliant, wonderful, beautiful, lovely *Henry*.

Charlotte Ward (8)

My Best Friend

Do you have a friend like mine?
They're sometimes around the bend
But my friend's not
She is great
She is always there for me
Looking out for me
She is never late
Because she is my mate

That's what you call a best friend!

Tanzeela Hanif (9)

Me And My Brother

Me and my brother
Go to school
Me and my brother
Play with each other
Me and my brother
Sing together
Me and my brother
Eat together
Me and my brother
Argue together
Me and my brother
Fight each other
Me and my brother.

Oliver Mas

My Favourite Person

I don't have a favourite person,
I have five.
They're joyful, happy and fun to be around,
But they can drive you around the bend at times.
They're messy, noisy and crazy,
That is why I love them.
Sometimes they're sweet, sometimes they're mean,
But they're my little sisters,
And that is why I love them.
No one can have a favourite person like them!

Stephanie Browne (14)

My Favourite Person

My favourite person is my mummy
Even since I was in her tummy
She is loving, gentle, caring and kind
And embarrassing sometimes
But I don't mind.

She cooks my dinner
And washes my clothes
She helps me through
The highs and lows
She cleans the house
From head to toe
How does she do it?
Only she knows.

Haydn Lewis (13)

My Dog Polo

Your face lights up an entire room,
Making people happy when they feel gloom,
Cheering people up when they're feeling down,
Everyone's happy when you're around.

Every time I walk through that door,
You come to greet me, each time even more,
You wag your tail as hard as you can,
At that moment, I know you're my biggest fan.

You're the one I love to love,
Love to be with, love to hug,
Love to be with when I'm down,
Love to see when I frown.
Love to play with when I feel crazy,
Love to cuddle when I'm feeling lazy,
Love the time we spend together,
Love to love you for now and forever.

You bring a smile to anyone's face,
You make it fun, no matter what place,
Life with you is never a bore,
You're even fun when you sleep, and snore.

Whenever, wherever, you always have time,
To listen to me and what's on my mind,
No matter how hard my day has been,
I always feel happy after you I have seen.

You're the one I love to love,
Love to be with, love to hug,
Love to be with when I'm down,
Love to see, when I frown.
Love to play with when I feel crazy,
Love to cuddle, when I'm feeling lazy,
Love to love you, that much I know,
Love to love you, my dog Polo.

Madeleine Helme (14)

My Best Friend

C aring and clever, that's my good friend
H appy and helpful, my friend to the end
A lert and active, waiting for the catch
R eady and reliable, goalkeeper of the match
L iveliness and laughter, as we play together
O ne and only, we're best friends forever
T imid and trendy, she's my best star
T eam of two, that's what we are
E veryone knows she's my best friend by far!

Rosanna Gilmour (10)

My Friend Victoria

My friend Victoria
She will give me a present
She will give me a motorbike
She will give me a toy
She will give me a guitar
I will sing.

James Hunt (6)

My Favourite Person

My favourite person is my brother
I love to play with him
We play on the PS2
And we do it every day.

Richard Cornall (6)

Manchester United

Manchester United
are the best
they are better
than all the rest
I love their goals
and I love their kit
Manchester United
are fit.

Ben Smith (6)

My Mum

My mum is the best person ever
In the whole wide world
I give her cuddles
I love her
She likes to make me pancakes.

Jennifer Kenyon (6)

Robyn Is My Best Friend

Robyn is my best friend
She is very funny
And she makes me laugh very much
I like Robyn because
She never ever hurts me
That is why I like Robyn
She is very nice
I really do like her
I do, I do, I do
I really like Robyn
She is my best friend
That is why I like Robyn.

Anastasia Measures-Wardle (6)

My Best Friend

I like Katie M
I like her so
She really is good
At her work
She gets lots of house points!

Emma Lonican (6)

My Favourite Person

My friend is my mum
She helps me play
My mum sends photos
When she is away.

Alex Varley (6)

My Favourite Person

My little sister Shannon
Is sweet as pie,
She has bright blue eyes like an owl,
I would describe her as jolly, kind, cute and very playful,
She will always make me smile,
My littl e sister is one year old,
But very active for her age,
I will always care and share with her.

Tracey Browne (13)

My Little Pussy

My little pussy
Has a very pink nose,
A black back as smooth as silk
And big, green eyes the size of saucers.

She lies in the garden
Under an apple tree
And stretches out with all fours
And stays there till tea.

She sits on my lap
And purrs perfectly
As I stroke her gently
While she plays with a mouse.

My little pussy
Eats and snoozes
But although she is lazy
I love her oodles and oodles.

Rosanna Sasson (10)

Angels

Mums are angels with loving faces,
They work so hard in so many places,
Why can't people see,
How special my mum is to me?
Since I was born she's given me so much,
Added hope to my life with a single touch,
She's filled my life with so much love,
She really is an angel from above,
This poem is written to say,
Thank you, in every way.

Amie Sandell (17)

My Great Granny

My great granny is fantastic,
I love her all the world.
When you see her she's always smiling.
If you're down and have a frown,
She'll turn it round as quick as she can.

My great granny is caring,
She's as kind as she could be.
My great granny is my favourite person,
And she's everything to me.

Chantelle Packman (10)

Friends Forever

For Daniella,
Who has love and care.
For Chloe,
Who is always there.
For Sophie,
Who knows you well.
For Charlotte,
Who is there to help.
For Georgia,
Who is understanding.
For Sarvarna,
Who you can tell anything.
For Shelly,
Who's really cool.
For Suzie,
Who is a real dude.
For Angel,
Who doesn't live up to her name.
But the nicest one of them all, we'll all agree,
Is Jade, because she's always filled with glee.

Ayla Meerveld (11)

My Favourite Person

My favourite person doesn't have to be
Tall, small or skinny,
Or to have brown or blond hair,
He/she can be just perfect,
Unless, of course, they're me!

But I must confess,
He is the only one,
My kick-boxing instructor,
Who puts me through hell!

Eve McMahon

My Favourite Person

I have to say that when my younger sister
Is away for the day, I really miss her,
Although I find it hard to believe,
I love her to bits, so she must be relieved.
Her favourite game is hide-and-seek.
In the quiet night, when I go for a leak,
She jumps out in front and I let out a shriek
And she laughs till she weeps, what a terrible cheek.
She gets me in trouble and laughs on the double,
Without a second thought, asks for a cuddle.
That terrible person who is just trouble.
Before she goes to bed, when I am tired like a zombie,
A voice calls out to me, 'Make some Rice Krispies for me.'
If it wasn't for Mum, I would tell her, 'No!'
But instead I go, yet I'm angry you know.
She's not all bad, my little sister,
When I'm sad or in trouble, she gives me a cuddle.
And even though she's only five years old,
She means more to me than the purest of gold!

Sakinah Thomas (12)

Super Mum

My mum is great,
She is the best,
She's so much better
Than the rest.

She has a secret
Of her own,
She flies helping mums
From home to home.

She'll show them how to cook and clean,
The best super mum I've ever seen.
She'll tuck me in and say goodnight,
Before the morning bright sunlight.

She'll rush off to her super mum school
And teach the other mums how to be cool,
Then they will help her throughout the night,
But they have to get home before daylight.

My mum is a super mum,
Haven't you heard?
Well you have now,
So spread the word.

Jessica Walsh (11)

My Dog Nannook

My favourite animal is a dog,
Mine is called Nannook.
His favourite thing to chew is a log,
We nearly called him Luke.

He loves to have me at home.
Some people say he looks like a wolf.
He can't stand being alone,
He stands proud and sometimes aloof.

When the postman comes down the drive,
He barks the whole house down.
The postman puts the letters in the door
And Nannook takes a big dive,
And chews Mum's dressing gown.

Victoria Evans (13)

Sophie

(This poem is dedicated to my special baby niece, Sophie)

Through her eyes there's a whole new world,
A place where no one's ever been,
She's an individual,
Her own sweet self.

She's my favourite person.

She learns new things every day
That passes through her life.
Her soul such a special thing,
Her smile makes your day,
A heart so warm and loving.

She's my favourite person.

Elisabeth Dean (13)

My Cat Gizzy

She is a fluffy powerball,
As cheeky as a monkey,
As alert as a satellite.
Her ears are always scanning for new sounds,
She is as fast as a train,
Always playful and soft.
She's a monster to birds.
That's my fluffy cat Gizzy!

Sam Wedley (10)

My Mum

My favourite person is my mum,
She's never moody or glum.
Mum is always cheery and great.
She is always on time and never late.
My mum is wonderful and a brilliant cook,
I don't think she has ever needed a cook book.
Mum is fantastic at maths and art,
Whenever you need her she'll be there like a dart.
My mum is humorous and funny,
Her favourite pet animal is a bunny.
My amazing mum will always make you smile,
Not forever, but for quite a while.
I love my mum, she's the best in the universe,
If my mum was angry she'd be under a curse.
My mum is never sad
And that's what makes me glad.
I really love my mum, as you can see,
Obviously my mum with that loves me.
My awesome mum is beautiful,
She's very colourful and never dull.
She's never mean and never shouts.
The only thing I dislike is when she cooks sprouts.

Jasryan Rai (10)

My Dad

When my sister is mad at me
I go to him because he always shouts at her.
When I fall over, he always helps me.
My dad is very loud when he is mad.
I think he loves me more than my sister.
He laughs really loud as well,
He has a sense of humour.
He lets me stay up when I can't go to sleep.
I love my dad.

Francesca Gutteridge (10)

Paddy And Alfie

Paddy is my teddy bear,
he's soft and honeycomb.
I buy him lots of clothes to wear
and he's never left alone.

Alfie is my other bear,
he's very soft as well.
He needs lots of taking care
and has a yummy smell.

Larissa West (11)

Tye

Tye, your eyes so brown,
White as milk neck,
Brown coat, like Mum's handbag!
Your orange curly toy,
Bright as a mango,
(They call it Tough Toy,
But nothing is tough
For Tye) -
You shred it, tear it,
Rip it apart!

I crouch down
With the toy underneath me,
You burrow, scratch and paw me
To get at it!

You tire me out, Tye,
You wear me out
Till I lie on the floor, panting.
Dad shouts, 'Stop that!
Something might break!'
But I simply can't stop.

I'm writing a poem about you, Tye.
You leap at me.

Tom Gripper (10)

Tracy Beaker

My hero is called Tracy Beaker,
She made a game called Tracy Speaker.
She has behaviour problems,
But she loves drawing goblins.
She lives in a care home,
But she calls it the Dare Home.
I love Tracy Beaker, do you?
Let's all stick like glue.

Tracy Beaker is her name,
Daring people is her game.
Up, 2, 3, 4 ...

Aimee Lee (11)

God's Gift

My mother raised me until today
Now it's time for me to repay
She means everything to me
She is God's gift for me

Every time that I become sick
She helps me like a magic stick
Everytime that I cry
She comes and shows love, I don't know why
But I know that
She's a God's gift for me

Oh my dear mother
There's no one like you on this Earth planet
You'll mean a lot to me
Until the day I die
Because:
You are God's gift for me.

Saziye Mehmet (16)

My Dad

My dad's the best,
He towers above the rest.

He's six-foot-four
From head to the floor!

He's blond, green-eyed and slim,
And doesn't need to work out in the gym!

My dad takes me out every Sunday,
But is back to work on Monday.

He gets up at four to milk his cows,
And never gets a rest!

My dad's the best!
He towers above the rest!

Megan Jones (12)

A Poem For My Nan!

She's a robin at my window, she's a sparrow at my door,
My nan will always be with me, everywhere I go.
And although you can't see her, she'll be there when you call,
She's better up in Heaven, than suffering in pain.
God brought her up in Heaven and we'll soon see her again,
But until then, goodbye and God bless,
We all love you, Nan.

Lauren Reynolds (9)

Ruby Red

Ruby's favourite colour is red,
Cherries are red, apples are red and her bed is red.
Her hair is light brown and she's got an orange gown.
She has a yellow towel
With the word on 'growl'.
She has green whipped-up cream
With a cherry on top.
There's a blue colour too.
There's a purple fur ball
On the purple floor.

Jade Hill (8)

My Daddy

My daddy is ...

Loving and kind,
Helpful too,
If he was your daddy
He'd do that to you.

He plays with me
At the weekend,
If you were a man
You'd be his friend.

Everybody likes him,
He's really lots of fun,
His best friend would be
My mum!

Everything's funny
When he's there,
We'll sit down comfortably
In a chair.

Everything's fun,
Everyone's glad,
He's always happy,
That's my dad!

Sarah Hunt (9)

My Mum

My mum's the best, the best in the universe,
She takes me out everywhere,
Like the zoo, the park and more,
She's the best, the best in the world.

She lets me on the PlayStation and on the computer,
She lets me go round people's houses after school,
And lets me walk to the postbox all on my own,
She's the best, the best in the world.

And when I feel ill she's always there to give me a helping hand,
She's the best, the best mum in the world!

Andrew Cowley (10)

My Family

I cannot choose who's the best
In my family.

They're all so great
I cannot choose one from another.

They're so cool though,
And they're the people I like most.

Amy Scaife (8)

Saskia

Saskia is one of my little sisters - I have three,
And she looks nothing like them or me.
She has sapphire eyes,
Kissable cheeks,
Impish grin,
And always chuckles when we play hide-and-seek.

My sister has a giant marshmallow tummy,
Yummy little hands.

Sweet fairy-sized feet,
In mini pixie shoes,
Short baby apricot hair,
Tiny dresses to wear, so many to choose,
Everlasting friendship is what we have,
Right through our lives it will always be Saskia and Tash.

Natasha Jones (10)

My Favourite Person

My favourite person is as special as a colossal, chocolate fluffy pillow,
When they hug me I feel like a golden smile,
Their hair brushes on the surface of my soft cheek,
They work like a non-stop machine,
My feelings for them are incredible,
So incredible I stop to think,
This special person is my mum.

Jessica Blyth (11)

My Best Friend

My mum makes me smile
All day long
I say goodbye when I go to school
But I always miss her

I give her a kiss before I go to bed
And wake up telling her my dreams
It's not right without my mum
She will never leave me

My mum is my best friend
My bestest friend in the whole wide world
Without my mum I wouldn't know
What to do ... I would be lost

She is there by my side
Every day and every night
She is very sweet and kind
I'm glad she is *my mum!*

Saffron Carter (10)

My Friend Kristy - Haikus

The terrible two
That would be me and Kristy
The bestest of friends

Having loads of fun
No one will split us apart
The funniest pair

Eating yummy treats
Shoving chocolate down our throats
Blowing bubblegum

We sit together
Every day, all the time
Whispering our jokes

Walking to the shops
Buying honeycomb and sweets
Eating all day long.

Sally Nicholas (9)

Jesse

Big brown eyes and a cheeky smile
I can't believe he's here, right here, right now
I've waited for such a long, long while
Then when I saw him I really thought, *wow!*

Who can she mean?
I hear you guess
Well since you are so keen
It's my baby cousin Jess

I can't wait for him to get older
So we can have lots of fun
I enjoy burping him on my shoulder
Cos when he smiles, he brings out the sun

I love him so much
Even when he scrunchies up his face
While he is waiting for his feed
At my auntie's place.

Ruby Simon (9)

Miss Jackman

Miss Jackman is my Year 2 teacher
She's sometimes very strict
And other times she makes me laugh
And giggle into fits.

She's taught me all about dinosaurs
And that has been great fun
Now I'm sad it's over
I wish it had just begun.

I now know how a sunflower
Grows from such a tiny seed
And how the Great Fire of London
Spread from street to street.

So thank you dear Miss Jackman
For teaching me so much
Now my brain is packed with things
Including goodbye and good luck!

Annie Mitchell (6)

Good Boy

Bullet's my best friend,
He's a dog, yeah I know,
He keeps himself busy,
Frightening his foe.

His foes may be birds,
And cute little cats,
But it keeps him occupied,
So a hats off to that.

He is a bit lazy,
And he lounges around,
He pretends to sleep,
Not making a sound.

He's really cheeky,
You can see it in his eyes,
He can't stop being naughty,
And he can't stop telling lies.

He is a bit dopey,
I have to admit,
But he's really obedient,
Well, he knows how to sit.

He always gets hyper,
When he sees another dog,
But when the dog is gone,
He sleeps like a log.

But don't worry guys,
He's not all that bad,
He's kind and unselfish,
He's really a good lad.

Amardeep Singh Bhaker (11)

My Favourite Pony

I have a favourite pony
Her colour is dark brown
She acts just like a princess
But she's missing a crown

I have a favourite pony
She's brilliant to ride
She is very comfy
'Cause she has a lovely stride

I have a favourite pony
Her name is Honeycomb
I am thrilled that I own her
And have given her a home

I have a favourite pony
She is 10 years old
I will keep her till the day she dies
So she will never get sold.

Shannon Lima (9)

My Mum

My mum she has the loudest voice,
She shouts from dawn to dusk.
At eight she starts when school I go,
Her voice, a rhino's tusk.

She makes me jump when she calls me,
While in my bed I lay.
'Get out from bed,' she shouts to me,
'It's school you go today.'

I bath, I dress, I eat breakfast,
Then telly do I see,
And then my mum she shouts again,
'You'll be the death of me.'

To school I go, at peace I'll be,
The work I do enjoy,
I run, I jump and play about,
I wish I'd been a boy.

At 3.15 my peace does end,
My mum is at the gate,
Her voice I hear, before I see,
'Quick Mollie, I'll be late.'

Then home we go and tea I eat,
And play, my friends in tow,
'Tis then I hear that dreaded voice,
'It's time for bed you know.'

But when I'm in my bed at night,
All warm and snug and curled,
It's then I realise I've got
The best mum in the world!

Mollie Jones (8)

My Favourite Person Is My Teacher

My favourite person is my teacher,
I like every one of her features,
From her friendly reflection,
To her rosy complexion.
My favourite person is my teacher,
She always gives me a hand,
To help me understand,
Yes, shouting she does,
But it's only because
Some people never respect her,
She has such a good nature,
Mrs Wilkinson - our teacher.

Rachel Buttery (9)

My Aunty

My aunty is so caring,
I love her so much just like my mam and my nan.
She gives me lots of stuff, my aunty is such fun,
Once before we had a water fight, we had lots of fun.
Whenever I go up there I make crispy cakes
And whenever my uncle Blake is up there he tries to eat them all.
So face it, my aunty is the one that is *f-u-n,* fun.

Ellie Harris (8)

The Best Mum

My mum is the best
My bedroom a mess
Oh no! Oh no!

She cleans it all up
My dog's had a pup
Oh yeah! Oh yeah!

My mum is the best
She beats all the rest
She is the best! She is the best!

Jack Harvey (10)

My Dad's Mirror Poem

My dad!
He's a cool man
Of that I'm sure
An excellent cook
He should write a book
He works in a window company
Once he showed me around that company
He's great on the computer too!

He's great on the computer too!
Once he showed me around that company
He works in a window company
He should write a book
An excellent cook
He's a cool man
My dad!

James Lewis (10)

My Rabbit Tommy

My rabbit Tommy
he loves eating honey
He jumps on the spot
and bounces around

He is my best friend
I like him when he's sleeping
he's so cute

I like him when he looks cute
with his cute eyes
the way he looks at me
from a distance

I like him when he is eating his food
and best of all
he is the best

He's special to me
because he's my best friend.

Jordan Ricketts (10)

My Dog

My dog Buster is funny
because he digs up bones
He makes me laugh
with his funny bark.

We call him Buster
because he busts balls
He's fun
with you and me.

When we play
he jumps as high as the rain
Buster is so special to me
because *I love him.*

Kayleigh Robins (10)

My Best Friend Amy

She makes me laugh, she makes me cry
She always says I'm nice
We like to shop, we like to bop
She never lies

When I have a bad day
She is always there, straight away
And when she's fine, I'm fine
And that's the way I like it.

If ever we were parted
I would be broken hearted
She is my best friend
And our friendship will never end.

Sophie Howells (10)

She's My Inspiration

She's my inspiration
She helps me when I'm down
She knows that I love her
She never lets me see her frown.

Fighting through cancer and she's still strong
She is super cool
Not letting it take her down for long
And she's like a fish when she's in the pool.

Love and hope is all we have got
The cancer will not take her away
And yet she hasn't lost the plot
She is here and here to stay

My auntie Ann!

Katie Vaughan John (10)

My Dog Bandit

My dog is my best friend
His name is Bandit
I teach him how to sit
Lie down and fetch
I talk to him when I'm sad or happy
And tell him what I do in school
I love my dog.

Alex Hollett (10)

My Mum

I love my mum very, very much,
She has got such a gentle touch,
All her smiles bring me lots of joy,
Lucky she had Ian and me, a girl and a boy.

She cares for my dad,
And when it comes to cooking she isn't half bad,
She is always there for me,
And classical music is her cup of tea.

My mother is super cool,
And she doesn't like people calling her a fool,
She is always right in every single way,
She is also awesome every day.

That is my mum,
I love her so much,
She is my one and true joy,
She will never go,
My mother, I love her so.

Laura Billington (10)

Sophie And Me

Sophie is my very best friend
She and I will never end
She makes me laugh, she makes me cry
My friend Sophie will never lie.

We like shopping and gossiping
We like walking and talking
She says I'm nice
And I give her advice

If we ever parted
I would feel down hearted
Sophie and me
Like a family tree.

Amy Bissett (10)

My Twin

My mum is like my twin
I love her so much
Her kindness and care touches my heart
I couldn't bear if we were torn apart.

My mum is a lot of fun
And when it comes to cleaning, she is the one
The one who is the best
She is better than all the rest.

Dancing, we've got all the grooves
Yeah baby, we have all the moves
Cooking every meal time
It's delicious, it's mine, all mine.

Working, caring, loving me
Shopping, she is the funniest one
I can face it, she is the one.

Jessica Harris (10)

Untitled

My favourite person is my best friend Emma
She's fun and cool, but not like a mule
I tell her my secrets and she never tells
She knows who I fancy and she says he acts like a pansy
She's my best friend Emma, forever.

Amy-Jo Marsden (13)

My Hero

Alan Smith is fairly tall,
He always scores brilliant goals.
Alan Smith! Alan Smith!

He runs so fast,
He's gone in a flash.
Alan Smith! Alan Smith!

His skills are great,
And his heading is cool,
He always has lots of fuel.
Alan Smith! Alan Smith!

Anthony Moore (13)

All About My Family

My favourite person is my mum
She buys me things and she is fun
I also like my brother
But not as much as my mother
Sometimes I like my dad
'Cause I'm his favourite lad
I don't like him when he's mad
But I love him when he's glad
I really love my dog
But not when it needs the bog
He scratches at the door
To make me play more
We roll round on the floor
My mum comes home and says,
'Why are you so mucky?'
''Cause I've been playing with my Lucky!'

Ben Dobbie (13)

My Sis

My favourite person may be dead,
When she died it filled me full of dread,
She died when I was 4,
Which made me cry more and more.

Heather's the name of my sweet big sister,
Heather my sis, oh how I miss her,
I took it worse when she died,
I saw her every day when she was alive.

The day she was 6, her last birthday I remember
She died so close, so close to September
My mother said, 'Hey, remember the day ... '
That me and Heather used to play.

Adam Uttley (13)

My Dad

My favourite person is my dad,
He is never sad,
He is never mad.

He works all day,
He works all night,
But he's always there to say goodnight.

Naomi Culshaw (13)

My Brother

My favourite person is my brother,
The person who loved is my mother,
He is a smoker which is bad,
He is happy never sad.

He has a girl daughter,
He didn't buy her,
He is her real dad,
She got spoilt that's why she's bad.

The age of him is twenty-three,
He is as sound as you and me,
He also has a daughter called Dianna,
She's a nuisance, that's why he calls her a spanner.

Robert Cadwick (13)

Untitled

My favourite person is my mummy
She is a lovely dovey
She works till 6 to give me money
She treats me like her honeybee
She is so cool, she acts like a fool
In my house just me and my mum
Dad has gone with his new family
Looks like he's not coming back
That's why I love my mummy.

Emma Barry (13)

My Friends

My friends are always there
Whatever happens they care
Friendship can be powerful
But also can be showerful
I have fun with my friends
And hope our friendship never ends.

Ruby Etches (12)

Shanakay

S is for Shanakay
H appy most of the time
A lways honest with my friends
N ever let them down
A nd good at
K eeping secrets
A nd by the way, my favourite colour is
Y ellow,

Shanakay Alexander (12)

I Have An Angel

I have an angel
she looks after me
she shines a light
so I can see

I have an angel
she looks down from above
she kisses me
and gives me love

I have an angel
I love her so
she watches
she is the kindest person I know

I have an angel
do you know who it is?
It's my mum
my lovely mum.

Esme Winter-Lockwood (12)

My Dog

M y dog
Y ells and barks

D igs holes in the mucky mud
O verly huge and very big
G ives you wet, sticky licks

That's my dog!

Oliver Claridge

Kumi - My Cat

Long day at school
Long walk home
Raining all the while
I feel like a moan.

Take out my key
Turn it in the lock
Step in the cold, dark house
And my knees begin to knock.

But here she comes
Streaking through the gloom
With a miaow and a purr
To brighten up the room.

I'll cuddle her close
She'll feel strong and warm
And there I will stand
Throughout the raging storm.

Finn Bulman (12)

Family

Family, the cushion we fall on,
to soften our landing.

Family, the wings that we use,
to reach up to our targets.

Family, the writers,
that help us shape our destiny.

Family, the one thing we need.

Kiah Tasman (12)

In My Heart

Every day, me and my mate,
Meet together at the gate,
A place for just him and me,
A place for no one else to see.

The one empty space in my heart,
Is filled with him, just one part,
He's the only one for me,
He's just part of the family.

He is brave and to me he gave
A photo of him and me,
Climbing up our favourite tree,
And in my eyes I can see,
That we are one happy family.

Just me, my mum, my dad and he - my brother,
The one happy family.

Jess White (12)

Stormy Jack

S tormy Jack a psycho cat,
T ail swishing, ready to pounce,
O verreacting, killing a mouse.
R ed blood spurting, from the prey,
M y cat's basis every day.
Y elling at him, I want him to stop.

J ack's prey's death is hard to top,
A ll of the birds cowering in their nests,
C atches them, seconds flat, eats and rests,
K ing of the felines, my cat, Stormy Jack.

Kai Johnson-Smith (12)

My Gran

I wish I knew her as she was,
I wish I had the chance,
I wish I could turn back the clock,
And see her wrinkled glance.

I wish I knew her as she was,
I wish she could remember,
I wish she could have been 84,
And made it until September.

Theo Roseland (13)

Lady Of My Dreams

I see you galloping along
On your great white horse
Your golden hair streaming behind you
Lady of my dreams

You weave in and out of every dream
Nearly close enough to touch
Bells around your ankles and knees
Lady of my dreams

You make me so very happy
Every night I want to sleep
Just to see you in robes of white
Lady of my dreams

Your horse has ribbons plaited in its tail
Your horse looks like it doesn't touch the ground
Your golden crown always upon your head
Lady of my dreams

But every day when I wake
I wish you were real
You are my only one true friend
Lady of my dreams.

Anna Heath (13)

Micheal Anthony Green

Great in many ways was a beautiful face
Lightened with creativity
Darkened by race
A personality warm and gentle
Broad minded
In body small
Ambitious and demanding
Determined to achieve
What his heart is set to do
And his mind to believe
For you I collect these words
I think you, they define
I can always make clear for you
In my mystery of a mind
You were embarrassed to tell me your name
I couldn't understand why
Micheal Anthony Green
There was no need to lie
For you are a good boy
Quickly becoming a man
Rise tall and overcome
On your two feet you will stand.

Tatum Campbell (13)

Amanda

A manda you're so funny,
M an you can be silly,
A nd you're just like the one on TV,
N ever call me static again
D one your school days already,
A nd now you're 19 so you better get going.

Kieran Sutherland (12)

My Favourite Person

She is like a lion catching a deer
Whether the prey is far or near
She is like a monkey in a tree
Having no fear of getting stung by a bee
She messes about as much as she can
Jumping up and down like a gingerbread man
Lying there without a thought in her head
As at last she goes to bed
Yeah, she might give me blisters
But deep down she is my sister Sophia.

Laurent Vaughan (10)

My Teddy

I love my teddy very much
When I sleep he's in my clutch
I toss and turn
I flinch and twist
But all the night he's at my fist.

Through thick and thin
Through this and that
Always at my side for a chat
I love my teddy very much
He's always there for me.

My teddy is from Australia
He lived in trees and ate a lot
But now he's here
He lives with me
Sometimes I find him ...
Still climbing trees!

Annie Avery (10)

Obi-Wan Kenobi

Obi-Wan Kenobi
With a blue lightsaber
Sighting the dark forces of evil
While he gets stronger.

Oh no!
This is disastrous
Who has done this? The clones!
Throwing away Jedi bones

But Obi-Wan Kenobi
He is the best
He destroyed the fat old clones
And was able to save the rest.

Jack Morgan (9)

Molly

My favourite person would have to be
Molly the Westie dog
Molly's fur is as white as snow
She is loveable from head to toe
Her tongue is the shape of a fish tail
Her teeth are as sharp as a nail
Molly's eyes are the colour of the sea
She really fancies cups of tea
She likes to chase a cat
I love my Westie dog and that is that!

Hannah Dudley (9)

My Favourite Person

My favourite person's name is Ryan
We met in nursery before school,
He's been my friend for many years
He's never mean, he's never cruel.

When I left that town a few years back
He was the friend hardest to leave,
We moved to Bath and got sorted out
But I was happy and didn't grieve.

St Mary's school is the place where we went
To go to school a few years back,
Although he didn't like school a lot
All his SATs were in the sack.

My favourite person's name is Ryan
We met in nursery before school,
I haven't seen him since a few years back
But he's a friend for me and all.

Laurence Murray (13)

My Favourite Person

My favourite person's called Leo
He's never been to school
He murders rats
And fights with cats
And that's what makes him cool

He's not always happy
And sometimes is really sad
Teddy bears
And fold-up chairs
Always make him mad

He miaows when he wants food
And scratches up the mat
Oh can't you see
Obviously
Leo is a cat!

Ryan Bamsey (13)

My Favourite Person

My favourite person is my dog
Although that's not quite right,
For a dog is not a person at all
But he fills me with delight.

He is the breed of otter hound
Not Labrador or beagle,
But he is very rare now
Hunting otters is illegal.

He's a hungry dog with massive teeth
But some things he can't eat,
And as we've found he's not so strong
He has to leave the meat.

He has a pair of big green eyes
Which come in very handy,
For getting things off people in streets
Like doughnuts, crisps and candy.

So I'm going to see my dog again
But I am in a muddle
'Cause I bet he's chewing my favourite shoes
While I'm giving him a cuddle.

Kit Jones (13)

My Favourite Person

My favourite person has to be,
Someone who's almost the same as me,
Playing tennis is so much fun,
With this person under the sun.

This person can also be very funny,
But is not spoilt with tons of money,
We laugh and have a good time at school,
But sometimes he acts like a bit of a fool!

We share the same interests,
We go to the same school,
Out of my friends, they are the best,
Because they're just so cool!

Alistair Davies (13)

My Favourite Person

My favourite person
Is my mate Joe,
We like to play together
Especially in the snow.

He really likes the summer
But I prefer the spring,
In football I play striker
And he plays on the wing.

We've also got things in common
Like playing catch at school,
We both like to play rugby
And would both like a swimming pool.

When we are together
We could play all day long,
But if we're not too careful
Something could go wrong.

We could break something precious
Which would annoy my mum,
But when we are together
We are always having fun.

Joshua Abbott (13)

My Favourite Person

My favourite person is a hero
He really started off at zero
At school committing a sinner
Grows up to be a World Cup winner.

He kicked for hours at a park
For posts he used the trees' bark
From a young age he slotted them over
Smashing the window on an old lady's Rover.

He started off with football
He could always kick a ball
At a young age he started rugby
Liked to get his hands all dirty and grubby.

Number ten he ran the game
To his house the selectors came
England really needed Jonny
He became Newcastle Falcons' Sir Bobby.

To the World Cup he went
Helping England to build a dent
In Australia's hopes to win the cup
Jonny's golden boot is on the up!

Charlie Grey (14)

My Favourite Person

My favourite person is Danny Grewcock,
In the line-out he is a winner,
Also at scrumaging and open play,
He'll knock anyone over that gets in his way,
Danny is unique in his position.

His fists are made of solid steel,
With one punch anyone would keel,
He is also extremely tall,
His fitness levels are very high,
Every day he trains for his next match.

In his second row position,
With his scrum cap on and his ferocious face,
Whether he plays for Bath or England,
He will never give up even if they're losing,
That's why he's my favourite person.

Dan Huntley (13)

My Favourite Person

My favourite person is my mum
She cheers me up when I'm glum
She gives me lifts when I need them most
Because if I was late I'd certainly be toast
She helps me when I'm stuck
She tells me how to improve my luck
My mum is always kind and sharing
She never ever stops caring
She works very hard and long
For very many hours strong
The good times we share together
I will always hope they last forever.

David Lacey (13)

549

Untitled

My favourite person is my dad
He does not make me sad or mad
He gives me lifts when I need them most
Because if I was late I would be toast
He also helps me when I am stuck
Gives me advice to improve my luck.

My dad is kind and sharing
He's very good at caring
He works hard and long
For many hours strong
The good times we share together
Will always last forever.

As well as a good parent he is a good friend
We laugh at funny movies until the very end
I hope he will always be a friend to me
Even though he is my family
When I grow up I'd like to be
Just like him for all to see
Strong and proud
He stands out from the crowds
A friend to me
He will always be
But most of all I am glad
That he is my very good dad.

Christopher Aruthan (13)

My Favourite Person

The one and only Michael Vaughn,
Drove the ball across the lawn.
Fours and sixes smashed about,
Until the scorers had lost count.
The very next ball he took one stride ...
'Hit it for six!' the crowd all cried.

Oh a captain's role he does play,
One of the greats, the fans do say.
If the England squad go downstream
It's always cos Vaughn's not in the team.
He can bat and bowl a bit
And there's never a ball he can't hit.

When it comes to playing, for some ash,
He can give the Aussies, a good old thrash.
His team can beat the unbeatables
And I'm sure this, will be repeatable.
He plays to win, and what does he do?
He wins, cos he is Michael Vaughn, that's who!

Nathaniel Scott (13)

My Favourite Person

My favourite person is my dad,
When I see him it makes me glad.
Even though, the truth be told,
I think he's getting kinda old,
He takes me to play football games,
And he's quite good at the same.
After that we go to the shops,
To buy some sweets and fizzy pop.
And when he takes me up to bed,
I think of all the things he's said.
I only see him at weekends,
So he tries (and fails!) to make amends.
But I love him anyway,
And he loves me come what may.

Jack Bailey (13)

My Favourite Person

My favourite person is really funny.
He is really cool and gives me money.

He got me a lift on a hot air balloon.
It was a wonderful flight in the afternoon.

Bristol Rovers are the best!
We watch them in our blue and white vest.

He gives me presents and real, cool stuff.
All these things that I really love.

He takes me to places like the cinema,
Bowling, football and the theatre.

Every tournament that I go into,
Whatever it is he'll tell me what to do.

So the next best thing after winning the lotto
Is knowing my brilliant uncle Otto.

Charlie Thresher (13)

Fishy!

My favourite person
Is my fish!
All it does is
Swim, eat, sleep.
It has to be
The coolest fish I know,
Swimming around,
Fins flapping
Head high,
Tail turning!
Oh what a life
I wish I was a fish!
I wouldn't swap my fish for anything
Except maybe another fish!

Sam Hollingshead (13)

Mum

My favourite person is my mum.
When I'm with her we have such fun.
Sunny, windy, rain or shine,
In her arms I know I'm fine.

We go for trips into town.
She picks me up when I am down.
Whatever the time is, day or night
She comforts me and makes things right.

Lots of kisses, lots of cuddles,
She helps me with maths if I'm in a muddle.
Cooking and cleaning through the week
But time with her is what I seek.

When it's late and time for bed
She says goodnight and kisses my head.
A hug, a smile, a special touch
Mum I love you very much.

Alex Jones (13)

My Cat

My favourite person is my cat
His favourite hobby is sleep
Resting upon the squashy sofa
While the sun shines in on him

After five or six long hours
Of sitting in the sun
He may rise up from his seat
And head out to the garden

Once he's out in the garden
He knows exactly what to do
He knows the bushes where the mice reside
He may even bring one in

Once he's finished with the mice
Some food is what he wants
He starts to miaow and rub around me
Until he gets his grub

I like my cat
For many reasons
He's always there for me
My favourite person is my cat.

Thomas Marshall (13)

My Favourite Person

My favourite person could be an elf,
But I would prefer it if it was myself.

Although I'm small you might debate,
Life like me is really great.

I have brown eyes and dark brown hair,
My pet is a fish, not a grizzly bear.

I like to read books and do tae kwon do,
But the thing I hate most is the fruit called a mango.

I like lots of food, like burgers and fries,
Ham and pineapple pizza, and crispy steak pie.

My favourite subject at school is art,
In which paints and pencils play a big part.

I like lots of gadgets like my cool plasma ball,
And my TV mounted on my bedroom wall.

Now you can see why I like myself,
And why I really don't want to be an elf!

Sam Bennett (13)

My Favourite Person

My favourite person is always there
My favourite person, he really cares
Whenever I'm down and want to cry
He is always by my side

He makes me laugh all the time
Making up his silly rhymes
Always happy, never sad
He is good, never bad

He always wants the best for me
He wouldn't mind if I could be
A person who is quite like him
Someone not big but neither thin

He wants to carry on with the family
He wants my sister and even me
To have a nice wife and lots of babies
He would call them, 'My lovely ladies.'

My favourite person, I am so glad
To say that that person is my dad.

Josh Hall (13)

My Favourite Person

Joy-bringer, clothes wringer, great singer,
Great love, gives me a shove,
Keeps me toe to the line to make me shine,
Produces a smile, all the while,
Gives me protection, a bit of redirection
If I'm in the wrong
She'll keep up a song, till I'm gone,
On a better path, or started to laugh
About the great skill that will
Come to nil for she'll
Stay with us, comfort us, chivvy us,
And do it all with a magnificence
That shines through pestilence,
All evil and sadness,
Is turned to gladness,
When my favourite person walks in the room
Dispelling gloom,
The most amazing fun,
My favourite person, my mum.

Daniel Hinchliff Walz (13)

My Favourite Person

My favourite person is my cat,
She's black and white and rather fat.
In the winter she lays by the fire,
Even my dog will lay beside her.

When we come downstairs in the morning,
We both hope a great day is dawning.
She miaows for food,
Because she knows she won't lose.

She sleeps through the day,
Then she may;
Sleep on my bed or she will fight
Till the night turns into light.

She is the best cat in the world.

Ben Anderson (14)

Jethro Is His Name!

My family has a guinea pig and Jethro is his name
He likes to hide in straw as if it is a game

He lives with my rabbit Dotty, she likes him you can tell!
He likes munching grass, he likes her just as well!

Jethro and Dotty live in a Dutch hutch
We don't care if they are naughty, we love them just as much

Jethro is a baby, he really is quite small
If he looks at Dotty, she looks really tall!

My family has a guinea pig
And Jethro is his name.

Sophie Palmer (10)

Untitled

My mum has blue eyes
She is small and cuddly
She gives me lots of hugs
and tells me every day she loves me
My mum is so special, caring and kind
I'm so very glad she is mine.

Emma Robertson (11)

Bracken!

B racken is my cuddly bunny
R abbits are very funny
A nd they love to chew
C arrots are not nice in Irish stew
K ittens are my friends
E ven though Bracken dislikes their furry ends
N ever will I trust a cat and Bracken will make sure of that!

Christina Paish (9)

My Sister Chloe

My sister Chloe is a lovely little thing
She always smiles when I start to sing.

She gurgles and coos
Trying to play with her shoes.

She makes a big splash,
When she plays in the bath.

She plays with her toys
Making lots of noise.

My sister Chloe
I love you.

Joshua Davies

My Best Mate Katie!

It's a big bright beautiful future,
Thank your lucky stars you're alive,
I've got my best mate Katie to talk to,
She's a friend that I can trust for life.

We've been on our own with no friendly time,
But those old, old days are gone,
We are two of a kind spending quality time together,
As Katie and Jess!

Jessica Gillibrand (11)

My Friend Ruby

She's funny,
She's nice,
She's cooler than ice ...
And her name is Ruby.

She cries,
And she laughs,
And she likes to have baths ...
And her name is Ruby.

She chuckles,
She clucks,
With tears and stuff ...
And her name is Ruby.

She's pretty,
She is funny,
She likes to earn money ...
And her name is Ruby.

She watches TV,
She watches movies,
Best of all she likes smoothies ...
And her name is Ruby.

She'll laugh,
And she'll cry,
She has that twinkle in her eye ...
And that's my best friend, Ruby!

Leigh Hookway (10)

My Favourite Pet!

I love my chicken, Maple,
She's really very sweet,
Her feathers are a chocolate brown,
She's always very neat.

Although she's full of mischief,
She flutters all around.
Jumps upon the table,
And knocks cups to the ground,
Maple, Maple, let me see,
If you can be good -
Lay an egg for me,
And I'll eat it with bread for tea!

Angelika-Rose Stangl (12)

My Favourite Person

When I first met her,
She was the best.

We made friends and now she is better than the rest,
She is one of the people I can trust.

She always cares about me,
She is always there when I need her.

That is my best friend ...
Ami Slater.

April Davies (11)

Young Writers Information

We hope you have enjoyed reading this book - and that you will continue to enjoy it in the coming years.

If you like reading and writing mini sagas drop us a line, or give us a call, and we'll send you a free information pack.

Alternatively, if you would like to order further copies of this book or any of our other titles, then please give us a call or log onto our website at **www.youngwriters.co.uk**

Young Writers, Remus House, Coltsfoot Drive, Woodston,
Peterborough PE2 9JX
Tel (01733) 890066